EMBATTLED
EROS

Thinking Gender
Edited by Linda J. Nicholson

Also published in the series

EMBATTLED EROS

SEXUAL POLITICS AND ETHICS IN CONTEMPORARY AMERICA

STEVEN SEIDMAN

ROUTLEDGE   NEW YORK AND LONDON

Published in 1992 by

Routledge
An imprint of Routledge, Chapman and Hall, Inc.
29 West 35 Street
New York, NY 10001

Published in Great Britain by

Routledge
11 New Fetter Lane
London EC4P 4EE

Library of Congress Cataloging in Publication Data

Seidman, Steven.
    Embattled eros : sexual politics & ethics in contemporary America / Steven Seidman.
       p.   cm. — (Thinking gender)
    Includes index.
    ISBN 0-415-90356-4. — ISBN 0-415-90357-2 (pbk.)
    1. Sex customs—United States—History—20th century. 2. Sexual ethics—United States—History—20th century. 3. Feminism—United States—History—20th century. 4 Intimacy (Psychology) I. Title.
II. Series.
HQ18.U5S428 1992
306'.0973—dc20   91-22944
                                     CIP

British Library Cataloguing in Publication Data

Seidman, Steven
    Embattled Eros : sexual politics & ethics in contemporary America.—(Thinking gender)
    I. Title II. Series
    306.70973

    ISBN 0-415-90356-4
    ISBN 0-415-90357-2 pbk

To my friends, Audrey, Brian, Carol, Cindy, the late Ernie, Re-augh, Harold, Keith, the late Jim Perry, Libby, Nathan, Richard, Sally, Sheila and the many other individuals whom I have had the good fortune to work with on the front line of sexual politics.

To my son, Andrew, with hopes that my moral and political struggles make your own sexual and intimate choices less socially weighty.

Contents

Acknowledgments

I have worked on *Romantic Longings* and *Embattled Eros* for about the last 10 years. Many individuals have contributed in personal and professional ways to my work. I would like to thank Jeff Alexander, Dennis Altman, Chris Bose, Ann Ferguson, Jonathan Katz, Stephen O. Murray, and Iris Young for commenting on some version of the latter text. In particular, I have carried on a conversation about issues of sex, gender and theory with Linda Nicholson for a good part of this time. She read and commented on every chapter; I feel lucky to have had the support and intelligent commentary of this dear friend. Without the patience, good will and insightfulness of Bob Cutler I'm not sure I would have had the psychic centeredness and enthusiasm to complete this project. To Aaron Roth, thank you for being there for me, so many times.

All authors should be blessed with an editor like Maureen MacGrogan. I wish to thank Maureen along with Max Zutty and Carla Sommerstein at Routledge for handling my books with such care and intelligence. As in my last book, the interlibrary loan staff at the State Univesity at Albany was enormously cooperative and efficient. Similarly, I relied heavily on the competence and good will of the administrative staff of the Sociology department, especially Louise Tornatore. I thank Xu Xun for gathering materials for me with care and promptness.

Preface

In *Romantic Longings* I traced the development of a unique culture of eroticism in the twentieth-century United States.[1] This culture constructed the body as a site of sensual pleasure and self-expression; it created an elaborate language of body parts, erotogenic zones, sex technique, sex acts, and pleasures. It was initially shaped by popular discourses and representations that framed sex as a sphere of love in the early decades of the twentieth century. To the extent that sex became a chief site for proving and sustaining romantic love, the giving and receiving of erotic pleasure acquired legitimacy. The development of the erotic aspects of sex was furthered in the post-World War II period by efforts to legitimate sex for its pleasurable, expressive, and communicative qualities, apart from its symbolizing of love. This differentiation of the erotic from the romantic aspects of sex greatly intensified the formation of an erotic culture. Sex, I concluded, was framed in middle America both as a way to express and maintain romantic love and as a medium of erotic pleasure and self-expression.

The intimate culture that evolved in twentieth-century America exhibited tensions around this dual construction of sexuality. For example, framing sex as a medium of love implies a person-centered orientation. Since sexual expression in this construction carries the imperative to treat the other as an end in itself, it is expected that lovers should never relate to each other as mere bodies or instruments of pleasure. Yet constructing sex as a medium of pleasure entails a body-centered orientation. Sex is projected as both a medium of romantic love with expectations of treating the other as a integrated individual, and as a site of self expression valued for promoting individualism. Thus, ambiguities surround sexual expression. Does mutual sexual satisfaction signify a fortunate meshing of organs and orifices, or does it prefigure a broader companionship or intimacy? Does sexual maladjustment symbolize merely sexual incompatibility, or a broader social and spiritual dissonance? Moreover, legitimating sex for its pleasurable qualities alone sanctions its uncoupling from intimate bonds. The splitting off of sex from intimacy and its legitimation as "recreational" may, as some critics contend, have a destabilizing impact on romantic bonds, but it also expands sexual choice and diversity. Finally, I argued that the tensions in contemporary American intimate culture give rise to social conflicts, for example, between those who wish to connect sex exclusively to intimate bonds and others who defend sex as a medium of pleasure apart from love and intimacy.

Beginning in the late 1970s, I detected a reaction to this culture of eroticism. Eros was often depicted in mass cultural representations as dangerous and destructive. I described efforts to place limits on erotic expression by those who emphasized the nonerotic—social and spiritual—dimensions of intimacy and by those who advocated the exclusive legitimacy of romantic, intimate sex. Constructions of sex that highlighted the social, spiritual and romantic aspects of sex began to dominant public attention in the 1980s. There were stepped-up assaults on representations and discourses that permitted a slippage between sex, love and intimacy. I thought of these movements as basically conservative, since they placed unnecessarily restrictive limits on lifestyle choices. I underscored the dangers, especially to sexual minorities, of this conservative social trend.

My main aim in *Romantic Longings* was to offer a broad historical perspective on the present intimate culture in the United States. I did not address the divisions and strains in contemporary American intimate culture until the epilogue. My concluding comments amounted to a cautious defense of an American intimate culture which allows some slippage between sex and love. I argued that such a culture promotes choice and diversity and can be productive of new identities and social bonds. As a gay man, I had good reason, especially in the mid-1980s, to fear that movements to restrict sexual expression would be repressive of nonconventional sexual lifestyles. My defense of this sexual culture was sketchy and largely rhetorical. Moreover, at the time I believed that I had to choose between a defense of choice—defending sex as an "autonomous" sphere of pleasure—or side with the party of restraint. Accordingly, I tended to simplify these trends by defining them as conservative or backlash movements. I saw challenges to the American culture of eroticism, too narrowly, as entailing a restrictive sexual ideology and politics.

In *Embattled Eros*, I begin where I left off in *Romantic Longings*—

namely in America in 1980. Although I draw on the historical perspective I sketch in chapter 1, my focus is on the late 1970s and 1980s. I intend to provide a novel understanding of current American conflicts. Specifically, I wish to go beyond seeing the present as divided between the friends of eros and the party of discipline and restraint. The heart of American sexual conflict is, I believe, less a battle between proponents of sexual expression and defenders of repression than a basic division over the meaning and morality of sexuality. Moreover, my intention to provide a sociological description of current sexual conflicts is perhaps less important than the moral impulse of this work. I intend to greatly elaborate on moral themes that were left underdeveloped in *Romantic Longings*. One of my chief aims is to stake out a moral standpoint that defends an expansive notion of sexual choice and diversity, but can articulate norms that can limit choice beyond that of mutual consent.

Notes

1. Steven Seidman, *Romantic Longings: Love in America, 1983–1980* (New York: Routledge, 1990).

Introduction

Sexual Conflicts in the Contemporary United States

The post-World War II years were a period of unprecedented economic growth and prosperity, but also national turmoil. Social unrest was, of course, a continuous feature of twentieth-century America. Conflicts between labor and capital were especially sharp in the early decades of this century; religious, racial, and ethnic tensions were never far from the surface in this century; the suffragist movement called attention to persisting gender discord. Yet the social tensions of the postwar years threatened to engulf the United States in a virtual civil war. Whereas the civil rights movement did not seriously challenge American liberalism, a militant black liberation movement advocated social revolution. The black civil rights and liberation movements served as paradigms for the New Left and for the women's, gay and lesbian, and ecological movements. By the mid-1960s, the spirit of social rebellion spread to wide circles of youth, and especially to students. Political rebellions were paralleled by social and cultural movements among the counterculture, the hippies, and the student protesters, all pressing for far-reaching social change.

The social movements of this period were unique not only because they had mass-based social support but because they were sweeping in their aims. These movements challenged not only racial and gender arrangements or facets of our national domestic and foreign policy, but criticized the middle-class, individualistic, consumer oriented, suburban ideal that was becoming dominant. America in the 1960s seemed like a nation under siege. The assault was being carried out not by a foreign enemy, or even by an alien domestic element, but by the sons and daughters of the parents who, after living through the

1

Depression and war, felt that their current lives were just rewards for earlier sacrifices.

A major site of social conflict in the postwar years was sexuality. In the various youth centered movements, from the 1950s rock n'roll phenomenon through the counterculture and women's and gay movements in the late 1960s, sexual rebellion was central. Whether protest in this sphere took the form of the sexually provocative music and gesturing of Elvis Presley or Little Richard, the free love ideology of the hippies, the feminist struggle to legitimate clitoral orgasm, or the battle for homosexual rights by feminists and gay activists, these movements placed the battle over the body and desire at the heart of their social rebellion. Indeed, sexual struggles over, say, control of the body or erotic expression were often intertwined with other struggles for social justice. Thus, the feminist struggle for equal civil and social rights pivoted around women's right to control their bodies, which included the right to define their sexual pleasures. The antiwar protesters and counterculture frequently connected their social critique with demands for a more sexually open, expressive, eroticized society.

The social conflicts of the period, especially those around sexuality, were often described as generational. Youth were said to favor expanded choice, democracy and equality; they were viewed as advocates of sexual freedom and diversity. They were opposed by an older generation who, it was said, represented a parochial, tradition bound power elite. This older generation was often publicly depicted as defending a regime of sexual discipline and restraint. The major sexual conflict was then said to exist between the youthful supporters of freedom and their elders, who presumably rallied behind a repressive sexual ideology. The battle lines were often drawn in stark, oppositional ways: young versus old; human liberation versus repression. This way of framing sexual conflicts was indicative of the tendency of many Americans during these years to wrap social divisions in millennial meanings. The struggles for civil rights, gender equality, and sexual freedom took on the character of a grand battle over the soul and destiny of America.

The portrayal of the postwar sexual and social conflicts as a generational battle between the youthful forces of freedom and the elderly defenders of the status quo is terribly misleading. Struggles for sexual liberalization, for example, extend back generations. From the early decades of this century, sex liberals and radicals fought for sexual liberalization and the legitimation of the erotic aspects of sex.[1] The hundreds of sex manuals written by liberals through the midcentury, the experimentation with intimate lifestyles by bohemians in Greenwich Village well before the beatniks or hippies, and the "New

Woman" who struggled to integrate an assertive, eroticized sexuality into her image of femininity, suggest that the postwar generation was less an historic break than a continuation of the past.[2] Moreover, at the vanguard of the sexual liberation movements of the 1960s were often the elders of the youth. It would be hard to imagine the sexual liberation movements without, say, Hugh Hefner and *Playboy* in the 1950s, Alex Comfort and the many other sex advice writers who brought an open eroticized sexuality into the mainstream, sex radicals like Norman O. Brown and Herbert Marcuse who served as spiritual leaders to the New Left, and the entrepreneurs of pornography who created space for the public exhibition of sexuality that was to become so pivotal to mainstream cultural production in this period.[3] In other words, the generation that came of age in the 1940s and 1950s, against whom the generation of the 1960s rebelled, was divided on issues of sexual meaning and morality.

The illusion perpetrated by some intellectuals in the 1950s of America as a culturally unified nation may have been shattered by the events of the 1960s only to be replaced by another: that of an America embroiled in a wrenching generational conflict. Initially, the youthful propagandists for these movements simply ignored or censored division in their midst. It was assumed that if the young rebels supported, say, racial integration, through quotas or affirmative action measures, they would be defenders of equal rights for women or homosexual rights. The new social rebels were imagined by some of its apologists as well as critics to be a sort of united front for social change.

This myth of a new youthful "progressive" bloc was able to be fostered with some public credibility to the extent that such events as Vietnam and the Nixon presidency continued to divide America. By the mid-1970s, however, it became abundantly clear that a unified youth movement fighting for social justice was an illusion.[4] Separatism and interest group politics had become the guiding spirit of the new social movements. In part, this reflected the dynamics of identity formation and interest group politics in the United States. Yet this separatist strain also reflected the perception that progressive attitudes in one sphere did not necessarily extend to other areas. Thus, just as many women felt oppressed in the civil rights movement by black men who were in power, many lesbians and women of color felt alienated and disempowered in the white, middle-class, heterosexual-dominated women's movement. Moreover, as political agendas went beyond the struggle for civil rights there was less ideological consensus within these movements regarding a social vision and strategy of social change.

In the course of the 1970s and 1980s conflicts broke out within and between these new social movements. Divisions surfaced not only over political strategies and social agendas, but over such fundamentals as the goals of separatism versus integration and the question of whether the ethnic model of identity and community was empowering or restrictive. The very notion of building a community and politic around a common identity—e.g., as a lesbian, gay man, woman, or African-American—was challenged. For example, conflicts surfaced within the women's movement as feminists contested one another's constructions of womanhood or female identity as normative and political.[5] Many feminists, as well as lesbians and gay men, high-lighted the repressive, politically obstructive aspects of the ethnic/separatist model of identity and community as coalition building became a condition of preserving past gains and moving forward. A postmodern language of multiple identities and community affilia-tions cohering around a politics of the body and desire challenged the ethnic/separatist model.[6] Questioning identity politics went to the very core of the new social movements.

As differences within and between these movements surfaced, con-flicts intensified and spilled into the public arena. One prominent site of discord was sexuality. This was not new. For example, the issue of the sexual objectification of women in the civil rights movement and the New Left had already made sexuality a source of tension among movement activists. Similarly, the lesbian issue was an important point of contention in the women's movement from the very begin-ning. Some feminists preferred to see lesbianism as a personal issue, if not a psychological problem, while others argued that it is a social and political condition. In the late 1970s and 1980s a series of social conflicts around sex occurred within and sometimes across these so-cial communities. Most prominent, among these, was a far reaching discussion among feminists, focused less on the question of lesbianism than on broader issues of the nature of female desire and the relation between sexuality, gender and politics.[7] Underlying many of the con-flicts over lesbianism, pornography, S/M or eroticism among feminists were basic disagreements regarding the meaning of sexuality. Some feminists saw an ideology of sexual liberation as an integral part of their agenda of liberation, while others looked to articulate a female-centered sexual ideology.

Similar divisions surfaced in the gay male community.[8] Even prior to AIDS, we can observe a division among gay men over the role of sex in the formation of a gay identity and community and over the meaning of sex as a sphere of pleasure or intimacy. Some gay men argued that an adventurous, free wheeling concept of sex was integral to a gay identity and a liberationist agenda, others criticized this position as reductionist and even homophobic. This discussion over the meaning and role of sex in the gay community intensified with the emergence of the HIV/AIDS epidemic.

These conflicts that occurred over sexuality in the feminist, gay male and lesbian communities were not confined to them but often entered into the cultural mainstream. This was particularly true as these minority communities, their discourses and points of view, received broader public attention. For example, writers like Andrea Dworkin or Barbara Ehrenreich carried the sexual conflicts from the feminist community into broader social arenas.[9] A more striking example is that of the Mapplethorpe exhibition, which traveled across the country in 1990, carrying into mainstream American culture images of a nonconventional, expressive, guiltless sexuality that was a product of the gay male culture. The conflicts in these minority communities were mirrored in the broader youth culture. Surveys in the 1970s and 1980s show, in general, youth to be more liberal along a number of sexual dimensions, while still revealing divisions around premarital sex, sex outside a romantic intimate context, homosexuality, nonmonogamy, teenage sex, etc.[10] The notion of an America enmeshed in a generational conflict between united youthful forces of change and an equally unified older generation defending order is far too simplistic.

Although the sexual conflicts in postwar America do not neatly fold into a generational division, I believe that the new social movements gave to the existing sexual oppositions a heightened social importance as they were now sharpened, connected to broader social conflicts, and often imbued with national significance. As we observe the debates over abortion, divorce, pornography, teen sex, illegitimacy, homosexuality and AIDS in the 1980s, we can appreciate the extent to which sex now functions as a key site of national conflict in the United States.

Sexual conflicts in America occur in diverse settings (e.g., in the mass media, popular culture, medical and scientific institutions, legal and religious forums, urban streets and bars) and range over varied issues, from abortion to teen sex to homosexuality.[11] Yet at the heart of contemporary American sexual conflicts is, I believe, a struggle over two broadly conceived sexual ideologies. In the various movements for sexual liberalization and liberation, a libertarian sexual ideology is advanced. Sex is viewed as a positive, beneficial, joyous phenomenon. Its expression is connected to personal health, happiness, self fulfillment, and social progress. Sex is said to have multiple meanings; it can be justified as an act of self expression or pleasure, a sign of affection, love or a procreative act. Sexual expression is said to be legitimate in virtually all adult consensual social exchanges, although most libertarians place sex in a romantic, loving bond at the top of their value hierarchy.

Opposed to this libertarian sexual construction is what I call sexual romanticism. Romanticists may very well affirm the sensually pleasurable and expressive aspects of sex while simultaneously emphasizing its dangers—from sexual objectification and dehumanization to promoting relational instabilities, unwanted pregnancy, violence, and exploitation. Whereas the libertarian wishes to release sexual expression from social constraints in order to activate its beneficient powers, the romanticist counsels controlling and sublimating eros to receive its self-enhancing benefit. The romanticist believes that to harness the beneficial aspects of sex, eros must be connected to and kept intertwined with emotional, social and spiritual intimacies. The romanticist holds that sex should always be a way to show affection and love. It should exhibit tender, caring, loving qualities, or qualities that are always respectful of the other as a integrated, whole person. Erotic pleasure should be limited and connected to social and spiritual feelings so as not to reduce the other to a mere body or vessel of pleasure.

The conflict between these two sexual ideologies is at the core of many sexual and social struggles. For example, the conflict over pornography in the postwar years reflects, at one level, a basic division among Americans over the meaning and morality of sex. Libertarians may object to some of the gender images in pornography or to its excesses (e.g., violent images or the use of children and adolescents) but they defend pornography for what they take to be its healthy, playful, eroticized sexual expressions. By contrast, romanticists view pornography as essentially dehumanizing and degrading by virtue of its separating erotic pleasure and expression from intimate loving feelings and social bonds. Similarly, libertarians and romanticists typically are at odds over teen sex. Whereas the former would generally defend, at least in principle, sex between adolescents if it were consensual and responsible (e.g., involved contraceptives), the latter would likely oppose it on the grounds that adolescents lack the maturity to approach sex in an intimate committed relationship.

The gulf between libertarians and romanticists has been seemingly unbridgeable. As a result, sexual conflicts often are polarized and bitter. Libertarians see romanticists as conservative prudes; behind every limit placed on sexual expression, they see an erotophobic impulse. Libertarians describe the 1960s as a time of progress in which sex was supposedly liberated from the restrictive control of the moral

guardians of a repressive order. Sex was accepted as a sensual pleasure; eros moved out of the bedroom into the public arena, thereby
losing some of its repressive mystique; tolerance for nonconventional
sexual practices and lifestyles expanded. For many libertarians, the
late 1970s and 1980s is viewed as a time of reaction, even backlash.[12]
Sexual freedom and diversity are seen as under attack; eros is being
blamed for social ills from AIDS to divorce. The forces of order and
repression are said to be swelling as they have successfully linked, in
the public mind, sexual freedom and permissiveness to social disorder
and decline.

Romanticists contribute to sexual polarization no less than libertarians. They describe libertarians as agents of chaos and moral breakdown, comparing them to children whose egocentric hedonism must
be domesticated and hemmed in to prevent self-destruction and social
disorder. Although romanticists might defend the 1960s for eliminat-
ing hypocrisy, abolishing some outdated fears, and for expanding
tolerance, they believe that this period did as much harm as good.
Sexual liberalization, they argue, went too far. The ideology of tolerance has undermined standards or norms that allow us to criticize or
limit sexual expression. The 1960s is believed to have placed too much
emphasis on erotic pleasure; individuals were reduced to mere organs
and bodies. This humanistic ideal of sexual fulfillment ironically produced a trail of maladies from herpes and AIDS to violence towards
women and the carcasses of loving relationships that simply could
not live up to the expectations of sexual joy. A new tyranny of orgasmic
pleasure is said to now reign.[13] Romanticists argue that American's
today recognize the excesses and illusions of the 60s; we have rediscovered the value of connecting sex to intimacy. The current period is
said to represent a new maturity as individuals are taking responsibility for their lives; we are, it is said, approaching sex with more healthy,
balanced attitudes.

As we move into the 1990s, America is at an impasse. We are divided
on virtually every issue surrounding sexuality. Libertarians and romanticists project antithetical sexual constructions. Sexual conflicts
rooted in these contrasting ideologies almost invariably deteriorate
into bitter rhetorical and social battles. Sexual differences seem to
automatically escalate into sex wars. The forces of liberation or chaos,
depending upon your vantage point, stand against the forces of repression or civilized morality. Sexuality has become a battlefield where
opponents rally their troops against a demonized enemy. These skirmishes on the sexual front escalate as sexual and intimate affairs get
entangled with nonsexual interests and conflicts. As sexual issues like
pornography, homosexuality, S/M and casual sex are interpreted as

signs or symptoms of the social and moral state of America, sexual conflicts assume a heightened moral and political interest. A virtual surplus of meanings and affect surround sex. Emotion and political passion have come to dominate a sphere which is clearly in need of calmer and quieter voices. Sex itself is entangled in a web of dense meanings, feelings, and social and political agendas. It has become virtually impossible to navigate this terrain without being forced to quickly decide whether one is a friend of choice or order.

My hope is to begin to move us out of this morass. I wish to clear away some of the noise that veils these conflicts in confusion. Building on my previous work, I aim to provide a perspective on the present that can clarify some of the major dynamics and patterns of contemporary American intimate culture, while helping us to grasp current sexual conflicts. I will show that at the root of these conflicts are two sexual constructions. I aim to clarify the strengths and limits of each ideology and to move towards a sexual ethic that goes beyond the current polarization.

Overview of the book

The theme of this book is that at the root of the diverse conflicts over intimate culture in contemporary America are two different constructions of sexual meaning and morality. I do not wish, of course, to reduce sexual conflicts to an ideational struggle. Ideas are personally and socially charged only to the extent that they are driven by affect and interest. For example, conflicts over the meaning and social role of homosexuality are emotionally and socially charged because the issue of homosexuality is connected to concerns of gender identity, familial and cultural order, and struggles between strata for social and political power. Conflicts over teen sex are similarly inseparable from issues of social control, family dynamics, considerations relating to pregnancy, abortion, economic growth, welfare, and so on. Yet these ideational struggles cannot be reduced to a mere battle over "material" interests. Individuals give meaning and purpose to their lives by drawing on publicly available values and beliefs. These meanings need to be analyzed in themselves because they orient and structure actions and conflicts.[14]

My aim is, at one level, to sketch out the social context of contemporary cultural conflicts over sexuality and intimate life in the United States. I intend to examine these conflicts not only as a social analyst interested in describing current affairs, but also as a participant in the ongoing public conversation about the meaning and proper role of sex in contemporary America. Hence, I intend to engage the current arguments over sexual ethics in America for the purpose of shaping their outcome.[15] This is the broad impulse of the book. I turn now to a brief resume of each chapter.

In chapter 1, I offer an historical perspective on the intimate culture of the post-World War II United States. The contemporary intimate culture emerged from the breakdown of Victorian intimate conventions. In response to the perceived crisis of intimate life in the early decades of the twentieth century, many Americans, especially the liberal wing of the new middle classes, campaigned for change. Broad changes in the patterns of twentieth-century American sexual culture occurred, in part as a product of liberal reformers' actions. In particular, I trace a process of the eroticization of sex. This relates to the legitimation of sex for its erotic—sensually pleasurable—qualities. In the early decades of this century, eroticism was legitimated as a medium of romantic love and later, in the postWorld War II years, as a vehicle of self expression and pleasure. This emerging culture of eroticism could not have occurred had there not transpired a process of sexual liberalization, revolving around the notion that sex is less a matter of strict public regulation than a right of individual choice. By the postwar years, the dominant discourses and representations projected a concept of sexuality as essentially a beneficial, joyful phenomenon that promotes self-fulfillment and the formation of social bonds. In short, in their struggle against Victorian elites, a strata of the new middle class—often assuming a liberal guise but at times appearing in a more radical version—helped to forge an intimate culture whose class ambitions, interest and hopes were often expressed in a concept of sexuality that carried strong resonances of personal salvation and self-fulfillment.

In chapter 2, I argue that by the mid-1970s we can observe a growing public discontent over the evolution of American intimate culture. The anticipation of sexual freedom and fulfillment that accompanied the evolving culture of eroticism had diminished. Indeed, far from ushering in a new era of freedom and fulfillment, the "sexual revolution" was held responsible for eroding intimate bonds, producing new performance anxieties, and promoting both sexual objectification and violence. AIDS, herpes, escalating rates of divorce, illegitimacy and teen pregnancy, loneliness, violence against women, child abuse and abandoned children were said to be the real and bitter fruit of our revolution in sexual conventions.

This critical reassessment of American intimate life should not be thought of as a backlash to a historical trajectory of social progress. This latter view, advocated by many liberals and leftists, presupposes the validity of their own concept of sexuality and ideals of sexual freedom. This, however, is exactly what is being challenged. Instead of framing current divisions as between the forces of sexual freedom and the forces of repression or, from the alternative vantage point, as between the forces of chaos and those of moral order, I suggest that we describe the current conflict as between two different sexual ideologies.

There is, moreover, a great deal of heterogeneity among critics of current sexual mores. Although conservatives have achieved a prominence in these public debates, equally cogent criticisms of American sexual culture can be heard from liberals (e.g., George Leonard and Willard Gaylin), leftists (e.g., Christopher Lasch), and feminists (e.g., Jean Bethke Elshtain and Andrea Dworkin). Despite disagreements on many particulars, these critics agree in opposing the trend towards highlighting the erotic aspects of sexual intimacy and permitting the separation of sex from intimate social bonds. They have rallied behind some version of a romantic sexual ideology. This chapter reviews the various efforts to rethink the meaning and social role of sex.

In Part Two my focus shifts somewhat from a principally sociological angle to a moral one. My primary interest is the critical analysis of moral arguments about sexual norms and practices. My site for moral engagement are the sex debates within feminism and the gay male community that have occurred from the late 1970s through the 1980s. This choice was not arbitrary. I believe that it is in these two settings that the debate over sexual ethics has proceeded in its most centered and elaborate form. For both of these groups, questions of sexual meaning and morality have been at the core of their construction of identity and community, as well as their political agendas. Moreover, in these communities we can observe the rise of critiques of a sexual liberationist ideology, as well as their defense. To the extent, finally, that the debate over sexual ethics among feminists and among gays divides between libertarians and romanticists, these two sites of debate are especially well suited to pursuing my moral inquiry.

Chapter 3 engages the feminist sexuality debates that have been pivotal to the women's movement, especially since the late 1970s. I argue that second-wave feminism developed ambivalent perspectives on contemporary sexual trends. One strain of the women's movement welcomed the trend toward sexual liberalization and eroticization, indeed celebrated sexual choice, pleasure and diversity, even if it was often wary of such tendencies being controlled and shaped from a male-centered standpoint. There was, however, a critical reaction on the part of some feminists, especially radical feminists, to emerging libertarian, hedonistic-expressive constructions of sex. They often described the "sexual revolution" as a movement by and for men, believing that the ideology of sexual liberation masked a conservative, even backlash, gender politic. By the late 1970s, these radical feminists grounded their critique of American sexual culture in an often essentialist notion of unique female-centered sexual values. This gynocentric sexual ethic was typically tied to a lesbian separatist political agenda. As this radical feminist perspective achieved prominence in the women's movement, many feminists began to react critically, some arguing that it did not describe their experience or values. These women took issue with the attempt to tie gynocentric sexual values to a feminist gender politic; they argued that this sexual construction reinforced conservative sexual trends. By the early 1980s, the minor skirmishes between radical feminists and their critics had escalated into a virtual sex war. I try to show that, notwithstanding the gender politics that inform these battles, the conflict is, at bottom, between romanticists and libertarians. I outline these respective moral positions in the course of reviewing the debates over pornography and S/M. I identify the strengths and limits of the two ethical standpoints, as part of my aim to push beyond this division.

In chapter 4, my attention shifts to the contemporary gay male community. I explore the topic of moral boundaries. What principles or standards do we invoke to limit forms of sexual expression, identity and community? The debate over homosexuality provides a useful site to examine the beliefs and normative standards Americans rely upon to circumscribe sexual expression. The centerpiece of this chapter is a section on AIDS. The HIV epidemic has heightened Americans' feelings about sexuality, and especially about homosexuality. In AIDS discourses, various moral standpoints make their appearance in unusually sharp ways. I try to sketch the wide range of moral positions Americans hold with respect to homosexuality as exhibited in the AIDS phenomenon. Positions vary from an exclusion of homosexuality from the realm of moral acceptability by appealing to absolutist rationales (e.g., nature, God, mental health) to constructions that legitimate homosexuality but only if it mirrors middle-class conventional romantic norms. Finally, I describe a variety of discourses that legitimate homosexuality, either by appealing to equally absolutist rationales (e.g., that it is natural, normal, healthy or sanctioned by God) or to a libertarian ideology. I claim, moreover, that the debate over homosexuality and sexual ethics that occurs within the gay male subculture reveals sharp divisions over the meaning and morality of sex and the social role of homosexuality. The discussion concludes by returning, once again, to the broad division between romanticists and libertarians—a division as sharp in this community as in the broader mainstream.

Chapter 5 brings into focus the moral considerations of this book. The discussions of chapters 1 through 4 lead to the conclusion that the major—though certainly not the only—division today is between the romantic and libertarian sexual ideologies. After sketching the strengths and limits of these two sexual ethics, I propose a way out of the current impasse. I criticize romanticists for limiting choice and diversity too much—without a compelling rationale. The essentialism of the romanticists is challenged, as is its residual "morality of the sex act." I wish to preserve libertarians' strong defense of choice and diversity—to preserve their concept of sex as having multiple meanings and legitimate social occasions. Yet, the minimalistic ethic of libertarians, an ethic that employs mutual consent as the only basis to limit sexual expression, is, I contend, sociologically naive and cannot afford us a sufficiently discriminating critical vantage point. I draw, in this regard, from the compelling argument of the romanticists that a sexual ethic ought to take account of the qualitative aspects of a sexual and social exchange for reasons relating to personal and social well being, as well as considerations of power and social inequities. As I see the current debate, the issue for sexual ethics is the following: the preservation of the expansive notion of sexual choice, diversity and pleasure contained in the libertarian ethic, while retaining multi-dimensional standards that allow us to offer social and personal criticisms of intimate life. I argue that the charge for developing a sexual ethic is not that of discovering some moral imperative or universal rationale. Rather it is a matter of articulating broad guidelines that draw on existing cultural traditions for their resonance and credibility. I offer a pragmatic ethic that revolves around the concept of sexual and social responsibility as a bridge concept between libertarians and romanticists. I try to articulate this concept so that it can provide at least one broad normative standard that can guide us in weighing issues of self-interest and social consequence.

Notes

1. Cf. Christina Simmons, "Marriage in the Modern Manner: Sexual Radicalism and Reform in America, 1914–1941," (Ph.D. Diss., Brown University, 1982); Gerald Marrimer, "The Estrangement of the Intellectual in America: The Search for New Life Styles in the Early Twentieth Century," (Ph.D. Diss.,

University of Colorado, 1972); John D'Emilio and Estelle Freedman, *Intimate Matters* (New York: Harper & Row, 1988); John Burnham, "The Progressive Era Revolution in American Attiudes Toward Sex," *Journal of American History* 59 (March 1973).

2. Seidman, *Romantic Longings*, chaps. 3 & 4; Also, Barbara Epstein, "Family, Sexual Morality and Popular Movements in Turn-of-the-Century America," in *Powers of Desire* ed. Ann Snitow et al. (New York: Monthly Review Press, 1983); Simmons, "Marriage in the Modern Manner"; Ellen Kay Trimberger, "Feminism, Men and Modern Love: Greenwich Village, 1900–1925," in *Powers of Desire*; Carroll Smith-Rosenberg, *Disorderly Conduct* (New York: Alfred A. Knopf, 1985).

3. See chapter 1.

4. See, for example, Sara Evans, *Personal Politics* (New York: Knopf, 1979) and *Born For Liberty* (New York: Free Press, 1989).

5. See, for example, Alice Echols, *Daring to be Bad* (Minneapolis: University of Minnesota Press, 1990) Currently, the chief site of the feminist conflict over gender is the debate over postmodernism. Many of the best essays in this debate are collected in *Feminism/Postmodernism*, ed. Linda Nicholson (New York: Routledge, 1990). In addition, see "Politics/Power/Culture: Postmodernity and Feminist Political Theory," *Differences*, eds. Kathy Ferguson and Kristie McClure 3 (Spring 1991).

6. See, for example, Jeffrey Weeks, *Sexuality and Its Discontents* (London: Routledge, 1985). Judith Butler, *Gender Trouble* (New York: Routledge, 1990); Shane Phelan, *Identity Politics* (Philadelphia: Temple University Press, 1989. For an overview of the discussion of identity politics, postmodernism and gay/lesbian theory, see Steven Seidman, "Postmodernism/Gay Theory: Towards a Politics of Desire," *Social Text* (forthcoming).

7. See chap. 3.

8. See chap. 4.

9. Barbara Ehrenreich, Elizabeth Hess and Gloria Jacobs, *Re-Making Love* (New York: Doubleday, 1986); Andrea Dworkin, *Intercourse* (New York: The Free Press, 1989).

10. For example, Morton Hunt, *Sexual Behavior in the 70s* (New York: Dell, 1974); Linda Wolfe, *The Cosmo Report* (New York: Arbor House, 1981); Carol Tauris and Susan Sadd. *Redbook Report on Female Sexuality* (New York: Delacorte, 1977).

11. For a theorization of sexual conflicts, see Gayle Rubin, "Thinking Sex: Notes for a Radical Theory of the Politics of Sex," in *Pleasure and Danger*, ed. Carole Vance (London: Routledge, 1984).

12. For example, Lawrence Birken, "The Sexual Counterrevolution: A Critique of Cultural Conservatism," *Social Research* 53 (Spring 1986); Richard Goldstein, "The New Sobriety," *The Village Voice*, Dec. 30, 1986; Scott Tucker, "The Counterrevolution," *Gay Community News*, Feb. 21, 1981; Larry Bush

and Richard Goldstein, "The Anti-Gay Backlash," *The Village Voice*, April 8–14, 1981; Pat Califia, "The New Puritans," *The Advocate*, April 17, 1980 and "Feminism vs. Sex: A New Conservative Wave?" *The Advocate*, Feb. 21, 1980.

13. For example, Willard Gaylin, *Rediscovering Love* (New York: Viking, 1986); George Leonard, *The End of Sex* (New York: Bantam, 1983); George Hendin, *The Age of Sensation* (New York: McGraw-Hill, 1975); Jason Epstein, *Divorce in America* (New York: E.R. Dutton, 1974); Christopher Lasch, *The Culture of Narcissism* (New York: W.W. Norton & Co., 1979).

14. For one overview of various statements on cultural analysis, see *Culture and Society*, eds. Jeffrey Alexander and Steven Seidman (Cambridge: Cambridge University Press, 1990).

15. In a series of essays, I have articulated a concept of postmodern social inquiry that informs this book. See "The End of Sociological Theory: The Postmodern Hope," *Sociological Theory* 8 (Fall 1991), "Postmodern Anxieties: The Politics of Epistemology," *Sociological Theory* 8 (Fall 1991) and "Postmodern Theory as Social Narrative with a Moral Intent," in *Postmodernism and Social Theory*, eds. Steven Seidman and David Wagner. (New York: Basil Blackwell, 1991).

Part One
SEXUAL POLITICS

1

Great Expectations:
The Quest For Sexual Fulfillment
in Twentieth-Century America

In the aftermath of the rise and fall of fascism, many Americans were exulted by the Allied victory. Interpreted through the prism of the American civil religion, our victorious role in this worldwide conflict seemed to many like a clear affirmation of America's divinely chosen status.[1] Through American intervention freedom and democracy would, it was hoped, prevail in the world. The moral superiority of the American way of life was thought to have been proven. Nationalism ran high in the United States.

The great national pride Americans felt after the war at times folded into conservative domestic attitudes. The massive loss of life and social disruption wrought by the war pressed many Americans to focus on putting their personal lives in order. Appeals to "the American way of life" were used to promote restrictive norms and ideals of personal and social life. A certain social intolerance set in that was further fueled by the emergence of a Soviet empire. Thus, women were encouraged, indeed pressured, to leave the paid workforce in order to return to their "primary" roles as wives and mothers. An idealized domestic life with women as its chief managers was promoted in advertisements and popular culture.[2] Many Americans in the 1950s were longing for a simple orderly world founded upon a consensus of basic social values that revolved around anti-communism, the free market, individualism, the value of marriage, the family, career success, and domestic tranquility.

While many Americans in the 1950s felt a need to turn inwards and a longing for social calm, there were many whose impulses strained in other directions. The war had, in fact, shaken up social conventions and encouraged individuals to evolve new social norms and codes of behavior. For example, many women had been forced to work for wages or to live alone for an extended period of time. They experienced themselves as competent in the labor force and independent.[3] People of color had fought alongside whites often experiencing degrees of equality absent in civilian life. They were not about to quietly accede to domestic conditions that denied them basic rights and opportunities. The war had taught them that tyranny in all forms should be fought—including the tyranny of a system of racial segregation and social disempowerment.[4] Similarly, homosexually inclined persons had found in the war years a time of relaxed social norms that encouraged them to experience same-sex intimacies. The military mobilization concentrated individuals in same-sex environments that were often tolerant of sexual experimentation. These years witnessed the formation of homosexual networks which in the late 1950s and 1960s evolved into elaborate homosexual subcultures.[5] Many homosexuals in the 1950s would no longer accept a life of marginality and social invisibility. In a word, the war years allowed many individuals to step outside conventional identities, roles and relationships to experience themselves in different social roles. For many of these individuals the social pressure to return to prewar social conventions was felt to be burdensome and restrictive. The 1950s witnessed a conflict between the inward, conservative cultural strains and a more innovative, change-oriented ethos.[6]

While this cultural tension was evident in the United States throughout the 1950s, it was not until the subsequent decades that these tensions erupted into a national struggle over the soul of America.[7] In the 1960s, a series of mass-based social movements materialized that challenged America to go forward. Yet, these movements had their immediate roots in the 1950s. Before the sit-ins and Freedom Rides of the 1960s, there was the Brown v. Board of Education decision prompted by the NAACP, the Montgomery bus boycotts of the late 1950s, the evolution of black organizations, and the emergence of leaders who subsequently achieved national prominence. Although the lead organizations of the women's movement were products of the 1960s, it was the cultural contradictions and discontents of the 1950s that generated much of the movement's initial drive. Many of the pioneering feminists, women such as Betty Friedan, Gloria Steinem and Susan Brownmiller, came of age in the 1950s. Similarly, while gay liberation emerged in the 1960s, the first homosexual rights organizations in the United States were created in the 1950s. The image of the 1950s as a conservative period is no more apt in the case of the American sexual culture.

This period laid the groundwork for many of the changes in American sexual mores and behavior in the 1960s. While the 1950s may lead us to recall the sexually innocent image of Ricky Nelson, Bobby Darin or Wally Cleaver, it also produced the provocative erotic styles of James Dean, Marlon Brando, Elvis Presley, Little Richard, and Jerry Lee Lewis. Unlike Paul Anka, who may have been celebrated for his "wholesome" image, Elvis Presley was celebrated in youth culture for his exuberant wild sexuality. The 1950s witnessed the liberalization of obscenity laws, as well as laws regulating the distribution of birth control information and devices. The conventional marriage-oriented culture, with its cult of virginity and monogamy, was under assault by a Beat culture that embraced sexual experimentation and a playful, adventurous, free-wheeling sort of sexuality. Let us not forget that *Playboy*, which represented a frontal attack on conventional intimate culture, was launched in the 1950s. It would be hard to imagine the counterculture and much of the youth culture of the 1960s and 1970s without the Beats and the *Playboy* libertarian ideology. Similarly, when liberal sex reformers in the 1960s and 1970s wrote sex manuals that stirred public passions, they were building upon the work of 1950s reformers such as Alex Comfort, Eustare Chesser and Hannah and Abraham Stone. Not only were the social conditions that spawned sexual liberation movements created in the 1950s, but the ideology of sexual purity and restraint was already under attack by liberal reformers, sex radicals, and segments of the youth culture.

It was, however, in the 1960s that the public began to describe contemporary America as undergoing a sexual revolution. No doubt, the general turmoil produced by the black, women's and gay movements, the New Left and hippies, along with the attention the media gave to the personal lifestyles of rock musicians and public countercultural figures like Ginsberg and Timothy Leary, encouraged people to think that our beliefs and values regarding sexuality were changing in a revolutionary way. Headlines in the major national newspapers and magazines announced a coming sexual revolution initiated by our youth.[8] Liberal reformers and sex radicals triumphantly declared a sexual revolution-in-process and projected themselves as its vanguard. Reporters like Gay Talese traveled across the states chronicling the liberation of the libido in middle America. Movies like *Easy Rider* or *I am Curious Yellow*, plays such as *Hair* or *Oh! Calcutta!* seemed to dramatize a movement to release eros from its repressive constraints. Academics wrote books and held conferences debating the meaning and reality of the sexual revolution, thus giving a kind of credibility to the concept. For the doubters and detractors, people had only to appeal to certain obvious facts—pornography in the local market, the Pill, higher divorce rates, unmarried men and women sleeping together, homosexuals coming out everywhere, billboards selling you anything you could think of with the aid of sexual imagery, massage parlors and sex shops proliferating in suburbs and cities alike. Didn't all this add up to a sexual revolution?

From the vantage point of the 1990s, it is difficult to defend the claim that the United States underwent a sexual revolution between 1950 and 1975. The notion that postwar America experienced an epochal shift from a repressive to a liberated sexual culture is much too simplistic and overdrawn to accept. This Whiggish view of history has been seriously questioned by the new historians of sexuality, who have uncovered in the prewar period a sexual regime that was neither repressive nor ascetic.[9] Moreover, scholars have found in the postwar liberationist ideology new forms of constraint tied to the notion of sex as self-defining and self-fulfilling.[10]

Even more narrow concepts of sexual revolution, suggested by contemporary sociologists and sex researchers, seem less convincing today. For example, many researchers proposed that the real sexual revolution involved the decline of the double standard and a leap towards egalitarianism in sexual attitudes and behavior between the two genders.[11] There is no question that important changes in public representations of female sexuality and in women's practices did occur. For example, women are now typically viewed as sexual beings who are sensually motivated as well as equipped to satisfy these desires; their rates of premarital sex and extramarital sex are almost equivalent to that of men. Summarizing the available data on premarital sex, Paul Gebhard of the Kinsey Institute remarks:

> The Kinsey data reveal that 8 percent of the females born before 1900 had premarital coitus by age 20 . . . and this percentage gradually rose until among women born between 1910–19 some 23 percent had had premarital coitus by age 20. . . . Our own 1967 college study showed that at that date 33 percent of the unmarried college females were no longer virgins by age 20. The slightly later *Psychology Today* survey reported 78 percent of their female readers had had premarital coitus. . . . Figures for males are higher than those for females, but the differences are decreasing with each generation. Ultimately, we shall arrive at the point now reached in Sweden where roughly 95 percent of both males and females have experienced coitus before marriage.[12]

Gebhard goes on to say that these changes began in the early decades of the twentieth century, indeed, many of the most dramatic changes in this regard occurred before World War II. Contemporary feminists have raised doubts about this alleged egalitarian trend, however, as they have disclosed a hitherto hidden reality of rape, assaults on women and wife-beating, as well as continued inequalities with respect to which gender plays the active, initiating and directing role.[13] Many feminists would argue—a point we will return to in chapter 3—that the really significant trend in the postwar period has been a heightened awareness of the continued differences and inequities in the area of sexuality between the two genders. Some radical feminists argue that the history of American sexual mores and behavior is not one of simple progress from a regime of restriction to expression, but a history of struggles between men and women to control women's sexuality, and to define and regulate their bodies and desires.[14] Progress in sexual culture would signify for many feminists the ability of women to define and regulate their own sexuality, which presupposes significant changes in gender identities, roles and relationships.

A sexual revolution did not occur in post-World War II America. The language of sexual revolution must not be taken at face value. Rather than interpret the claim of a sexual revolution as a descriptive statement, we should take it as symbolic. Employing the language of sexual revolution was a strategic action. At one level, it was a rhetorical strategy used by reformers and rebels to mobilize support for their social agenda. By appealing to the fact of a sexual revolution-in-process ushering in an era of freedom, sexual liberationists could claim history to be on their side. To stand for sexual revolution was to stand for social progress and freedom. In a context where social rebellion was tied to millenial hopes of a new order of peace and freedom, the announcement of a coming sexual revolution had great appeal for social rebels. Morever, a sexual revolution-in-process was a powerful symbol of generational rebellion, as it was the youth who most enthusiastically embraced the cause. While the language of sexual revolution may have been intended to elicit fear on the part of the defenders of the social status quo, the opponents of these sexual rebels used this same rhetorical trope to rally their troops. For them, the imagery of a sexual revolution evoked anticipations of libidinal chaos, the breakdown of family and moral order, and national crisis and social decline. They deployed the rhetoric of sexual revolution to mobilize resistance to sexual and social rebels. The language of sexual revolution is important for its symbolic and strategic meanings, not as a descriptive or explanatory account of what actually happened in the postwar years.

Important changes did occur in the post-World War II period. The rate of premarital sex, especially coitus, among women, increased significantly; surveys document an expansion of sexual experimentation with regard to sex techniques; pornography and explicit sexual images spread more rapidly into the public realm; women demanded a more female-centered sexuality, and homosexuals struggled to move from the margins into the mainstream. These are significant changes, but virtually all of them were clearly visible in the early decades of the twentieth century. If we wish to talk of a sexual revolution, we must speak of a century-long event or date it as beginning in the pre-World War I period.[15] But even this conception carries serious difficulties. Many twentieth century trends are continuous with normative and behavioral patterns in Victorian America. There has, in fact, been little change with regard to the persistence of a heterosexual, marital norm, the binding of sex to marriage, the emphasis upon coitus, the legitimation of sex for its procreative aspects, and so on. Does a mere quantitative increase in premarital coitus or an expansion of sexual technique amount to a revolutionary change? Does the penetration of explicit sexual imagery into the outer edges of the mainstream amount to a sexual revolution?

My own view is that it is more useful to describe these trends as entailing a process of sexual liberalization, not revolution.[16] What occurred, in part, in the twentieth century was the expansion of sexual choice and diversity. We need to understand this dynamic, though, in relation to changes in the very meaning of sex. The series of changes that occurred between roughly the nineteenth and twentieth centuries were not only of certain behavorial patterns (e.g., premarital sex, frequency of coitus, and orgasm), but changes in the meaning of sex and its role in personal and public life. Instead of thinking of sexuality as an essentially natural, fixed phenomenon whose dynamics vary only to the degree that social controls are severe or relaxed, it may be more useful to think of sex as something whose nature—form, meaning, social role—varies socially and historically.[17] For example, to describe changes in the status of same-sex desire and intimacy between, say, 1830 and 1960 as a trend towards the social acceptance of homosexuals would be historically incoherent. As many historians have documented, what was meant in the 1960s by homosexual is not what typically was understood in the Victorian period by same-sex sexual behavior.[18] In the twentieth century, homosexuality became a primary self-identity; in the 1970s, to the extent that homosexuality was transfigured into being gay or lesbian, it accquired a much more social and political meaning.[19] My point is that sex changes not only in its quantitative aspects but in its qualitative-meaningful dimensions as well.

Between the nineteenth and twentieth centuries, some key changes occurred in the meanings many Americans attached to sex. In at least middle-class Victorian culture, sexuality was already viewed as a powerful instinct.[20] The sexual instinct could determine the physical, moral and mental health of the individual and society. Its abuse or misuse could have ruinuous consequences—ranging from serious health problems and career failure to the spread of crime, vice, and national decline. To harness its benevolent powers, the Victorians thought it necessary to control and channel sexuality in the right direction. Most essentially, its erotic aspects needed to be sublimated into spiritual, moral or social projects in order for the individual to avoid its ruinuous effects and benefit from its self-enriching qualities. By the early decades of the twentieth century, sex was seen less as a tightly compartmentalized, discrete instinct than a sort of diffuse energy that saturates all feelings, motivations, desires, wishes, and acts. It was an unconscious power infecting everything individuals thought, felt or did. Moreover, the benevolent, life-enhancing qualities of sex were seen to lie not in sublimation of its carnal aspects, but in their expression and enhancement. The release of the carnal powers of sexuality was like an elixir, bringing health, fulfillment, happiness, love, and success. The twentieth century witnessed the legitimation of the erotic aspects of sex. Sex was legitimated by its sensually pleasurable and expressive qualities.

I propose the concepts of "liberalization" and "eroticization" to organize my historical sketch of the formation of contemporary American sexual culture. I am not saying that only the twentieth-century United States can be described in these terms. These terms could perhaps be applied to Victorian America and before. Nevertheless, I believe that the twentieth century, especially the postwar years, has seen a clear trend towards intensifying these liberalizing and eroticizing processes. Indeed, by the 1960s these processes were no longer confined to marginal groups or particular locales, but were societal-wide and had achieved more or less full public acceptance. This social and sexual environment made possible the appearance of sex radical movements. This historic juncture produced important public debates about sexuality, and especially sexual ethics, that we will review. The intensification of these liberalizing and eroticizing processes in the postwar years, along with the movements for radicalization and the discourses of sexual politics and ethics they engendered, is, I believe, historically unique. Before we turn to a discussion of these two concepts, I want to sketch what I take to be a critical juncture in the development of twentieth-century intimate culture.

The Crisis of Victorian Intimate Culture & the Modern Response

White middle-class nineteenth-century intimate culture, the configuration that commonly goes under the rubric of Victorianism, was not sex-negative or sqeamish about sex. As Foucault, among others, has argued, the Victorians produced volumes of discourses on sexuality; they named, classified, and explained every possible feature and manifestation of what they called human sexuality.[21] Historians have uncovered, moreover, in both public and private documents, an intimate culture that frankly thought about sex, and was sexually expressive.[22] Indeed, the evidence suggests that while the fertility rate diminished significantly throughout the nineteenth century, sexual activity did not—suggesting that sex had acquired an expressive or nonprocreative meaning.

My own view is that the chief tensions of Victorian intimate culture revolved around two conflicting beliefs. Many Victorians held that sexuality is an enormously powerful, life-giving-and-enhancing force that must be expressed. Yet, they were equally convinced that sexual expression automatically elicits lust, which carries serious personal and social dangers.[23] The Victorians responded to this dilemma by organizing an intimate culture that attempted to control and spiritualize lust or sublimate it into productive social projects. Sexual expression was legitimated only within a heterosexual, coitus-centered, marital norm. As the campaigns against masturbation and the moral reform efforts to spiritualize sex and marriage indicate, Victorian intimate culture sought to affirm sex expression while purging it of its carnal aspects. Ironically, it is likely that this sexual regime contributed to stimulating the very carnal desires it sought to control.

By the late nineteenth century the failure of this regime was evident. Sensuality was not so much extinguished or sublimated as it was split off from legitimate heterosexual marriage. A separate sexual underworld was created which threatened the very intimate ideal that the control of lust was supposed to protect.[24] As the proliferation of pornography, prostitution,and sexual disease occurred in a context of significant social change, this occasioned a public perception of a crisis of intimate culture.[25]

Between roughly the 1870s and the 1920s, two social responses can be observed to this perceived crisis. The first response tried to preserve the Victorian intimate ideal by purifying the social and moral environment.[26] This strategy promoted a politics of sexual restriction. It sought to limit sexual choice by severely circumscribing the socially available opportunities for sexual expression and by stigmatizing nonconventional sexual expression. The state was called to take the lead in the fight against obscenity, birth control, divorce, and prostitution. This signaled a change in sexual politics. Throughout most of the nineteenth century, explicit sexual imagery and birth control, including abortion, was not subject to strict governmental regulation.[27] Divorce laws, for example, were quite liberal, although divorce was fairly uncommon.[28] Similarly, birth control information was easily accessible in popular medical and advice literature, advertisements and through both regular and nonregular physicians.

This began to change dramatically by the late nineteenth century. The Comstock laws outlined a broad concept of obscenity that gave the state wide latitude in censoring public expression. It also prohibited the production and distribution of birth control information, even by licensed physicians. Vice commissions cropped up in many cities across the country to fight prostitution and obscenity. Restrictive divorce legislation was passed in numerous states. For example, South Carolina banned divorce; other states permitted divorce only in cases of adultery. Coupled to these efforts to cleanse the environment of corrupting elements and restrict choice were efforts to enlist the state and church to assume the role of moral guardian, especially with regard to sexual regulation. Social hygiene and purity groups thought that as urban migration expanded sexual opportunities, the state should assume more responsibility for regulating intimate life. Private religious agencies like churches, the YMCA, and various moral reform groups were expected to assist the state by educating individuals in the high ideals of Victorian culture.

By at least post-World War I, the campaign to enlist the state and church in a restrictive sexual politic was widely perceived as unsuccessful. Divorce rates continued to climb in each decade; survey after survey reported that contraceptive use was almost universally practiced; a birth control movement with considerable social support challenged the restrictive politics of sexual control; there was no let-up in the availability of obscene materials, despite its confiscation by vice squads; perhaps the biggest success of these purity groups was in the case of the control of prostitution. Red light districts were purged from many cities. Yet, the implications of this campaign were complicated for Victorian intimate norms. It suggested that sensuality must be sublimated and extinguished, or incorporated into the culture of love, romance, and marriage. The former seemed unlikely, given social trends; the latter suggested a sexualization of love and marriage quite alien to the Victorians and, indeed, pointed to the birth of a culture of eroticism that Victorians could only react to with horror.

By the 1920s, the question of the success of a restrictive sexual politics was, perhaps, irrelevant, since Americans were less and less hospitable to it. The United States was now a fully urban industrial bureaucratic society. Although the politics of sexual restriction resurfaced after World War I, its effect has been socially marginal.[29] Even in the restrictive strains of the 1950s, organizations like the League of Decency had little social support.

There was a second, alternative response to the crisis of Victorian intimate culture. Instead of trying to purge the social environment of suspect opportunities and practices in order to preserve a Victorian intimate ideal, a reformation of our intimate culture was proposed.

Beginning in the late nineteenth century, and especially prominent by the 1920s and after, reformers argued that the problems of our intimate culture lie with Victorian ideals and conventions.[30] Victorianism itself was held responsible for America's sexual anomie and malaise. At times, this critical reassessment turned into an assault on Victorianism that exaggerated its dangers; this is one source of the myth of the repressed Victorian.

These self-styled modern reformers attacked the effort by the heirs to Victorianism to separate the sensual aspects of sex from its social and spiritual dimensions. They enjoined their contemporaries to reject the Victorian notion of the evils of sensuality; they urged that sensuality could be enlisted to promote not only the health and success of the individual, but the enrichment of romantic love and marriage. By transfiguring sensuality into a self-enhancing, socially productive, benevolent power, these modern reformers contributed to the birth of a culture of eroticism.[31] By that I mean a culture that legitimates the production of sensual pleasures and therefore encourages the concentration on the body, desire, sex acts, and technique. Furthermore, these reformers attacked the effort to enlist the state bureaucratic apparatus to purify the environment of its so-called undesirable aspects. This restrictive sexual politic, they argued, only contributed to producing vice such as prostitution, homosexuality, and sexual disease. They recommended relaxing state and social controls or liberalizing America's intimate culture.

Underlying the modern reform agenda was a shift in the meaning of sex and intimacy. The Victorian emphasis upon the dangers of eroticism had given way to its affirmation. A restrictive politic centered around control, sublimation and the spiritualizing of eroticism passed into a sexual code emphasizing individual choice and the production of sensual pleasures, although the essentially heterosexual, marital, familial ideal remained dominant. More generally, the movement of sex and eroticism into the center of intimacy signaled a broader change in intimate values and ideals. Although a companionate ideal was evident in educated, white middle-class Victorian culture, love and intimacy leaned heavily on a system of mutual obligations, role expectations, and social and economic interdependencies. It is only in the late nineteenth century that the notion first appears

that individuals should look to love and intimacy for personal fulfillment and happiness—because it promotes their self-development and
happiness, not because it is socially or economically necessary, or
expected because of familial or social obligations. As love and intimacy were framed as a realm of personal choice and happiness, sex
could be explored for its self-fulfilling and bonding capacities.[32]

The crisis of Victorian intimate culture was met with two public
responses. The first was a restrictive sexual politic which sought to
preserve a Victorian ideal by controlling the social environment. Ultimately, this ideal was forced to adapt to changing social circumstances. Nevertheless, artifacts of this sexual politic persist to this
day. The second response sought to alter the intimate ideal both
because of its inherently undesirable features and because changing
social conditions required cultural accommodation. I have described
this proposal for change under the dual concepts of eroticization and
liberalization. Although the reformers were a heterogeneous group
differing along a number of dimensions, they supported the agenda I
have suggested above and will elaborate upon below. Moreover, they
were, in the main, reformers, not revolutionaries. They advocated
changes in order to protect and strengthen a basically heterosexual
marital and familial norm. Nevertheless, I argue that the defense of
eroticism and liberalism, even by reformers who wished to avoid
intense social conflict and substantial change, gave a certain legitimacy to sex rebels who wished to promote their own radical sexual
politic. Much of the discussion between the 1960s and 1980s has
moved between the effort of sex rebels, to radicalize the project of
sexual reform, liberals, to defend choice and eroticism but avoid radicalization, and conservatives, who sought to discredit eroticism and
liberalism by pointing to its excesses and troubling aspects. Before
we can review this discussion, we need to complete this sketch by
elaborating on the concepts of eroticization and liberalization.

Reforming America's Sexual Culture: The Making of a Culture of Eroticism

The reformers believed that America was in the midst of a crisis of
intimacy. The proliferation of red light districts, the spread of venereal
disease, the sharp increase in divorce rates and the growing public
awareness of homosexuals evoked a sense of widespread social disorder. The source of these social ills was said to be the restrictive Victorian culture. Liberal reformers charged that it was the sex-negative
attitudes of Victorians, especially the banishing of sensuality from
sex, love and marriage, that was the major source of current social

ills. As sensuality was disassociated from love and marriage, it was said to resurface in a sexual underworld of vice and excess that threatened healthy intimate bonds. The enemy was not thought to be sensuality, but its repression and its uncoupling from sex, love, and marriage.

Reformers surmised that a healthy intimate culture required bringing sex back into the core experience of love and marriage. This meant changing sexual attitudes and shaping a new intimate culture. Sex was to be framed less as a symbol of love or a marital obligation than as a sensual basis of love and marriage. In fact, what occurred in the twentieth century, in part because of the efforts of sexual reformers and rebels, was a process of the sexualization of love and marriage which, in turn, contributed to the birth of a culture of eroticism.[33]

By the early decades of the twentieth century we can observe a liberal reform movement centered on changing intimate beliefs, values and conventions. Reformers, such as the social scientists Ernest Groves, Ernest Burgess, E.A. Ross, and Stuart Hall, sex researchers and psychologists, such as G.V. Hamilton, Robert Dickinson, and Laura Beam, and public figures, such as Judge Ben Lindsay and Margaret Sanger, played a pivotal role in shaping the American intimate culture. In the forefront of liberal sex reform were the hundreds of marital and sex advice writers and advocates, most of whom were physicians and scientists who wrote popular books and lectured widely. Hannah and Abraham Stone, Margaret Sanger, Eustare Chesser, Maxine Davis, and more recently Mary Calderone, William Masters and Virginia Johnson, Alex Comfort, and David Reuben carried enormous public prestige.

The intent of the early liberal reformers was clear: to secure the exclusive legitimacy and stability of marriage. This required a series of changes in intimate conventions ranging from greater access to birth control to enhancing companionship through improving spousal communication and sharing social interests. However, their chief proposal for reforming intimacy centered on making sex more basic to the experience of love and the success of marriage. They advocated bringing sex into the very center of love and marriage. This entailed, first and foremost, abandoning the Victorian antithesis between sensuality, love and marriage. In *Woman, Her Sex and Love Life*, an early popular text that went through seventeen editions in a little over ten years, William Robinson comments: "Some writers attempt to make a clear distinction between sensual and sentimental love; . . . . The first is called animal love or lust; the second pure love or ideal love; the first variety of love is said to be selfish, egotistic, the other—self-sacrificing, altruistic. . . . There is no distinct line of demarcation between the two varieties of love, and one merges imperceptibly into the other. . . . In other words, there are not two separate, distinct varieties of love."[34] In direct opposition to Victorian intimate ideals, Robinson proposed that sex and, indeed, eroticism, was not alien to love, but was an integral, defining aspect of it. Robinson rendered sex the virtual ground of intimacy: "The foundation of, the basis of all love is sexual attraction."[35] Love was reconfigured in these reform discourses to render sex its original motivating force and foundation. Maxine Davis identifies erotic attraction as the driving force behind love. "In early marriage, sexual love is dominant. . . . [It is] at once the life force and the catalyst for merging two separate human beings."[36] Davis goes on to say that not only is erotic longing the initial motivating force behind love but its most "complete expression of love."[37] The "mutual enjoyment of sexual intercourse [is] the most intimate and exclusive way to express love."[38] Sex is not, however, simply a symbol of love but a core experience of it. "Nothing in all their married fellowship can contribute more toward the growth of their love," says another advice text, "than this beautiful and sacred contact[i.e. sexual intercourse]."[39] The very success of conjugal love was said to depend on a satisfying sex experience. Love must continually be redeemed through realizing mutual sexual satisfaction. "The winning of love is but the first stage of a long adventure. Its maintainance calls for more thought and skill than its gaining. And all the means of stimulating [sexual] desire must be enlisted in the task."[40] It follows that sexual maladjustment, or the lack of sexual satisfaction, signaled a crisis in love. "When sex deserts the bed, love flies out the window. With the breakdown in the sexual relationship comes a corresponding breakdown in every other aspect of love."[41] The fate of conjugal love, says Ms. Davis, turns on "the physical, mental and spiritual intimacy sexual love generates."[42]

Sexual fulfillment was thought necessary to keep love vital and to sustain a successful marriage. "The basic marriage bond is sex attraction, the sex urge; and this being an inborn drive, its normal satisfaction becomes . . . a condition for sustained harmony and mutual satisfaction in all the other areas of the marital relationship. . . . Harmony and mutual satisfaction in the sexual sphere is likely to be the sustaining vital health of the marriage as a whole," wrote Mr. Exner in a popular 1932 marriage manual.[43] Reiterating this belief, Isabel Hutton insists that "no matter how ideal the partnership in every other way, if there is want of sex life or abuse of it, marriage cannot be a success."[44] Almost thirty years later the well-known advice author, Mary Calderone, echoes the belief that sex is the underpinning of marriage. "Marriage consists . . . of many demands. . . . Like the radiating spokes of a wheel, most of these demands spring from and return to the hub of the marriage itself. This hub is the sexual relationship. Attitudes, values, decision-making and most other aspects of marriage are colored by the climate of marital sex."[45] If love and a successful marriage depend upon mutual sexual fulfillment, the production of sensual pleasures through the acquisition of sexual skills and the right attitudes is essential. "Sexual . . . incompatibility must be guarded against. . . . It is possible if . . . both parties . . . are attentive . . . to one another's needs; and [this is possible] by [learning] a culture of erotic technique."[46]

As sexual satisfaction became the site where love and marriage succeeds or fails, it acquired a new importance. In particular, a heightened value was placed upon the erotic aspects of sex. The giving and receiving of sexual pleasure became a chief standard by which to judge love and marriage. The valuing of the sensually pleasurable and expressive qualities of sex acquired legitimacy in a context of love and marriage. Accordingly, a new emphasis was placed on the body as a site of pleasure and on sexual skills and knowledge.

In the advice literature of the early twentieth century(1890–1940s), reformers specified some general conditions for making sexual fulfillment possible. In particular, they advocated a norm of mutual sexual satisfaction. Sex was supposed to be cooperative, mutually respectful and involve shared responsibilities. This presupposed an acknowledgment of women's sexual needs and desires. These texts affirm a view of women as men's sexual equals. Victorian images of female sexuality had by no means disappeared; women's sexuality was still often defined as "more coupled with feelings of tenderness and maternity."[47] This discourse of gender difference, however, was not joined to a Victorian framework which posited female sexuality as lacking sensual desire. Sensuality was not viewed as antithetical to femininity. Hannah and Abraham Stone may have still imagined female sexual nature as different, but they insisted on equality with respect to erotic desire. "It is rather generally assumed at present that the woman's erotic desires are just as strong as those of the male, although the manifestations of the sexual urge may vary considerably in the two sexes."[48] Similarly, Maxine Davis didn't deny that female sexual nature is more romantic but she was adamant that "men and women are equally capable of sexual desire and each is physically fully provided with the means for gratifying that desire."[49] Furthermore, although these authors believed that female sexual desire was less genitally localized than in men, the clitoris was characterized as the principal site of carnal desire. "The clitoris is perhaps the main seat of the woman's sensuous feelings," wrote the Stones' in 1939.[50]

Liberal reform discourses routinely describe female sexuality as similar to male sexuality at least with regard to erotic feelings and capacities. This equality of eros between the two genders grounded a norm of reciprocity which was embraced by virtually all liberal reformers. "The sexual embrace," remarks Abraham and Hannah Stone, "should become . . . the expression of mutual desire and passion. . . . In other words, the joy of sex is increased for both when it is mutual."[51]

Good sex entailed, then, a norm of mutuality. This required being empathetic, caring, and overcoming sexual fears and inhibitions. Nevertheless, no matter how sexually enlightened a husband and wife might be, without the proper knowledge and skill, sexual fulfillment would elude them. Ignorance of sex technique was singled out as a major source of sexual unhappiness in marriage. Theodore Van de Velde, author of the bestseller, *Ideal Marriage*, recommended the mastery of sex technique as the path to sexual fulfillment and a happy marriage. Acquiring erotic expertise entails, to begin with, understanding the complexities and sequential logic of good sex. Van de Velde described good sex as a developmental process involving distinct phases, each of which must be fully mastered. In all phases of the sex act "equal rights and equal joys in a sexual union" is essential.[52] In stage one, the "prelude," erotic desire is awakened. Sexual interest is displayed in words, looks, and smell, not in touch or taste. The prelude is a kind of erotic conversation that prepares the couple for the second phase—"love-play." Here the center of the erotic drama shifts from verbal and visual to sensual play. Love-play begins with the mouth to mouth kiss but gradually extends to the "body kiss" (kissing all the non-genital body parts) and the "genital kiss." The love expert knows all the possible ways to yield pleasure from the kiss. In love-play the hands are equally effective as an instrument of sensual pleasure. Van de Velde described in detail the various erotic zones and how they may bring pleasure from various touching strategies, e.g., pressing, gripping, stroking, caressing. As sexual excitation builds up the couple enters the third phase, "coitus." This is the sexual climax. It is "the consummation of sexual satisfaction which . . . concludes with the ejaculation—or emission—of semen into the vagina."[53] The orgasm initiates the final phase, "after-glow" or "after-play." In the after-glow of mutual orgasm, the couple experiences a spiritual union as "their souls meet and merge. . . ."[54]

Throughout Van de Velde's description of good sex, he underscored the point that sexual expertise involves not only mutuality and skill but a spirit of experimentation. The husband and wife were encouraged to explore every possible way to enhance their sexual satisfaction. He implored his readers to experiment not only with sex acts and positions, but also with their voice, body odors and secretions, environmental sounds, and lighting to augment sexual pleasure.[55] Only "cruelty and the use of artificial means for producing voluptuous sensations" were proscribed.[56]

As we shift to advice texts in the 1960s and 1970s, the culture of eroticism is much more prominent as these discourses center on the mechanisms for producing and expanding sensual pleasures. Indeed, whereas the earlier advice texts focused on sex as definitely linked to making love and marriage successful, in the more recent texts it is the sex act itself and its expressive and sensually pleasurable possibilities that is the dramatic center.

The sex act is abstracted from considerations of time, place and social locale that are thought to be irrelevant to erotic play and pleasure.[57] Individuals are typified in a one-dimensional way so that attention is focused on erotic body parts and behavior. Social interaction is emptied of its thick emotional content as it is narrowed to a bounded erotic exchange. The focus on intensifying erotic pleasure entails a heightened concern with the body and sex technique. Every conceivable organ and orifice is to be explored using every possible stimulant for the sole end of maximizing pleasures, exploring feelings and expanding communication. These discourses urge a rich, diffuse body eroticism. A preoccupation with genital sex, and especially vaginal intercourse, is criticized. For example, the authors of *Joy of Sex* complain that sex today is "over-genital" and "too focused on vaginal intercourse."[58] They insist that "to have good sex . . . we need the total acceptance of our whole body as a source of pleasure."[59] Similarly, David Reuben advises his readers to utilize "all the available erotic pathways to reinforce and add to the 'cumulative gratification' of the sex experience."[60] "M" urges the Sensuous Man to use his hands and mouth, not his penis, as his primary sex organ and to make "his entire body an instrument of sexuality."[61] Exercises and sensitizing regimes are suggested to re-eroticize dulled body regions and to make one sexually adept at giving and receiving pleasure.

Sex can, the reader is told, legitimately be approached with an eye to pleasure and fun. The reader is encouraged to put aside all his/her inhibitions. Erotic fulfillment requires that one be adventurous and experimental. Variety with regard to act, position, place, and role-playing is crucial to enhancing erotic pleasure. Nor should we be deterred from erotic experimentation by anxiety over the normality of our behavior. Indeed, Dr. Reuben proposes that the very term "sexual perversion," which functions to stigmatize and inhibit harmless sexual pleasures, be replaced by the morally neutral phrase "sexual variation."[62] These manuals aim to expand the range of legitimate sex acts to include all types of body rubbing, voyeuristic and fetishistic behavior, oral-genital sex and anal eroticism. "J" encourages the Sensuous Woman to use "dirty sex talk" to enhance sexual excitement. "Whispering 'I love you' to the average man doesn't have nearly the exciting effect on him that 'your cock makes me so hot I can hardly stand it' does."[63] *The Joy of Sex* recommends exploring aggressive feelings. Flagellation games and bondage are referred to as "harmless expressions of sexual aggression and a venerable human resource for increasing sexual feeling."[64] Eroticizing aggression and games of power pushes sexuality deeper into the realm of fantasy. These discourses encourage the reader not to resist, since the sexual sphere is said to represent an ideal setting for probing tabooed wishes and fears. "This [sex] is the place to experience things you can't possibly act out, and to learn your partner's fantasy needs. These fantasies can be heterosexual, homosexual, incestuous, tender, wild or bloodthirsty—don't block and don't be afraid of your partner's fantasy; this is a dream you are in."[65]

Liberal reformers looked, then, to sex to provide an anchor for love and marriage. If individuals could acquire the right attitudes and skills, sex could sustain love and marriage while providing self-fulfillment and personal happiness. One implication of this reform agenda was that the development of the erotic aspects of sex acquired value and legitimation. Liberal reformers were, in my estimation, a key social force in shaping an intimate culture that entailed a concentrated focus on the body and techniques for maximizing erotic pleasure.

To be sure, these texts count, at best, as evidence of a cultural shift in sexual norms, not behavior. Yet, there is evidence that behavioral changes have occurred that are consistent with these normative trends. For purposes of brevity, I highlight some broad behavioral and attitudinal changes that are repeatedly evidenced in sex surveys and research.

Kinsey's *Sexual Behavior of the Female* compared an older generation born before 1900 with one born after 1900 along a number of dimensions. Confining ourselves to his findings on marital sex, his research found that while the frequency of marital coitus was more or less constant, there was a heightened attention to the erotic aspects of sex. The younger generation engaged in more foreplay for longer periods; oral-genital sex increased significantly; there was more experimentation with coital positions; couples were more likely to perform deep kissing and to manually stimulate the genitals; and marital couples were more likely to have sex naked.[66] These findings suggest that erotic pleasure was valued and legitimated at least in marriage.[67]

In 1974 Morton Hunt published *Sexual Behavior in the 1970s* which sought to document changes in sexual attitudes and behavior between the generation born between 1900–1920 and the generation born between 1930–1950. Hunt found that in comparing a younger generation, born roughly after 1940, and an older generation, in almost all respects the former were more accepting of eroticism, and this was reflected in their behavior.[68] For example, whereas Kinsey reported that oral-genital sex and manual stimulation of genitals were rare among the generation that came of age in the 1940s, Hunt found these practices had become common among the generation that matured in the 1960s.[69] The rate of approval of oral-genital sex among the younger generation was almost double that of the older generation.[70] Again, whereas Kinsey found that among males who had not attended college 60 percent said they had practiced oral-genital sex at some time, Hunt found among the same population that between 80 and 90 percent reported regularly practicing oral-genital sex.[71]

Hunt's survey was done in the late sixties and early seventies. Subsequent national surveys are even more revealing. *The Cosmo Report* found that contemporary women (the generation born between 1940–1950) take their erotic pleasures as seriously as men. About 50 percent of these women said they found "sexy talk" a pleasant accompaniment to sex. Almost one-quarter of these women said the same about pornography. The overwhelming majority reported practicing fellatio regularly. Even more striking is that almost 15 percent of these women said regularly participate in anal sex; about 7 percent said they routinely take pleasure in fetishes.[72] These findings are reiterated in *Redbook Report*. This national survey found that most women surveyed regularly use clothing as a sexual stimulant, vary locations or settings of sex "to make sex more exciting," and regularly use devices and aids (such as pornography) for sexual stimulation.[73]

The point need not be belabored: a culture of eroticism materialized in twentieth-century America that valued sex as a sphere of pleasure and self-expression. This culture was initially wedded to a heterosexual marital norm. It had as one of its sources the sexualization of love and marriage that occurred in the early decades of the twentieth century. As a way to experience, demonstrate, sustain and revitalize love and marriage, sex, and especially the enjoyment of its erotic aspects, gained legitimacy. The giving and receiving of pleasure became a way to give and receive love and to make marriage succeed.

The Making of a Liberal Sexual Culture

The development of a culture of eroticism was possible in twentieth-century America only because it occurred concomitantly with social liberalization. It presupposed, for example, a social structure that permitted a wide latitude in talking and writing about sex; having easy access to birth control information and devices; having greater access to information on sex techniques; and having fewer obstacles to the production and distribution of explicit sexual materials. In fact, as I have already suggested, such a liberal sexual and social environment was forming in the early decades of the twentieth century. The failure of the late Victorian sexual regime was appealed to by reformers to legitimate a politic of eroticization and liberalization. A restrictive politic, it was argued, unintentionally promoted vice and pathology. A positive attitude towards sex combined with a more relaxed social environment would, it was thought, encourage the beneficial qualities of sexuality to promote our personal and social welfare. If sexual expression were significantly less regulated, and if sexual expression were subject to positive moral education, its naturally beneficial powers would, it was assumed, prevail.

By the early decades of the twentieth century, sex was constructed in many cultural media as a positive, life-enhancing, benevolent power. Although there were still risks associated with sex, it was believed that they were not of the magnitude assumed by many Victorians. The personal benefits of sexual expression were celebrated— from bringing individual health to enhancing love and marriage. Because sex was primarily viewed as a personal affair with individual consequences which were largely beneficial, state bureaucratic controls could be relaxed. Indeed, excessive state regulation or restrictive social controls were said to turn a benevolent power into one that produced excess, vice, perversion and pathology.

By the 1920s and 1930s, a liberal sexual culture was in the making. Central to this process was state deregulation of sexual representations and behavior. This was paralleled by the continuing decline of the family and the church as agents of social control. Furthermore, stimulated by the shift to mass consumerism and a culture emphasizing individual expression and hedonistic values, there occurred between the 1920s and the 1970s a noteworthy expansion of sexual choice and diversity. To be sure, as the state, church, and the family lessened their controls, the medical, scientific and psychiatric institutions, along with mass culture (television, radio, film, popular music), stepped in as agencies of sexual regulation. These controls were not, however, as imposing and directive. Morever, the sexual meanings and directives they carried were quite ambiguous. Although a heterosexual, monogamous, marital norm continued to be authorized by the dominant cultural discourses, the rendering of sex as a private, individual matter and the demand for state deregulation of sexual expression helped to shape an environment conducive to expanded choice and tolerance for difference. It made possible the movements for sexual radicalization which further pushed for expanded sexual choice and diversity by challenging the heterosexual, monogamous, and marital norm.

Indicative of state deregulation were changes in laws regulating "obscene materials." The Comstock Law in 1873 placed severe restrictions on the publication and distribution of such materials. One historian has observed that prior to the 1870s there were few cases of obscenity, in spite of federal and state laws prohibiting it. "But in the last quarter of the nineteenth century groups of citizens began calling for censorship action. Fiction of all types became suspect, classics as well as dime novels. Books dealing with the sexual facts of life . . . were considered invidious. . . . [There] seems to have suddenly crystallized . . . an organized censorship movement."[74] By the turn of the century, and through the 1920s, a steady barrage of legal action restricted sexual expression. Although censorship has continued into the present, the 1930s marked a break in state legal regulation. The ruling that James Joyce's *Ulysses* was not obscene signaled the liberalization of obscenity laws, a trend accelerated in the post-World War II period. The barriers against the public presentation of explicit sexual images were rapidly removed. "Between 1957 and 1967, the [Supreme Court] justices heard a series of obscenity laws. Though rarely achieving unanimity, the Warren Court progressively contracted the domain of obscenity, in large part by affirming the appropriateness of sex as a matter for public consumption."[75]

Indeed, this narrowing of state regulation of sexual expression was simply confirming a reality: sexual representations had, by the 1960s, penetrated the public sphere. For example, the 1970 United States Commission on Obscenity and Pornography issued a massive report that noted the enormous growth and diversification of pornography. It was readily available in mass-circulation magazines, popular paperback books, and in film. The Commission estimated that 85 percent of all American adult men and 70 percent of all adult American women had been exposed to pornography.[76] Resonating with this liberal social environment the Commission recommended the repeal of all existing local, state and federal statutes that prohibit the sale, exhibition and distribution of obscene material.[77] Further reinforcing this liberalizing trend was the deregulation of the mass production and distribution of contraceptive and birth control information and devices. The passage of the Comstock Law had set off a wave of anti-contraceptive statutes through the 1920s. With the struggles of the birth control movement, led by Margaret Sanger and backed by liberal reformers and radicals, many of the legal and social barriers to birth control were eliminated by the 1930s. Birth control clinics sprang up across the country in the 1940s and 1950s. By the 1960s, with the appearance of "the Pill," the legal barriers to contraceptive information and use were all but abolished,[78] and sexual imagery further introduced into the public realm. Finally, capitalist development favored the movement of sexual representations into the public sphere. For example, the shift to mass consumerism in the early decades of the twentieth century promoted the integration of sexual imagery into mass advertising.[79] Spurred by capitalism's search for expanded domestic markets, sex was used to sell every possible commodity, and soon filled the marketplace and the public sphere. Entrepreneurs seized on sexuality as a potentially new market and site of economic profit and growth. A virtual sex industry developed in the 1960s, producing sex aids, manuals, erotica and pornography as well as creating businesses oriented to sexual behavior, e.g., massage parlors, gay baths, sex retreats, escort services, and sex shops. Between the 1920s and 1970s, public sexual imagery moved from the margins to the social center, from a ghettoized, stigmatized sphere of representation to a legitimate multi-billion dollar business.

The reduction of state legal restraints on sexual expression encouraged not only the sexualization of the public sphere, but the expansion of sexual choice. The liberalization of divorce laws, of the production and distribution of birth control information and devices, and the increased access to erotic representations encouraging sexual pleasure provided a favorable context for expanding sexual choice and diversity. Sexual expression was viewed as an individual choice.

The liberalization of sexual attitudes and behavior in twentieth-century America has been amply documented. Briefly and quite schematically, I'll refer to some of this literature. My baseline of comparison is the Kinsey research, since there is really no research on the generation born in the mid-nineteenth century. Comparing the generation born before 1900 (roughly 1870–1890s) with the one born between 1900–1920 in terms of premarital sex, Kinsey and his associates found significantly higher rates of premarital sexual activity among men and women. With respect to women, Kinsey writes: "This increase in the incidence of premarital coitus, and the similar increase in the incidence of premarital petting, constitute the greatest changes which we have found between the patterns of sexual behavior in the older and younger generations of American females."[80] Some twenty-five years after Kinsey began his research, Morton Hunt's survey of sexual behavior and attitudes in the 1970s compared the generation that came of age in the 1920s and 1930s, which Kinsey interviewed, and the generation that matured in the 1950s and 1960s. He found a continuous process of liberalization with respect to sexual attitudes and behavior in general. "Our data shows a dramatic shift towards permissiveness . . . and more generally towards sexual liberalism (by which we mean both attitudinal permissiveness and freedom to include certain formerly forbidden acts)."[81] For example, comparing the generation that matured in the pre-World War II period with the one that matured after the war, Hunt reported the latter to be significantly more accepting of premarital coitus and having significantly higher rates of premarital coitus. Other researchers have found that the liberalization trend did not stop in the 1950s and 1960s, but continued into the 1970s. For example, comparing premarital sexual expression among college females in 1958, 1968 and 1978, two sociologists found that "the number of women having premarital coitus while in a dating relationship went from one in ten in 1958, to about one in four in 1968 and to one in two in 1978."[82] Other researchers confirmed these findings. "Two major changes in the nature of premarital behavior and attitudes were found in this study. First, although a considerable liberalization in premarital sexual behavior and attitudes had taken place in the latter 1960s,(especially among females), liberalization was accelerated in the early 1970s. Second, due to the great liberalization in female premarital sexual behavior and attitudes, the difference between male and female behavior and attitudes has greatly diminished."[83] Summarizing the relevant research done between 1930 and 1970 that bears on sexual attitudes and behavior, J. Roy Hopkins writes:

> The following phenomena are elements in the liberalization of sexual behavior: (a) a major shift in attitudes regarding acceptability of premarital intercourse, (b) a discontinuous increase in incidence of premarital coitus, (c) a shift toward earlier participation in coitus in the adolescent years, and (d) a liberalization in patterns of sexual expression—including coitus; with a number of different partners, increased frequency of intercourse, less insistence on a context of emotional attachment, and willingness to experiment with variation in sexual technique.[84]

If we take attitudes towards premarital sex as one indicator of expanded sexual choice, the evidence overwhelmingly points towards sexual liberalization.

Liberalization, however, entails both expanded choice and enhanced public tolerance for sexually diverse lifestyles. A process of liberalization took place not only with regard to attitudes and behavior, but also with regard to lifestyle choices. Between the 1930s and 1970s a wider range of options gained public credibility. Although the heterosexual, marital ideal continued to be the dominant norm, tolerance grew for alternative lifestyles, especially in the post-World War II period. I'll briefly allude to three indicators of these expanded options.

First, not only was premarital sex approved of by many more Americans than in previous generations, but sex that was not oriented to marriage gained widespread legitimacy. In the youth culture, sexual expression unrelated to love or marriage had become widely accepted.[85] Many youth in the 1960s and early 1970s approved of sexual expression unrelated to romance, intimacy or love. Somewhat disconcerted, Morton Hunt found evidence of tolerance of deromanticized sexual meanings by postwar youth.

> [T]he acceptability of premarital sex in the absence of strong affection—also seems to be gaining considerable ground. . . . We find it noteworthy that 60 percent of our males and 37 percent of our females consider premarital coitus acceptable for men, even where no strong affection exists, while 44 percent of our males and 20 percent of our females find it acceptable for women under the same circumstances. . . . A growing number of young men and women are no longer willing to condemn premarital intercourse even when the context is one of very mild affection, or none; they themselves may strongly prefer sex associated with love . . . but they do not criticize or find fault with casual sex in other unmarried males or females, nor do they rule it out altogether for themselves. This is, indeed, a remarkable and epochal change in attitude.[86]

In the post-World War II years, there were visible trends towards loosening ties between sex, love and marriage. One such effort, which I will return to shortly, involved rendering sex a sphere of pleasure, needing no further justification than its expressive or individuating qualities.

A second challenge to the exclusive marital norm came in the 1970s with the social acceptance, especially among the young, of cohabitation. The demographer Paul Glick reported that between 1960 and 1970 the number of adults living in cohabiting arrangements increased almost tenfold. According to the 1970 census, about 11 percent of the adult population were living with a partner of the opposite sex with whom they were not legally married.[87] In a 1977 study, two researchers found that 18 percent of the men surveyed said they had lived with a woman for six months or more outside of marriage. Even though the actual percentage of those living in a cohabitating arrangement at any given time was comparatively small (about 5 percent), the significant fact, according to these researchers, was that in the 1970s the rate of cohabitation tripled.[88] Research revealed that between 20 and 35 percent of college students surveyed reported having lived in a cohabiting arrangement.[89] These studies document the widespread public approval of cohabitation, at least among the youth in the postwar years. This had the effect of weakening marriage as the only legitimate intimate arrangement.

The slight weakening of the marital norm signaled by this increased tolerance for diverse lifestyles undoubtedly contributed to the expanded tolerance for homosexuality. Hunt found that nearly 50 percent of all men and women surveyed responded that homosexuality should be legal.[90] Norval Glenn and Charles Weaver analyzed seven national surveys and found a slight trend towards tolerance in attitudes towards homosexuality in the 1970s.[91] Survey data is of limited value, though, since public awareness of homosexuality is fairly recent and there is little, if any, relevant data to compare the present with the past. Nevertheless, a multitude of empirical indicators suggest that between 1960 and the mid-1970s there was a widening tolerance towards homosexuality. First, a review of mass-circulation magazines in the heterosexual press reveals a sympathetic, often strongly supportive bias. Not only was it legitimate to publicly discuss homosexuality as newsworthy, but a good deal of the coverage was critical of prejudices against homosexuals.[92] A second indicator is the successful repeal of sodomy laws in numerous states and the passage of "gay rights" ordinances in dozens of cities, as well as the numerous other legal, political and legislative victories that signal social acceptance.[93] Finally, the 1970s witnessed a visible community building effort in the lesbian and gay male community. In small towns and cities across the country, lesbians and gay men created their own institutions, culture and political organizations that typically had a visible social presence, suggesting enhanced tolerance of homosexuality.[94]

A process of sexual liberalization occurred in the United States in the twentieth century. The retreat of the state as a social control agency, simultaneous with the weakening of the church, family and local community as agencies of control, permitted an expansion of sexual choice. Individuals had more options regarding the social context and meaning of sex. They could now choose, with a good deal of social approval, to have sex before or after marriage, outside of marriage, while dating or even more casually, in a same-sex context, or to go solo. Prior to the postwar years, there was little or no public support for such intimate lifestyle choices. These broad processes, sexual liberalization and with eroticization, decisively shaped the American sexual culture in the twentieth century.

Sexual Reformers and Rebels; Liberating Eros

In the course of the twentieth century, the intimate culture of the United States underwent crucial changes. In particular, I've commented on a trend towards liberalization, or the expansion of sexual choice and tolerance for diversity. As the state retreated from intimate affairs, the individual was given more sexual choice and reponsibility. This liberalization occurred in a context in which the very meaning and role of sex in personal and social life was changing. Sex was, for example, becoming a major source of identity alongside gender, work, religion, or ethnicity. The abstract categories of sexual identification developed by sexologists and psychologists in the late nineteenth century (e.g., the concept of the homosexual and the heterosexual) were being absorbed into public culture, rendering sexuality a language of identity and social regulation. Moreover, sex was being reconceived as a self-enriching, joyous phenomenon. And it was precisely its erotic aspects that were said to hold great potential for promoting successful intimate bonds while enhancing personal happiness. The legitimation of eroticism entailed framing the body as a site of pleasure and self-expression.

These changes in intimate culture were markers, if you will, of broad shifts in American society. Central is the dramatic commercialization of everyday life that has been so consequential in the twentieth-century United States. This shift towards a consumer-oriented, leisure-centered culture, which seized on sexuality as both a marketing strategy and as a new market, was pivotal in altering American sexual conventions.[95] Expanding individual sexual choice, tolerating sexual diversity and legitimating eroticism opened up vast new market possibilities for entrepreneurs. For example, the increasing social acceptance of homosexuality in the 1960s and 1970s occurred simultaneous with the realization of the enormous commercial prospects of this population. The building of gay and lesbian communities would hardly have been imaginable without the role of entrepreneurs in, say, promoting gay bathhouses and bars, and in exploiting new markets for clothes, music, dance clubs, pornography, fiction, and travel. In short, entrepreneurs found in the evolution of a gay community a lucrative market which they exploited, in part, by marketing eroticism in everything from gay bathhouses and gay porn to gay S/M equipment and sex aids.[96]

The shift to a more consumption-oriented economy in the twentieth century was one key social force contributing to changes in intimate mores. Equally significant, if less obtrusive, were changes in gender roles. Although Victorian middle-class women were frequently powerful as public figures involved in the church, schools or moral reform movements, such as abolitionism or the women's movement, they had little economic and political power. This greatly circumscribed their autonomy, particularly in the realms of intimacy and sexuality. While historians have noted that at least some middle-class Victorian women had the option of intimacy with women without any disapproval or stigma, these involvements were, in the main, permitted only because they were not threatening to the heterosexual marital norm.[97] The development of same-sex intimacies were, moreover, impeded by the reality of intimates living apart and often at great distances, and by the absence of institutional and legal authorization for such relationships.[98] Furthermore, middle-class Victorian women gained autonomy to the extent that they were seen as moral guardians of society. The cult of true womanhood in middle-class Victorian America merged femininity with spiritual and moral purity.[99] While this gave women authority in the household and beyond it, it rendered eroticism dangerous, as a lustful woman was defined as "fallen," and forfeited her claims to virtue and power.

By the early decades of the twentieth century, the cult of true womanhood was losing social credibility. Women began entering the paid labor force and, by the post-World War II period, many women were economically independent. The contradication between their growing economic empowerment and their political subordination prompted women's demands for social and sexual autonomy, including the legitimation of eroticism.[100] No less significant for the American sexual culture was the assault on the ideology of feminine moral purity and virtue. The perception hardened that Victorian intimate culture, with its de-eroticization of femininity, was responsible for the crisis of intimacy and marriage. The companionate intimate ideal, in which love and marriage were to be anchored in sexual fulfillment, presupposed a woman for whom carnal desire was consistent with her femininity. The cult of true womanhood, with its idealization of feminine purity, gave way to a notion of femininity which included erotic desire. This eroticization of womanhood made possible the American culture of eroticism.

Capitalism, changing gender roles, technological changes in contraception and birth control, the formation of a hedonistic and expressive culture, and the broader processes of social and political liberalization contributed to the making of twentieth-century American intimate culture. Yet, social change is not the result of abstract social processes, but is made by people. Individuals, groups, and social movements may be shaped by social forces, but these social processes are given form, coherence and articulation by human agents. The role of sex reformers and rebels were critical to sexual change in twentieth-century America. They stepped forward as the chief creators of sexual meanings and ethics, and the principal defenders of liberalizing and eroticizing trends. The reformers led the assault on the ideology of restraint; promoted a new ideology of sexual expression; celebrated the power of eroticism, and advocated for an ideology of choice and diversity. They saw themselves as a vanguard of a new era of sexual freedom and happiness bringing personal health and success in love and intimacy.

At the center of this movement were the liberal reformers. From the end of the nineteenth century to the mid-1970s, these individuals produced discourses and representations that celebrated sexual choice, variety and pleasure, at least within a heterosexual, romantic, and marital context. They were a heterogeneous group made up of physicians, psychiatrists, journalists, social scientists, feminists, birth control advocates, and an assortment of public officials and figures. In the early decades of the twentieth century Judge Ben Lindsey, feminist birth control advocate Margart Sanger, psychiatrists G.V. Hamilton and Robert Dickinson, social scientists such as Stuart Hall and Ernest Groves, and physicians such as Abraham and Hannah Stone were at the forefront of the liberal reform movement. In the post-World War II period, sexologists Alfred Kinsey, William Masters and Virginia Johnson, psychiatrist David Reuben, physicians like Mary Calderone, journalists like Gay Talese, and advice authors like Alex Comfort, "M" and "J" carried on a tradition of liberal sex reform. Often figures of public stature, whose talk and discourse carried public authority, these reformers shaped public sexual meanings—sexual beliefs, values and norms—through their writings, speeches, and public authority.

They saw themselves as the forces of reason, enlightenment, and progress battling one of the last vestiges of ignorance and superstition in the modern world. Their struggle was against the power of religion which, they thought, stifled the healthy sexual education of the public. Armed with scientific and medical knowledge, they intended to liberate Americans from the crippling superstitions that have wrought havoc on our intimate lives. Liberal reformers did not see themselves as revolutionaries. In their view, sexual and intimate malaise was caused by ignorance and fear perpetuated by anachronistic attitudes and beliefs. Their aim was to promote the modernization of sex by substituting rational beliefs and attitudes for outdated ones. In part, the power of reformers rested upon their appeal to the mainstream—to basic liberal values and beliefs. They were not, in the main, critics of American society as a whole; they did not advocate massive social change. They proposed reforming sexual attitudes without, for the most part, challenging existing intimate conventions and social institutions.

Liberal sex reformers found support, even if quite ambivalent, from sex radicals and some political radicals. Paralleling the liberal tradition are various sex radical strains in the United States. One thinks, for example, of the bohemian and radical culture of the early twentieth century, associated with such public intellectuals as Max Eastman, Crystall Eastman, Randolph Bourne, Mabel Dodge, Emma Goldman, Floyd Dell, Hapgood Hutchins, Edgar Lee Masters, and Keith Boyce.[101] This bohemian radical culture found continuing expression in the "Beats" of the 1950s and New Left critics of the 1960s such as Paul Goodman, Herbert Marcuse and Norman O. Brown, as well as in certain currents of feminism and gay liberation.[102] These sex rebels supported the liberal assault on Victorianism and its advocacy of sexual choice, variation and pleasure. They too believed that there were sexual trends in America that promised a new era of freedom and happiness which they associated with expanded choice and eroticism.

These sex rebels diverged from the liberal reformers in important ways. They embedded their criticisms of sexual conventions and their agenda for reform within a broader social critique and project for social change. For example, they linked their critique of the Victorian intimate culture to criticisms of its social institutions. Similarly, although they endorsed many liberal concepts of sexuality and intimacy (e.g,. a companionate ideal, the sexualization of love and the value of eroticism), sex rebels typically linked their proposals for changes in intimate life to changes in gender relations, political economy, and the family. Although many sex rebels endorsed a heterosexual, romantic norm, they exhibited a broad tolerance towards sexual diversity. Sex radicals leaned more than liberal reformers towards a consistent libertarian sexual ethic where individual choice and consent were the guiding norms. Needless to say, this greatly circumscribed the legitimacy of state intervention into intimate affairs, while expanding or maximizing the individual's range of legitimate sexual choice. This libertarian strain is apparent in the *Playboy* philosophy of Hugh Hefner, in the Freudo-Marxism of Marcuse and Brown, in the anarchic sexuality of Allen Ginsberg and the counterculture, and in the gay subculture and feminism.

These liberal reformers and sex radicals may have been a heterogeneous group but they had, in my view, enormous impact. Many were prominent public figures or members of a cultural elite. Moreover, the media often highlighted their nonconventional sexual beliefs or lifestyles, functioning inadvertently to give their views a public authority. One thinks, for example, of the Ginsberg trial around the publication of *Howl*, which made the poet and his expressive vision of sex widely available to Americans.[103] Again, think of Hugh Hefner's self-promotion as a sexual libertarian, made possible both by his own proprietorship of *Playboy* and the media attention given to him. These reformers and radicals gave shape and moral sanction to the trends towards liberalization and eroticization. They fashioned the inchoate feelings and impulses prompted by capitalism, consumerism, and other social forces into a sexual ideology that valued sex for its pleasurable, expressive and communicative or socially bonding qualities.

I have been speaking of changes in sexual meanings and mores that span a century. Sexual liberalization and eroticization were long-term processes visible as early as pre-World War I. Liberal and radical sex discourses and representations accompanied and indeed preceded these changes—both as cause and effect. The debunking of the myth of a sexual revolution between 1950–1970 does not require that we deny any historically unique shifts in this period.

Two features of the sexual culture of the postwar years are crucial to an understanding of contemporary sexual politics and ethics. First, the defense of sexual choice, variation and pleasure gained mass social support, at least among the middle class. The ideology of sexual expression, to use a shorthand term, went mainstream in this period. Even as late as the 1930s, the defense of birth control and divorce, the advocacy of a companionate marital ideal with its sexualized intimacy, was, if not confined to the social margins, vigorously resisted by core groups in the social center. By the 1960s and 1970s, it was the resistors and detractors who were marginal. The legitimation of birth control, the Commission on Pornography's recommendation to abolish all laws regulating adult pornography, the saturation of the public sphere with sexual images, and the mainstreaming of liberal sexologists like Masters and Johnson suggest the broad social appeal of this new sexual ideology.

A second development in the postwar years that departs from previous trends relates to challenges to the heterosexual, romantic and marital norm. To the extent that reformers endorsed this dominant intimate ideal, their advocacy of sexual change was not threatening. Indeed, part of their appeal rested upon their claim that they sought to strengthen heterosexual and romantic intimacy. Yet, there surfaced in the postwar years a defense of an ideology of choice and pleasure that was less tied to this norm.

The challenge came mostly from sex radicals. This was a truly diverse group. There were the highbrow discourses of Herbert Marcuse's *Eros and Civilization* and Norman O. Brown's *Life Against Death* and *Love's Body*. These social critics not only championed eroticism for its individuating, bonding, and solidaristic powers, but they, at times, celebrated a diffuse playful eroticism unrestrained by heterosexual, romantic or marital boundaries.[104] A libertarian sexual ethic, which valued sex not only for its procreative and intimate functions but for its pleasure-producing and socially bonding role, was endorsed by many of the leading spirits of the counterculture.[105] One thinks, say, of Allen Ginsberg, Timothy Leary, Ken Kesey, and of rock n'roll and counterculture idols such as Mick Jagger, Jim Morrison, Andy Warhol and the "Factory"—all of whom represented and, at times, advocated an expressive-hedonistic sexuality that defended sex in varied social contexts. Though not necessarily radicals in any broader ideological sense, Hugh Hefner and the *Playboy* philosophy defended a libertarian sexual ethic that justified sex in nonromantic, nonmarital contexts.[106]

These sex radical currents were promoted by two key social movements: the women's and gay movements. Although many feminists were ambivalent towards an ideology of sexual choice and pleasure that was not sensitive to the dangers it carried for many women (e.g., unwanted pregnancies, rape and physical assault, the stigma of a loose woman), they were consistent in their defense of sexual diversity.[107] Moreover, for many feminists the women's movement was defined as a sexual liberation movement; they endorsed a strong libertarian ethic. Leading feminists such as Kate Millet in *Sexual Politics*, Shulamith Firestone in *Dialectic of Sex* and the feminist collective that authored *Our Bodies, Ourselves* viewed an ideology of choice and eroticism that went beyond a heterosexual, romantic and marital norm as a pivotal part of their feminism. "A sexual revolution would require," says Kate Millet, "an end to traditional sexual inhibitions and taboos, particularly those that most threaten patriarchal monogamous marriage: homosexuality, illegitimacy, adolescent, pre-and extra-marital sexuality. The negative aura with which sexual activities have generally been surrounded would necessarily be eliminated, together with the double standard and prostitution. The goal of revolution would be a permissive single standard of sexual freedom. . . ."[108] The feminist defense of choice and eroticism found echoes in the mainstream writings of Erica Jong, Nancy Friday and Lonnie Barbach.[109]

This feminist defense of sexual choice and variation found substantial support within the gay and lesbian community, whose members had, of course, to defend diversity to promote their own interests in social acceptance. Nevertheless, although discourses within this community did at times insist upon a romantic and "marital-like" norm, this was overshadowed, especially in the gay male community, by discourses endorsing a view of sex as having multiple meanings and occasions of legitimate expression. In major gay male newspapers, magazines, fiction and nonfiction, in advertisements and in the culture of gay baths and bars, the dominant ideology viewed sex as legitimate for both romantic and pleasurable, expressive and communicative reasons, in contexts entailing commitment as well as ones involving only consent.[110] The spirit of the 1970s was clearly articulated by Dennis Altman, a reliable barometer of trends in the gay male culture of the 1970s. "Sex can be a very significant and intimate expression of love, but it can also be fun, pleasure, release, adventure and a good way to establish contact with someone from whom one's otherwise separated by class, age, education and interests. Sex is not a unitary phenomenon with one meaning, one appropriate form, or one correct context."[111] Indeed, many gay men saw themselves as pioneering an adventurous, luxuriant, pluralistic and playful sexuality where there was a good deal of slippage between sex and love.

Although sex radicals pioneered the critique of a heterosexual, romantic and marital norm, there was, in fact, growing support among mainstream liberal reformers. For example, although the sex advice texts I have previously analyzed privileged a heterosexual, marital, romantic norm, they often defended forms of sexual expression and intimate lifestyles that deviated from this ideal. Postwar sex advice discourses construct sex as an activity that has three legitimate meanings: procreation, romance and recreation or an expressive, pleasure-inducing hedonistic role. *More Joy of Sex*, for example, states: "Sex in humans has three functions. It can be reproductive (producing babies), relational (expressing love and bonding adults together), or recreational (play and fun)."[112] To the extent that sex is valued for its pleasurable, expressive and communicative qualities, it can be legitimated in a variety of nonromantic, nonmarital social contexts. Alex Comfort, editor of the bestselling *The Joy of Sex* and *More Joy of Sex*, put the matter as follows: "The adult of today has all three options—sex as parenthood, sex as total relationship, and sex as physical pleasure accompanied by no more than affection. . . . Since sex is now divorced from parenthood, there are many more relationships into which it can enter if we choose."[113] Moreover, if sex need only be consensual and reciprocal to legitimate it as a realm of pleasure and communication, this would extend the range of legitimate sexual expression to include hitherto variant or "deviant" sexualities, e.g., homosexuality and S/M. Thus, *Joy of Sex* describes bondage and flagellation games as harmless sex play, the exploiting of fantasy and aggressive feelings to heighten eroticism.[114] Many liberal discourses of the 1960s and 1970s perhaps inadvertently endorsed a defense of sexual choice and diversity that contradicted a restrictive heterosexual, romantic and marital norm.[115]

In the course of the twentieth century, a culture was forming that framed sex as a private, individual sphere. The individual was given great latitude in fashioning a sexual and intimate lifestyle. A process of state deregulation of private intimate life encouraged this liberalization. In part, liberalization was justified by an increasingly popular view of sex as a beneficial, self-enhancing, socially productive power. Reducing social controls would allow its natural beneficence to be released. By the 1960s, discourses proliferated not only in the periphery but in the social center that imbued sexuality, especially eroticism, with expectations of self-fulfillment. These discourses viewed sex as having multiple meanings and functions: a symbol of love, enhancement of social communication, unifying basis for romance and intimacy, source of individual pleasure, mode of self-expression, and vehicle of social bonding. For most liberal reformers, and radicals, these trends towards liberalization and eroticization were signs of social progress. A new intimate culture was materializing that was said to expand freedom, enrich individuality, and promote sexual and social diversity while creating a multitude of social bonds and solidarities. America was moving, so it seemed to many reformers and radicals, towards a new age: eros unbounded and liberated.

Notes

1. The concept of the American civil religion has been developed by Robert Bellah, *The Broken Covenant* (New York: Seabury Press, 1975).

2. See, for example, Elaine Tyler May, *Homeward Bound* (New York: Basic Books, 1988); Betty Friedan, *The Feminine Mystique* (New York: Norton, 1963); Lynn Weiner, *From Working Girl to Working Mother* (Chapel Hill: University of North Carolina Press, 1989).

3. On the impact of the war on women, see William Chafe, *The American Woman* (New York: Oxford University Press,1972); Susan Hartmann, *The Homefront and Beyond* (Boston: Twayne, 1982); Sara Evans, *Born for Liberty* (New York: The Free Press, 1989).

4. On the impact of the war on African-Americans, see Landon Jones, *Great Expectations* (New York: Ballantine Books, 1980); Harvard Sitkoff, *A New Deal For Blacks* (Oxford: Oxford University Press, 1978); *Roots of Rebellion*, ed. Richard Young (New York: Harper and Row, 1970).

5. On the impact of the war on homosexuals, see Allan Berube, *Coming Out Under Fire* (New York: Free Press, 1990) and John D'Emilio, *Sexual Politics, Sexual Communities* (Chicago: University of Chicago Press, 1983).

6. On the complex strains of the 1950s, see May, *Homeward Bound*; William Chafe, *The Unfinished Journey* (New York: Oxford University Press, 1986); Marty Jezer, *The Dark Ages* (Boston: South End Press, 1982); William O'Neill, *American High* (New York: Free Press, 1981); Jospeh Veroff, Elizabeth Douvan, Richard Kulka, *The Inner American* (New York: Basic Books, 1981); Lawrence Wittner, *Cold War America* (New York: Praeger, 1974); Eugenia Kaledin, *Mothers and More* (Boston: Twayne, 1984).

7. Useful overviews of the 1960s and 1970s can be found in Godfrey Hodgson, *America in our Time* (New York: Doubleday, 1976); Landon Jones, *Great Expectations* (New York: Coward, McCann and Geoghegan, 1980); William O'Neill, *Coming Apart* (Chicago: Quadrangle, 1971); Jack Newfield, *A Prophetic Minority* (New York: New American Library, 1966); Milton Viorst, *Fire in the Streets* (New York: Simon and Schuster, 1979); Allen Matuson, *The Unraveling of America* (New York: Harper & Row, 1984); James Gilbert, *Another Chance* (Chicago: Dorsey Press, 1986).

8. See, for example, "The Second Sexual Revolution," *Time*, Jan. 24, 1964; Francis Canavan, "Reflections on the Revolution in Sex," *America*, March 6, 1965; Kermit Mehlinger, "The Sexual Revolution," *Ebony*, Aug. 1966.

9. See, for example, Carl Degler, *At Odds* (New York: Oxford University Press, 1980); Peter Gay, *The Bourgeois Experience*. Vol. 1, *Education of the Senses* (New York: Oxford University Press, 1984); Ellen Rothman, *Hands and Hearts* (Cambridge: Harvard University Press, 1984).

10. See Michel Foucault, *The History of Sexuality*, vol. 1, *An Introduction* (New York: Pantheon, 1978).

11. See the essays in *Changing Boundaries*, ed. E. Allgeier and N. McCormick (Palo Alto.: Mayfield, 1983); Robert Bell, *Premarital Sex* in a Changing Society (Englewood Cliffs, N.J.: Prentice-Hall, 1966); Ira Reiss, *The Social Context of Premarital Sexuality* (New York: Holt, Rinehart and Winston, 1967).

12. Paul Gebhard, "Sexuality in the Post-Kinsey Era," *Changing Patterns of Sexual Behavior*, ed. W.H.G. Armytage et al. (New York: Academic Press, 1980), pp. 47–48.

13. See Allgeier and McCormick, *Changing Boundaries*; also see chap. 4.

14. Mary Ryan, *Womanhood in America* (New York: New Viewpoints, 1975), pp. 47–48; Linda Gordon, *Woman's Body, Woman's Right* (New York: Penguin Books, 1977). For a more extended discussion of the feminist critique of the notion of a sexual revolution, see chap. 3.

15. Cf. Daniel Scott-Smith, "The Dating of the American Sexual Revolution: Evidence and Interpretation," *The American Family in Social-Historical Perspective*, ed. Michael Gordon (New York: St. Martin's Press, 1973); John Burnham, "The Progressive Era Revolution in American Attitudes Toward Sex," *Journal of American History* 59 (Mar. 1973); Rosiland Rosenberg, *Beyond Separate Spheres* (New Haven: Yale University Press, 1982).

16. Cf. John D'Emilio and Estelle Freedman, *Intimate Matters* (New York: Harper & Row, 1988). D'Emilio and Freedman speak of sexual liberalization in much less precise terms than I. For them, it refers to a general cluster of beliefs including an emphasis on sexual pleasure, sexual fulfillment, a heterosexual norm, the value of marriage, and so on. I emphasize the relaxation of state legal controls as part of the extension of individual choice. In addition, I differentiate the expansion of choice and diversity, as my central concept of liberalism, from a process of eroticization.

17. Cf. Foucault, *The History of Sexuality*; Jeffrey Weeks, *Sexuality and Its Discontents* (London: Routledge 1985); Jonathan Ned Katz, ed., *Gay/Lesbian Almanac* (New York: Harper & Row, 1983); Carole Vance ed., *Pleasure and Danger* (New York: Routledge, 1984).

18. Cf. Katz, *Gay/Lesbian Almanac*; Carroll Smith-Rosenberg, *Disorderly Conduct* (New York: Alfred A. Knopf, 1985); Lillian Faderman, *Surpassing the Love of Men* (New York: William Morrow and Co., 1981).

19. Cf. Dennis Altman, *The Homosexualization of America* (Boston: Beacon Press, 1983); Seidman, *Romantic Longings*, chap. 6.

20. This discussion draws on Seidman, *Romantic Longings*.

21. See Foucault, *The History of Sexuality*.

22. See n. 9. Also see Karen Lystra, *Searching the Heart* (New York: Oxford University Press, 1990).

23. Seidman, *Romantic Longings*.

24. Cf. Steven Marcus, *The Other Victorians* (New York: Basic Books, 1966); Walter Kendrick, *The Secret Museum* (New York: Viking, 1987).

25. Seidman, *Romantic Longings*, chap. 3; James Reed, *From Private Vice to Public Virtue* (New York: Basic Books, 1978); Barbara Epstein, "Family, Sexual Morality and Popular Movements in Turn-of-the-Century America," in *Powers of Desire*, ed. Ann Snitow et al.(New York: Monthly Review Press, 1983); Christina Simmons, "Marriage in the Modern Manner: Sexual Radicalism and Reform in America, 1914–1941," (Ph.D. diss., Brown University, 1982).

26. See Paul Boyer, *Purity in Print* (New York: Charles Scribner's Sons, 1968) and *Urban Masses and Moral Order in America, 1820–1920* (Cambridge:

Harvard University Press, 1978); David J. Pivar, *Purity Crusade* (Westport, Conn.: Greenwood Press, 1973).

27. See Felice Flannery Lewis, *Literature, Obscenity, and Law* (Carbondale, Ill.: Southern Illinois University Press, 1976); Gordon, *Woman's Body, Woman's Right*; Reed, *From Private Vice to Public Virtue*.

28. See William O'Neill, *Divorce in the Progressive Era* (New Haven: Yale University Press, 1967).

29. See Robert Wiebe, *The Search for Order, 1877–1920* (New York: Hill and Wang, 1967); Gilman Ostrander, *American Civilization in the First Machine Age 1890–1940* (New York: Harper & Row, 1970); Louis Galambos and Joseph Pratt, *The Rise of the Corporate Commonwealth* (New York: Basic Books, 1988).

30. Cf. Seidman, *Romantic Longings*, chap. 3; Simmons, "Marriage in the Modern Manner," and "Modern Sexuality and the Myth of Victorian Repression," *Passion and Power*, ed. Kathy Peiss and Christian Simmons with Robert Padgug (Philadelphia: Temple University Press, 1987).

31. Ibid.

32. Ibid. Also Paula Fass, *The Damned and the Beautiful* (New York: Oxford Univerity Press, 1977); May, *Great Expectations*.

33. Seidman, *Romantic Longings*, chaps. 3 and 4.

34. William Robinson, *Woman, Her Sex and Love Life*, 17th ed. (New York: Eugenics Publishing Co., 1929 [1917]), p. 368.

35. Ibid., p. 363.

36. Maxine Davis, *Sexual Responsibilities in Marriage* (New York: Dial Press, 1963), p. 27.

37. Ibid., p. 184.

38. Ibid.

39. Oliver Butterfield, *Sexual Harmony in Marriage* (New York: Emerson Books, 1953), p. 22.

40. Eustare Chesser, *Love Without Fear* (New York: Roy Publishers, 1947 [1940]), p. 104.

41. Robert Chartham, *Sex for Advanced Lovers* (New York: New American Library, 1970), p. 9.

42. Davis, *Sexual Responsibilities in Marriage*, p. 20.

43. M.J. Exner, *The Sexual Side of Marriage* (New York: W.W. Norton and Co., 1932), pp. 19–20.

44. Isabel Hutton, *The Sex Technique in Marriage* 3rd ed. (New York: Emerson Books, Inc., 1932), p. 26.

45. Mary Calderone, *Release from Sexual Tension* (New York: Random House, 1960), p. 166.

46. Theodore Van de Velde, *Ideal Marriage* (Westport, Conn.: Greenwood Press, 1950 [1930]), p. 17.

47. Hutton, *The Sex Technique in Marriage*, p. 47.

48. Hannah and Abraham Stone, *A Marriage Manual* (New York: Simon and Schuster, 1939), p. 217.

49. Davis, *Sexual Responsibilities in Marriage*, p. 110.

50. Hannah and Abraham Stone, *A Marriage Manual*, p. 77.

51. Ibid., p. 215.

52. Van de Velde, *Ideal Marriage*, p. 101.

53. Ibid.

54. Ibid.

55. Ibid., p. 178.

56. Ibid. Cf. Hannah and Abraham Stone, *A Marriage Manual*, p. 222.

57. See Steven Seidman, "Constructing Sex as a Domain of Pleasure: Sexual Ideology in the Sixties," *Theory, Culture & Society* 6 (May 1989).

58. *The Joy of Sex*, ed. Alex Comfort (New York: Simon and Schuster, 1970), p. 10.

59. Ibid., p. 11.

60. David Reuben, *Everything You Always Wanted to Know About Sex (But Were Afraid to Ask)* (New York: Bantam, 1969), p. 60.

61. "M," *The Sensuous Man* (New York: Dell, 1971), p. 14.

62. Reuben, *Everything*, p. 24.

63. "J," *The Sensuous Woman* (New York: Dell, 1969), p. 149.

64. Comfort, *The Joy of Sex*, pp. 54–55.

65. Ibid.

66. Alfred Kinsey et al., *Sexual Behavior in the Human Female* (Philadelphia: W.B. Saunders Co., 1953), pp. 268,392–393,400.

67. This was an underlying motivation in Kinsey's research which he believed confirmed the centrality of sexual fulfillment for marriage. See Kinsey, *Sexual Behavior*, pp. 11–12.

68. Morton Hunt, *Sexual Behavior in the 1970s* (New York: Dell, 1974), pp. 20, 35–38.

69. Ibid., pp. 85–88.

70. Ibid., p. 197.

71. Ibid., pp. 197–199.

72. Linda Wolfe, *The Cosmo Report* (New York: Arbor House, 1981).

73. Carol Tavris and Susan Sadd, *Redbook Report on Female Sexuality* (New York: Delacorte, 1977).

74. Lewis, *Literature, Obscenity, and Law*, p. 9.

75. D'Emilio and Freedman, *Intimate Matters*, p. 287.

76. U.S. Commission on Obscenity and Pornography, *The Report of the Commission on Obscenity and Pornography* (New York: Random House, 1970), p. 24.

77. Ibid., p. 85.

78. Reed, *From Private Vice to Public Virtue*; Gordon, *Woman's Body, Woman's Rights*; D'Emilio and Freedman, *Intimate Matters*.

79. See, for example, Stuart Ewen, *Captains of Consciousness* (New York: McGraw-Hill, 1979); *The Culture of Consumption*, ed. R.W. Fox and T. J. Jackson Lears (New York Pantheon, 1985); Roland Marchand, *Advertising the American Dream* (Berkeley: University of California Press, 1986); Wolfgang Haug, *Critique of Commodity Aesthetics* (Cambridge: Polity Press, 1986).

80. Kinsey, *Sexual Behavior in the Human Female*, p. 298.

81. Hunt, *Sexual Behavior in the 1970s*, p. 20.

82. Robert Bell and Kathleen Coughey, "Premarital Sexual Expression Among College Females, 1958, 1968, and 1978," *Family Relations* 29 (July 1980), p. 354.

83. Karl King, Jack Balswick and Ira Robinson, "The Continuing Premarital Sexual Revolution Among College Females," *Journal of Marriage and the Family* 39 (Aug. 1977), p. 458.

84. J. Roy Hopkins, "Sexual Behavior in Adolescence," *Journal of Social Issues* 33:2 (1977), p. 77.

85. See Fass, *The Beautiful and the Damned*; Rothman, *Hands and Hearts*; Robert Bell, *Premarital Sex*; Ira Reiss, *Premarital Sex Standards in America* (New York: The Free Press, 1960); Robert Coles and Geoffrey Stokes, *Sex and the American Teenager* (New York: Harper & Row, 1985).

86. Hunt, *Sexual Behavior in the 1970s*, pp. 118–119.

87. P. Glick, "Some Recent Changes in American Families," *Current Population Reports*. U.S. Bureau of the Census, Special Studies, Series P–23, No. 52, (Washington: GPO 1975).

88. Richard Clayton and Harwin Voss, "Shacking Up: Cohabitation in the 1970s," *Journal of Marriage and the Family*, 39 (May 1977).

89. Charles Lee Cole, "Cohabitation in Social Context," *Marriage and Alternatives*, ed. Roger Libby and Robert Whitehurst (Glenview, Ill.: Scott Foresman, and Company, 1977); Eleanor Macklin, "Heterosexual Cohabitation Among Unmarried College Students," *Family Coordinator* 21 (Oct. 1972) and "Nontraditional Family Forms: A Decade of Research," *Journal of Marriage and the Family* 42 (Nov. 1980); Paul Glick and Graham Spanier, "Married and Unmarried Cohabitation in the United States," *Journal of Marriage and the Family*, 42 (Feb. 1980); Paul Glick and Arthur Norton, "Marrying, Divorcing, and Living Together in the U.S. Today," *Population Bulletin*, 32 (1977).

90. Hunt, *Sexual Behavior in the 1970s*, p. 22.

91. Norval Glenn and Charles Weaver, "Attitudes Toward Premarital, Extramarital, and Homosexual Relations in the U.S. in the 1970s," *The Journal of Sex Research* 15 (May 1979).

92. I've examined a large number of articles on homosexuality from the mid-1960s to the mid-1970s. See, for example, Gene Phillips, "The Homosexual Revolution," *America*, Nov. 14, 1970; Jack Star, "The Homosexual Couple," *Look*, Jan. 26, 1971; "The Militant Homosexual," *Newsweek*, August 23, 1971; "Gays on the March," *Time*, Sept. 8, 1975.

93. D'Emilio, *Sexual Politics, Sexual Communities*.

94. Cf. Altman, *The Homosexualization of America*.

95. On the link between capitalism and sexuality that best reflects my own view, see Weeks, *Sexuality and its Discontents*. Also, see Alan Soble, *Pornography* (New Haven: Yale University Press, 1986); Haug, *Critique of Commodity Aesthetics*.

96. See Altman, *Homosexualization of America*; Jeremy Seabrook, *A Lasting Relationship* (London: Allen Lane, 1976).

97. See Faderman, *Surpassing the Love of Men*.

98. E. Anthony Rotundo, "Romantic Friendship: Male Intimacy and Middle-Class Youth in the Northern United States, 1800–1900," *Journal of Social History* 23 (Fall 1989).

99. Barbara Welter, "The Cult of True Womanhood; 1820–1860," *The American Family in Social-Historical Perspective*, ed. Michael Gordon.

100. For an attempt to place women at the center of the changes in American sexual patterns, see Barbara Ehrenreich et al., *Re-Making Love* (New York: Doubleday, 1987).

101. See, for example, Gerald Marrimar, "The Estrangement of the Intellectuals in America: The Search for New Life Styles in the Early Twentieth Century,"(Ph.D. diss.: University of Colorado, 1972); Ellen Kay Trimberger, "Feminism, Men, and Modern Love: Greenwich Village, 1900–1925," *Powers of Desire*.

102. Excellent reviews of the Beats are available, for example,in Dennis McNally, *Desolate Angel* (New York: Random House, 1979); Bruce Cook, *The Beat Generation* (New York: Scribner, 1971); Louis Simpson, *A Revolution in Taste* (New York: Macmillan, 1978).

103. See Barry Miles, *Ginsberg, a Biography* (New York: Simon and Schuster, 1989).

104. Herbert Marcuse, *Eros and Civilization* (Boston: Beacon Press, 1955). Norman O. Brown, *Love Against Death* (New York: Vantage, 1959) and *Love's Body* (New York: Vantage, 1966).

105. On the sexual culture and ideology of the counterculture, see *The Sixties Papers*, ed. Judith Clavir Albert and Stewart Edward Albert, eds., (New York: Praeger, 1984); Gene Anthony, *The Summer of Love* (Ca.: Celestial Arts, 1980); Ralph Benton, *Psychedelic Sex* (Canoga Park, Ca.: Viceroy 1968);

Counter Culture, ed. Joseph Berke (London: Peter Owen, 1968); Mitchell Goodman, *The Movement Toward a New America* (New York: Knopf, 1970); Martin Lee and Bruce Shlain, *Acid Dreams* (New York: Grove, 1985).

106.   See Seidman, *Romantic Longings*, chap. 5. Also, see Barbara Ehrenreich, *The Hearts of Men* (New York: Doubleday, 1983).

107.   See chap. 3 of this book.

108.   Kate Millet, *Sexual Politics* (New York: Ballantine, 1978 [1969]), p. 86. See chap. 3.

109.   Seidman, *Romantic Longings*, chap. 5. Also see chap. 3 of this book.

110.   Ibid., ch. 6. Also see chapter 4 of this book.

111.   Dennis Altman,"How Much Do Gay Men and Lesbians Really Have in Common," *The Advocate*, April 16, 1981.

112.   Comfort, *More Joy of Sex*, p. 96.

113.   Alexander Comfort, "Sexuality in a Zero Growth Society," *Current* Feb. 1973, pp. 30–31.

114.   Comfort, *Joy of Sex*, p. 153.

115.   See Seidman, *Romantic Longings*. A similar thesis has been suggested but in a less systematic way by Paul Robinson, *The Modernization of Sex* (New York: Harper & Row, 1976).

2

False Promises:
Reconnecting Eros and Romance

In 1970, the Commission on Obscenity and Pornography issued a report documenting the penetration of pornography into mainstream America.[1] While most adult men and women and many teenagers had been exposed to pornography,[2] it appeared to have little or no relationship with crime and deviance.[3] Indeed, the Commission maintained that pornography played a beneficial social role, as a medium of sex education and communication, and stimulant of fantasies which enhanced sexual satisfaction.[4] The Commission recommended the elimination of virtually all federal, state, and local statutes prohibiting the production and distribution of pornography.[5]

In 1986, the Attorney General's Commission on Pornography released a massive statement on the meaning and morality of pornography.[6] Like its predecessor, this Commission documented the spread of pornography into daily life: in local drug stores, food markets, videoshops, on cable television and so on. Unlike its predecessor, the Meese Commission considered Americans' increasing exposure to pornography as alarming. Despite some disagreement, this Commission insisted upon the dangers of pornography. It was thought to lead directly to deviance, nonconventional behavior, violence, and contempt for basic American institutions and values like love, marriage and the family.[7] The Meese Commission recommended legislation that would greatly restrict the production and circulation of sexually explicit representations, stricter laws regulating pornography, and harsher penalties for violating these laws.[8]

The different interpretations of pornography by the two Commissions are indicative of a shift in American culture. The 1970 document represents a defense of an expansive notion of sexual choice and pleasure. From the perspective of this Commission, pornography exhibits a concept of sex as a joyous, beneficial power. Legalizing it goes hand in hand with an ideology that identifies sexual freedom with expanded sexual choice and celebrates eroticism as a sphere of pleasure and play. On the other hand, for the 1986 Commission, pornography evokes the dangers of unrestrained desire. An eroticism released from intimate social bonds is said to be destructive of personal integrity and healthy intimate relations; it promotes social deviance and violence toward women.

The Meese Commission recommended the strict regulation of pornography. It did so less because the Commission was offended by its nudity or eroticism, than because many of its members were convinced that the hedonistic-expressive celebration of sex and the joys of eroticism were misplaced. They believed that sex needed to assume its fundamentally social and spiritual role as a romantic, intimate bond to realize its beneficient capacities.

Between the mid-1970s and the 1990s, a discourse celebrating the liberating and self-fulfilling power of sexual expression came under critical scrutiny. Critics of this liberationist ideology highlighted the dangers and undesirable consequences of a free-wheeling, pleasure-centered desire, from depersonalization and sexual objectification, to the destabilization of intimate bonds and exposure to disease, exploitation, and violence. Although these critics did not speak with one voice, they generally called attention to the absences and silences in the liberationist celebration of sexual choice, diversity and eroticism. They urged a renewal of restrictions on choice while disclaiming an endorsement of sexual repression. They wished to reconfigure the very meaning and morality of sex.

This shift should not be described as a backlash reaction to a movement of social progress. I am not describing a trajectory of revolution and counterrevolution. Between the 1960s and 1980s, the defense of sexual choice, diversity and eroticism remained prominent in mainstream American culture. For example, while Anita Bryant's "Save Our Children" crusade against homosexuality in 1977 may have initiated a wave of antigay politics, it would be wrong to assume that this was evidence of a societal-wide movement against choice and diversity. In the course of the 1980s, the gay community was able to include a gay rights plank in the 1980 Democratic presidential platform which was written into the charter and bylaws governing the National Democratic Party; national gay and lesbian organizations like the National Association of Gay and Lesbian Democratic Clubs and the Human Rights Campaign Fund, a gay Political Action Committee, were created; and gay public officials from city councilpersons to mayors and United States senators were elected. While an organized antigay movement did crystallize in the late 1970s, it did so in reaction to the substantial movement towards the social inclusion of lesbians and gay men which continued, however unevenly, through the 1980s.

A noticeable shift did occur, however, in sexual meanings between the mid-1970s and late 1980s, but this did not amount to a radical break with the past. Moreover, the shift cannot be described as a conservative return to a repressive sexual ethic. Critics of the liberationist ideology raised serious questions about the morality of an expansive concept of sexual choice and a pleasure-centered sexual ethic that were typically neglected by its advocates. Does a hedonistic ethic present unique concerns for women? Does a pleasure-centered ethic create a tension between eros and romance, and between individualism and social bonding? Does investing sex with expectations for self-fulfillment create a new tyranny of performance and orgasmic ecstasy? Does making sex a natural, profane act strip it of its mysterious and enchanting qualities?

Critics of a liberationist ideology spanned the ideological spectrum. Some critics advocated a conservative sexual politic while others sought to defend a politic of choice and eroticism within a post-liberationist framework. Yet, two overarching themes surface prominently in these sex discourses. First, post-liberationist discourses emphasized the social and spiritual meaning of sex, challenging the notion that sexual fulfillment meant simply removing social restraints and allowing for the proliferation of sexualities and pleasures. Sex should be positioned within a social framework that embedded it in rituals of dating, courting, romance and intimate bonding. Second, post-liberationists contended that the celebration of choice and diversity had ambiguous moral implications. They claimed that it weakened bonds of intimacy that depend on commitment and fidelity, leaving many individuals, especially women, vulnerable to abuse, exploitation and loneliness. Thus, post-liberationists generally advocated placing more restrictions on sexual expression.

This chapter aims to document the rise of post-liberationist sex discourses to a position of public authority between the mid-1970s and the late 1980s. I will argue that though this cultural shift was prompted by important social and moral concerns, and though it speaks in multiple voices, a conservative sexual politic has often controlled the public discussion of sexuality. This has had some unfortunate consequences. In an effort to legitimate their own sexual values, conservatives have produced a caricature of the sexual liberationists as promoting an agenda of unrestricted sexual expression. They have held liberationists accountable for a range of current social ills, from high rates of divorce and illegitimacy to herpes and AIDS. As liberal and Left defenders of a liberationist ideology were put on the defensive, they, in turn, caricatured their critics as stalwarts of sexual repression. The result is that the debate over sexual politics and ethics has often been described as polarized between advocates of sexual expression and defenders of sexual restraint. As a common ground for discussion disappears, sexual political conflicts tend to become closely intertwined with broader social divisions which make a more pragmatic mode of conflict resolution virtually impossible. To avoid this simplistic opposition of friends of choice versus friends of restriction, it is necessary to recover something of the complexity and range of post-liberationist discourses. Accordingly, although I begin with a discussion of conservative responses to a liberationist ideology, I intend to review liberal, Left and some feminist critical reactions as well. To begin this discussion of post-liberationist sex discourses, we need to at least sketch its social setting.

Social and Sexual Crisis: The Costs of Liberation

Just as the politics of liberal democracy were initially a response to a social crisis in the 1920s, a conservative political drift from the mid-1970s on was a reaction to a perceived social crisis. This time, however, it was a crisis of liberalism that was at the heart of postwar social conflicts.

The 1960s began in a national mood of optimism and liberal consensus. It was a time of economic growth and relative affluence, a period of growing United States prestige in the world. A consensus, at least among middle-class whites, coalesced around the notion of the United States as a basically beneficent world power; that economic productivity required a free market; that economic growth created the conditions of a free and egalitarian society; and that there were no major social divisions in the United States, only local social problems to be dealt with by the appropriate coalition of experts, citizens and elected officials. By the end of that decade, however, many Americans saw their country in a state of crisis. The liberal consensus had apparently collapsed; the legitimacy of key institutions was being called into question; America seemed like a divided, strife-torn nation.[9]

It is not often appreciated that social discontent in the 1960s was not confined to liberals and the Left, but was felt among conservatives too.[10] The support garnered by Wallace in the 1968 presidential primary and the spirited backing of Spiro Agnew by many Americans between 1968–1973, as well as the spread of fundamentalism in the 1960s and early 1970s suggests that discontent had spread across the ideological spectrum. We should not forget that while we often think of liberal and radical protesters as the symbols of the time, it was Richard Nixon, and not George McGovern or Eugene McCarthy, who was President during these turbulent times. For every leftward push there was a social push in the opposite direction.

Nevertheless, the movements in the 1960s that favored liberalization and democratization were more visible and appeared to many Americans to be more socially defining of the period. The Vietnam War, the student protests, the New Left, and the movements around black, women's and gay liberation became national symbols of a breakdown in the liberal consensus. These were mass-based movements which assailed the central myth of America: that we are a nation divinely chosen to lead humanity to a better future. Far from being the land of liberty and progress, America was often portrayed by these movements as corrupt, bigoted, greedy, militaristic and oppressive of many of its citizens. These movements not only demanded expanded liberties and opportunities for individuals to design their own lives, but pressed for far-reaching changes; they offered social visions that were post-liberal.

With their radical agenda for social change, these new social movements alone could have stimulated a conservative reaction. But these attacks on American liberalism occurred in a social setting that seemed to many Americans to suggest a national crisis.

The preeminent global presence of the United States as a world power seemed shaken in the early 1970s. As the influence of the Soviet Union successfully expanded into Cuba, North Korea, parts of Africa and the Middle East in the postwar period, the United States experienced a major defeat in Vietnam and Cambodia. This blow to our world status was reinforced by the oil crisis in the early 1970s; many Americans felt that we were being held hostage by weaker Third World powers. The overthrow of the United States-backed backed Shah Palavi regime in Iran and the humiliation many Americans felt during the hostage crisis, along with the signing of the Panama Canal treaty, was taken by many Americans as signs of the loss of our national nerve. These symbols of social crisis were reinforced by the forced resignation of Richard Nixon and the subsequent weak presidential regimes of Ford and Carter.

The perception of a United States falling from global dominance seemed further evidenced in its economic decline in the 1970s.[11] During these years, the United States economy suffered a steady decline in the rate of corporate profit, a pyramiding of short-term debt, a constant rise in inflation and interest rates, high levels of unemployment, a decline of one-fifth in real wages, and other signs of economic deterioration. This decline did not appear, moreover, to be a response to a situational event or short-term development. Economists underscored one major fact: the internationalization of the United States economy. Between 1970 and 1980, the percentage of United States goods exported rose from 9 percent to 19 percent, while the percentage of imported goods rose from 9 percent to 22 percent. Capital investment overseas was a full 10 percent of our total investment. By 1980 more than 70 percent of all goods produced in the United States were competing with foreign-made goods. Moreover, competition was not simply from Europe and Japan. In the 1970s, imports from developing nations increased tenfold, from 3.6 billion dollars to 30 billion. The developing nations now had advanced technology, sophisticated systems of transportation to distribute goods, access to specialized markets and cheap labor that allowed them to compete with high-volume, and labor-intensive industries (e.g., steel, automobiles, textiles) in advanced industrial nations.

These developments seemed to reveal a telling point: the United States economy was losing its competitive edge in this new world economy. The fate of the core industrial-manufacturing sector, for example, alarmed many Americans. By 1981, the United States was importing 26 percent of its automobiles, 25 percent of its steel, and 60 percent of its televisions and radios, whereas in 1960 such imports amounted to less than 10 percent. The considerable expansion in employment that transpired in the 1970s was concentrated in the service sector. Specifically, eating and drinking places, health services, and business services accounted for more than 40 percent of the new private sector jobs created. These new jobs were usually temporary, part-time, low paying, and lacked career possibilities. Slowed economic growth and productivity, high levels of unemployment, government deficits, and inflation followed the decline of the industrial base and the burgeoning of the service sector. These troubling economic signs seemed, at the time, linked to structural changes in the world economy that were less amenable to Keynesian strategies. There was a sense that our fate was less and less in our own hands.

By the end of the 1970s, the United States was perceived by many Americans as in the midst of a crisis as much social as economic. Domestically, the young and the masses of disenfranchised populations (people of color, women, gays) were in revolt; our political leaders and institutions seemed nonresponsive; the country was mired in an unpopular war; with our economy on a downward spiral, a sense of national decline spread. Kevin Phillips spoke of America as an "empire in retreat"; Christopher Lasch, in his bestselling *The Culture of Narcissism*, prognosticated the end of liberalism as he analyzed a nation drifting aimlessly; Robert Heilbroner sketched various scenarios of American decline in *Business Civilization in Decline*; George Gilder argued that the loosening of traditional gender and sexual codes symbolized a deep social pathology; and Daniel Bell portrayed contemporary America as morally exhausted and in the throes of a cultural crisis.[12]

The appearance of a conservative sexual political agenda in the mid-1970s was, in part, a reaction to this perception of national decline. Many conservatives thought the source of our malaise to be moral and cultural. Liberalizing social trends, which were accentuated by the liberation movements of the 1960s, were accused of undermining social restraints. The quest for self-fulfillment had turned destructive. Inspired by a liberationist ideology, many Americans, especially the young, were said to be mounting an assault on all institutional and normative constraints. Inevitably, those social institutions that were authorized to provide moral regulation and order (e.g., the church, school, family) became enfeebled. The breakdown in moral order was exhibited in a crisis of the family (high divorce rates), economy (low productivity, high turnover) and government (low voter turnout, party disaffiliation). In a word, our national crisis was seen by many conservatives, and some liberals, as originating in the breakdown of moral order and social discipline.

Many conservatives believed that national renewal hinged on restoring moral order. They wished to clarify normative standards, provide stricter regulation of behavior, and erect constraints upon desire. Social renewal was thought to require a regime of individual discipline and self-control. This entailed the restoration of the moral and social authority of our key institutions, especially the family. Strengthening the family required the reprivatization of social functions, many of which had been taken over by the state. Many Americans, both conservatives and liberals, believed that heterosexuality, marriage, and the family needed to be defended against feminists, gays, countercultural critics and an interventionist welfare state. Advocating the reinstatement of an autonomous private sphere centered around a refurbished family unit pushed conservatives and liberals alike into the politics of sexuality.[13]

In part, a conservative and, to a lesser extent, a liberal sexual politic was a response to a perception of national malaise and decline. Many conservatives and some liberals were led to challenge the dominant liberationist sexual ideology. For some, that meant advocating a restrictionist sexual politic at odds with social trends that continued to have a great deal of public support. Other conservatives and liberals sought to preserve some of the liberalizing trends of the postwar period while avoiding what they took to be its unhealthy aspects.

This critical response to a liberationist ideology was by no means confined to conservatives or some centrist liberals. Many Americans, regardless of their ideological persuasion, believed that something was terribly wrong with our intimate culture. Whatever the hopes of sexual liberationist movements, current realities were sobering.

Between the mid-1970s and late 1980s, many Americans perceived symptoms of a virtual crisis in sexual morality. America in the 1980s seemed to be reeling from a series of epidemics: divorce, illegitimacy, teen pregnancy, domestic and sexual violence, herpes and AIDS. Commentators of all ideological persuasions spoke of the endemic instability in relationships, a loss of commitment to marriage, and a "trend away from family living."[14] Psychologists spoke of a rising tide of anxieties associated with sexual performance, impotence, and loneliness; feminists highlighted an epidemic of child abuse and violence towards women stemming, in part, from an intimate culture encouraging the objectification of individuals as mere bodies to be exploited for personal pleasure and adventure. Cultural critics assailed American intimate conventions for promoting emotionally shallow and callous behavior, and for reducing individuals to mere bodies and organs. Many Americans thought the source of this malaise to be a liberationist ideology that was characterized as excessively permissive, that placed too much value on erotic pleasure, and that was so tolerant toward variant sexual expressions that it undermined moral standards. Although post-liberationist discourses surfaced in diverse ideological camps, it was conservatives, especially those who advocated a restrictive sexual agenda, who often controlled public debate through the 1980s. My discussion will begin with conservatives but will pursue this reconfiguring of sex, eros and romance in liberal, Left and feminist contexts.

Discourses of Restriction: Conservative Interventions

As the counterculture went mainstream and as the gay and women's movements became more politically effective in the 1970s, the voices of the detractors of change reached a higher pitch. Articles like "Is the American Family in Danger?" or "Will Liberalized Sex Kill Romantic Love?" captured the concerns and fears that many Americans felt towards the changes of the preceding years.[15] Did too much sexual choice threaten marital, familial and societal order? Did emphasizing sexual pleasure weaken the emotional, social and moral bonds of intimacy? Did too much tolerance of variant sexual and intimate lifestyles endanger the heterosexual, marital, and familial norm? As I will show, concerns about the proper balance of choice and control, of pleasure, variety and intimacy, were sounded across the ideological spectrum. Nevertheless, as social trends in the late 1960s and early 1970s leaned heavily in the direction of expanded choice, tolerance for diversity and the pursuit of pleasure, the greatest concerns were voiced by conservatives. They reacted sharply to liberationist movements by producing a discourse of restriction.

In the early 1970s, two key figures in this conservative discursive intervention were Midge Decter and George Gilder. The former, along with her husband, Norman Podhoretz, was a chief editor of *Commentary*; both played a pivotal role in shaping what was to be called neoconservatism. Mr. Gilder has likewise proved to be a key figure, serving as a bridge between the centrist conservatism of Eastern Republicans and the radical populism of the New Right. My discussion of the conservative discourse of restriction begins with Decter and Gilder.

In 1972, Midge Decter published a stinging critique of the women's movement entitled *The New Chastity and Other Arguments Against Women's Liberation*.[16] In fact, Decter's aim was not only to discredit this movement but to simultaneously attack a liberationist sexual ideology and politics.

Decter interpreted women's liberation as combining what she described as a radical strain—its premise that men and women are similar and therefore should share equally in social tasks—and a conservative position with respect to sexuality. The women's movement, Decter argued, was against the sexual revolution.[17] Decter argued that feminists viewed the sexual revolution as a movement by and for men. They held that in response to women's expanding social empowerment, men reacted by trying to impose new sexual definitions and roles that would leave women socially subordinate. Women's liberation, thought Decter, did not view the sexual revolution as expanding women's freedom and happiness, but as creating new forms of male social control and dominance. The subtext of the women's movement, according to Decter, was a call for a "new chastity." Feminists, said Decter, entreated women to withdraw from heterosexual relations into a spiritually conceived woman-centered life.

Decter agreed with feminists that the sexual revolution was bad for women, not because it imposed new constraints but because it gave women too much choice. "Women's liberation calls it enslavement but the real truth about the sexual revolution is that it has made of sex an almost chaotically limitless and therefore unmanageable realm in the life of women."[18] Decter believed that the liberationist ideology weakened a heterosexual, romantic, marital norm. Sexual liberationist movements greatly expanded the options for both men and women. Far from being rendered a sexual object, the contemporary woman was "a sexual subject par excellence."[19]

In contrast to sexual liberationists, Decter reasoned that this new sexual freedom was a source of unhappiness for women. Whereas men's sexuality was said to be governed by a biologically rooted carnal drive, which was given more opportunities for expression in a permissive environment, the same was not true for women. "The problem of her having been left to the operation of her own lust is that young girls do not lust in any way that gives proper drive or guidance to action."[20] Lacking strong biologically programmed sexual drives and clear social directives, sexual liberalization was said to leave women feeling sexually anomic and vulnerable to exploitation.

Decter's perspective presupposes a natural difference between men's and women's sexuality. Men are said to be carnally motivated; they are genitally-driven and oriented to orgasmic pleasure. By contrast, women are thought to be romantically and spiritually motivated; they are person-centered and oriented to love. A woman's "erotic fantasies are not of the penis but of the man, complete with identity and personality, who is able to create in her and minister to an evergrowing feeling of arousal."[21] Women's diffuse intimate longings cannot provide emotional or behavioral direction. "No longer expected to be chaste, and yet without the active force of lust to guide her, she finds herself without natural boundaries. . . ."[22] Moreover, the trend towards emphasizing erotic pleasure, variety and orgasm is at odds with women's essentially spiritual nature. "The truth is . . . that the pursuit of orgasm for a woman is an entirely irrelevant undertaking. . . . Her need for sex is diffuse. . . . And her pleasure in sex is . . . found in . . . the power to elicit affirmations of her worth and desirability, in the excitements of giving pleasure."[23] In short, by expanding sexual choice, by asserting the natural equality between male and female sexuality, and by imbuing erotic pleasure with expectations of self-realization, our liberal sexual culture is said to be at odds with a natural order.

Decter maintained that sexual choice and intimate lifestyle variation should be restricted if we wished to escape the escalating incidence of divorce, illegitimacy, teen pregnancy, homosexuality, and sexual disease. She appealed to a concept of a natural sexual and gender order. The differences between women's other-directed, diffuse, spiritual desires and men's inner-directed, genitally-driven, carnal desires must be respected. Central to the restriction of choice is the exclusive legitimacy of heterosexuality. Notwithstanding some biological, social or psychic disturbance, men and women naturally long for each other.[24] Indeed, Decter invokes the notion of a natural order to further restrict choice to a romantic, monogamous intimate arrangement. "She [woman] requires . . . in her nature . . . the assurance that a single man has undertaken to love, cherish, and support her. As a sexual being, her true freedom and self-realization lie in a sustained . . . emotionally intimate commitment to one man. . . ."[25] In a word, Decter appealed to a concept of a natural order to defend an intimate ideal that legitimates only a heterosexual, marital norm in which sex functions either as a medium of love—and in which sexual expression therefore exhibits romantic, loving qualities—or as a reproductive act.

A year after Decter's *The New Chastity* appeared, George Gilder published *Sexual Suicide*, a broadly conceived critique of contemporary sexual trends.[26] Like Decter, Gilder imbued sexual and intimate behavior with enormous moral and social significance. The fate of civilization, Gilder believed, was directly linked to the social management of sexual expression. "Sex is the life-force . . . of a people, and their very character will be deeply affected by how sexuality is managed. . . . When sex is devalued . . . and deformed, as at present, the quality of our life declines and our social fabric deteriorates."[27] In Gilder's view, current trends had become socially destructive. "What is described as the sexual revolution is . . . the sexual suicide [of our] society."[28]

Gilder's critique was aimed directly at sexual liberationists, whose celebration of the liberating, self-fulfilling power of eroticism was held responsible for the debasement of American culture.

> The women's movement, the *Playboy* theorists, the gay liberationists, the sexologists and the pornographers all tend to . . . present alternatives to loving sexuality. The pornographer . . . advertises the potential joys of promiscuity. . . . The sex manuals [promote the] abandonment of inhibitions. . . . The women's movement offers visions of a spurious sexual equality. . . . The Homosexuals romanticize a pattern . . . in which temporary gratification is paramount. These forces together create an undertow that threatens . . . the enduring structures of civilized sexuality.[29]

Liberationists were said to promote a hedonistic-expressive sexual ethic. Sex was viewed as "a completely separate mode of activity" and valued as a vehicle of "orgasmic pleasure."[30]

Contrary to the expectations of liberationists, Gilder maintained that the expansion of sexual choice and the celebration of eroticism had yielded neither enhanced self-fulfillment nor social progress. At a personal level, "when sex becomes a kind of massage . . . one's whole emotional existence is depleted."[31] Indeed, the quest for sexual pleasure and adventure is said to inevitably lead to "impotence . . . a widespread sense of pessimism and demoralization, a fascination with violence, revolution, drugs, . . . and a strangely desperate loneliness."[32] The liberationist dream of self-fulfillment turned into a nightmare of vicious sexual competition, with an abundance of lonely losers, high divorce rates, and a rising incidence of homosexuality. Employing a rhetorical trope that surfaced prominently in New Right discourses, Gilder traced virtually all the major social problems of the time to disturbances in the sexual order. "All these social problems are ultimately erotic. The frustration of the affluent young and their resort to drugs, the breakdown of the family, . . . the rising rate of crime and violence . . . spring from . . . a fundamental deformation of sexuality."[33] Our society was in serious trouble because, under the influence of liberationists, we celebrated a debased and anomic intimate culture. "When a society deliberately affirms these failures—contemplates legislation of homosexual marriage, celebrates women who denounce the family, and indulges pornography as a manifestation of sexual health and a release from repression—the culture is promoting a form of erotic suicide. For it is destroying the cultural precondition of a profound love and sexuality: the durable heterosexual relationships necessary to a community of emotional investments and continuities in which children can find a secure place."[34]

Underpinning Gilder's critique of sexual trends is a concept of a natural order. He presumed natural differences between men and women and an innate, biologically rooted heterosexuality. Drawing on a familiar Victorian symbolic configuration, Gilder proposed that men are by nature genitally-driven, carnally motivated, aggressive, and promiscuous. "Males almost everywhere show greater sexual aggressiveness, compulsiveness, and lack of selectivity . . . Men are overwhelmingly more prone to masturbation, homosexuality, voyeurism, gratuitous sexual aggression and other shallow and indiscriminate erotic activity."[35] While male desire is thought to provide the will power to build civilization and to move society forward, unless this desire is regulated it will turn destructive. Fortunately, thought Gilder, women are, so to speak, programmed differently. Their sexuality is organized around romantic and maternal needs. Women look to sex to express their need to love and be loved. Women need men to give form and specificity to their diffuse sexual feelings as well as to realize their innate maternal longings. Accordingly, women function as the moral guardians of civilization. Their chief social role is to "domesticate and civilize male nature."[36] Gilder thought that women get men to sublimate their carnal desires into a quest for heterosexual romance, marriage, family, and career.

Gilder, like Decter, appealed to a concept of an essential female and male nature to justify a restrictive sexual and intimate cultural norm. Both authors invoked the Victorian image of the carnal promiscuous male, who requires the regulating power of the spiritually pure female who, in turn, is fulfilled only by her relentless, lifetime love of one man. Within this Victorian gender framework, a fairly narrow sexual regime is promoted. Only sex that is embedded in heterosexual intimate bonds, that symbolizes love, and that exhibits tender and loving qualities, promotes a healthy and prosperous society. Sex between same-sex partners, sex that is uncoupled from intimate ties, sex that is pleasure-centered or nonmonogamous is viewed as dangerous to the well-being of the individual and society.

Conservative sex discourses in the early 1970s were not immediately translated into a restrictive sex politic. They did, however, provide a favorable ideological context for such a politic. By the late 1970s, an emphasis on restraint and discipline had become central to the sexual political agendas of both neoconservatism and the New Right. My comments will be confined to the latter.

The Politics of Sexual Restriction: The New Right Attack on Choice

The great protests and countercultural happenings of the 1960s had come to an end by the early 1970s. Yet the secular, liberal democratic drift of United States politics had assumed a palpable social, legislative and legal form. For example, Congress had passed the ERA in 1972 and sent it to the states for ratification; Roe v. Wade had, in effect, made abortion legal on demand; "gay rights" ordinances had been enacted in dozens of cities; affirmative action, quotas, and school busing were official policy in all states; the Federal Courts imposed severe restrictions on school prayer and municipal Christian displays while legalizing pornography; and SALT II was signed, as was the Panama Canal Treaty, much to the dismay of conservatives. The great happenings and explosive rhetoric of the 1960s had disappeared but much of its social agenda was enacted in social and legal reform in the 1970s.

For many Americans, these developments did not express truly national values and interests. They seemed instead to reflect the power of a new middle class to impose upon Americans a morality and politics that reflected their own strident liberalism, secularism and egalitarianism. Moreover, the carriers of this new politics and morality of choice and equality had enlisted the state to enact its social agenda. The new activist state, with its war on poverty, school busing and affirmative action policies, urban planning ideology, civil rights legislation, and its legalization of pornography and abortion, seemed, to many Americans, to have taken over the liberationist social agenda of the new social movements. In a context of growing Soviet power and in the face of the Western European drift into social democracy, many American's were alarmed that their country was losing not only its political, economic and military world dominance but its very soul.

A new grass-roots conservative politics began to surface in the early 1970s. Although it had ties to the anti-communism and free market ideology of centrist Republican conservatives, its main focus was on issues bearing on personal life, e.g., health, family, sexuality, education, and religion. A plethora of single issue organizations cropped up across the country, e.g., the Stop ERA movement headed by Phyllis Schlafly and the Right to Life movement. Out of this network of activists and organizations there emerged a new powerful grass-roots, based social and political force: the New Right.[37]

The New Right was a loose coalition of political, religious, and single-issue pro-life and pro-family groups which combined grass-roots mobilization with professional lobbying. Its lead political organizations included the Survival of a Free Congress, led by Paul Weyrich; the National Conservative Political Action Committee, led by John Dolan; and the Conservative Caucus, led by Howard Phillips. Their principal journal was the *Conservative Digest*, published by the direct mailing virtuoso Richard Viguerie. By the end of the 1970s, these political organizations had joined forces with a number of fundamentalist Christian groups. At least two umbrella groups were formed: the Moral Majority, headed by Jerry Falwell, and the Christian Voice chaired initially by Robert Grant. Allied further with the pro-family, pro-life movement, the New Right functioned through the mid-1980s as a powerful social and political force.

The New Right was a reaction to both the new social movements of the 1970s and to the activist state that was thought to promote a liberationist social agenda. Its proponents believed that the government had been literally taken over by the most extreme liberal, democratic and secular elements of society. Ironically, the New Right adopted the rhetoric of crisis that was widespread in the 1960s. Events such as the signing of the Panama Canal treaty and SALT II, Watergate and the resignation of Richard Nixon, and the Congressional passage of the ERA and Roe v. Wade, symbolized for many New Rightists a moral and political crisis of the republic. America was drifting away from its great heritage; national pride was damaged; key institutions were losing their moral authority; a great confusion and malaise seemed to blanket the country. New Rightists had no doubt about the source of America's troubles: the new activist state controlled by the social agenda of the liberation movements. Internationally, the politics of detente were rendering the United States weak and cautious, while on the domestic front, the activist state had produced a bloated bureaucracy that benefitted few beyond the new middle class. The New Right blamed the activist state for creating a large underclass of Americans dependent upon a paternalistic government. The new welfare state had spawned, they argued, a morass of social and economic regulations that had sapped America of its dynamic, creative source: the risk-taking, innovative, self reliant individual.

Central to this view of America in crisis was the belief that the family was under beseige. The combination of the state's assumption of social functions the family had controlled and its attack by the liberationist movements, were thought to have embroiled the family in a web of debilitating conflicts. The family was in a state of crisis, as evidenced by escalating rates of divorce, illegitimacy, teen pregnancy and widespread homosexuality. In as much as New Rightists were convinced of the family's role as the basic moral and social unit of civilization, they anticipated social chaos and turmoil so long as the unit was unstable.

The aim of the New Right was to restore America's national pride, to revitalize the economy, to regain our confidence in our leaders and institutions, and to reestablish our global stature. This entailed a multifaceted strategy that included pursuing a Realpolitik foreign policy, reinvigorating a culture of discipline and risk-taking, deregulating the economy and society, and restoring a Christian public morality. A central component of the New Right agenda was the reprivatization of the state. This meant the return to the private realm of social functions taken over by the activist state: in short, the abolition of many government regulations over industry and the reassertion of local community control. In particular, reprivatization meant restoring the vitality and power of the family as an agency of moral and social control.

Strengthening "the family" entailed reasserting patriarchal authority, reestablishing clear bipolar gender roles, and reaffirming a heterosexual, romantic, marital, and familial norm. The New Right campaigned to elect public officials who supported their agenda, lobbyied for judicial and excecutive appointments, and pursued social reform through legislation.

The anti-abortion campaign was central to New Right politics.[38] Although a human life amendment that would have declared a fetus a legal person was not enacted, in 1977 the first Hyde Amendment was passed by Congress. This legislation cut off federal Medicaid funds for abortion services. By 1979 no federal funds could be paid for abortion services except when a woman's life was in danger. The Supreme Court upheld the Hyde Amendment despite the evidence that it amounted to a national policy denying poor women access to abortion. By 1980, state and local laws began to require parental consent before allowing abortions to be performed on unmarried minors and spousal notification before abortions could be performed on wives.

Underpinning the anti-abortion campaign was a struggle to control sexual and intimate behavior by regulating women's sexuality. In her outstanding analysis of the social and moral meaning of abortion politics, Rosiland Petchesky observes:

> Increasingly, antagonism to abortion stems less from concern for protecting the fetus than from a desire to prevent teenage sexuality. 'Right-to-Life' advocates assume a causal relationship between legalized abortion and a rise in sexual promiscuity and illegitimacy. . . . Not only abortion but also birth control and sex education programs are seen as giving official government sanction to 'illicit' sex and therefore as interfering with parents' control over the moral behavior and values of their children. . . .
>
> It is important to note that 'right-to-life' ideology is not simply antisex; the point is not wholesale repression but the rechanneling of sexuality into patriarchally legitimate forms, those that reinforce heterosexual marriage and motherhood.[39]

The pro-life stance of the New Right was linked to a defense of a particular sexual and intimate ideal—the heterosexual, romantic, marital, monogamous, and familial norm. This is made explicit in one of the most comprehensive legislative proposals advanced by the New Right: the Family Protection Act. Initially introduced in both houses of Congress in 1979, and again in 1981, it was designed "to preserve the integrity of the American family, to foster and protect the viability of American family life . . . and to promote the virtues of the family. . . ."[40] "The family" that the FPA was intent on preserving was the heterosexual married familial unit in which the wife attends primarily to domestic tasks and the husband assumes the breadwinner, head-of-household role. Thus, the FPA encouraged women to be full-time homemakers through a variety of tax incentives. Another provision of the FPA sought to augment parental control over teen sexual behavior by denying federal funds to any agency that provided birth control-related services without first notifying the minor's parents. Perhaps its most startling provisions related to its policies towards homosexuality. The FPA would deny federal funds, including Social Security, veteran's benefits or student loans, to any individual, private and public organization which, in any way, could be said to advocate homosexuality or present homosexuality as an acceptable lifestyle.[41] In short, the FPA was an attack on the 1960s movements that sought to expand sexual choice and diversity, and to depolice desire and pleasures that are private and consensual.

While sweeping "pro-family" legislation like the Family Protection Act was not enacted in the 1970s or 1980s, many of the provisions of pro-life, pro-family legislation have become public policy. Thus, the right of parental notification prior to receiving contraceptive services to unmarried teens was issued as an executive regulation by the Department of Health and Human Services. And while abortion rights have not yet been rescinded through a constitutional amendment or a Supreme Court decision, federal funds have slowed, new constraints have been imposed on family planning agencies, and restrictive laws limiting abortion services have been enacted in many localities and states.[42]

The restrictive ideology and politics of sexuality advocated by the New Right gained social credibility in the 1980s. Defenders of choice and diversity, of erotic pleasure and expression, were put on the defensive. Indeed, although the politics of restriction was pioneered by the New Right and conservatives, restrictionist themes surfaced in liberal and Left, including feminist, sex discourses. Yet many of these discourses sought to reconfigure eros and romance in a post-liberationist framework that would preserve a defense of a strong notion of choice, diversity and eroticism. It is to these challenges to a liberationist discourse that I now turn.

Eros and Romance in Liberal and Left Discourses

For many conservatives an opposition to a liberationist sexual agenda was closely tied to a restrictive, somewhat backward-looking, sexual and social politic. Thus, Decter and Gilder defended a decidedly Victorian gender order under the banner of the "natural order" which was at odds with egalitarian social trends. Similarly, many conservatives rallied behind a norm of intimate life that centered around the nuclear family while ignoring the immense diversity of existing intimate arrangements, for example, single and single-headed households, and gay and lesbian lifestyles.[43] Many conservatives insisted upon an ideal that tied sex exclusively to love and marriage which was in tension with a century-long trend towards loosening this bond.[44]

Liberals frequently shared many of the ideals of conservatives, but wished to accommodate sexual conventions to liberalizing social trends. Their critique of liberationists was less reactive and restrictive; it was less tied to appeals to past realities. They sought to preserve the liberalizing aspects of current trends against what they interpreted as its excessive tendencies. In a word, liberals and many leftists sought to strike a balance between the liberationist celebration of eros and the conservative value placed on stable, intimate bonds.

In "Report From the Sexual Revolution," liberal social critic Joseph Epstein defended the struggle of the liberationists against ignorance, undue sexual restraint and hypocrisy.[45] The liberationists went astray, however, in constructing sex as a sphere of pleasure and identifying sexual freedom with the unrestrained pursuit of sexual experience. Ironically, the liberationist demand for self-fulfillment had, said Epstein, promoted dehumanization, as individuals were reduced to mere sex organs and mediums of pleasure; liberationists were accused of unintentionally sanctioning an instrumental sexual ethic.

The intention of the liberationists was noble. They wished, says Epstein, to make sex something we could approach as a natural, enjoyable part of human life. Instead, they unwittingly created a new oppressive sexual regime. Liberationists were accused of overburdening sex with expectations of pleasure, self-fulfillment, and marital happiness. This transformed sex into work; it created strains on the individual and on social bonds. "Instead of deepened and enriched relationships, instead of shedding guilt and developing inwardly, we have . . . the tyranny of 'performance,'unreal expectations and misplaced salvationism."[46] With its reign of technique and pleasure, liberationist sexual ideology drove out tenderness, weakened intimate bonds, and produced more despair and loneliness as we became enslaved to a insatiable pursuit of erotic pleasure.

Epstein did not call for the return to older sexual codes of repression; he did not join the chorus of conservatives who saw in liberalizing trends only anomie and malaise. He was not against choice or eroticism. He wished to put sex in its place. This meant, above all, embedding sex in relationships in which "tenderness and sensuality find a confluence, each flowing into and strengthening the other."[47]

The claim that the liberationist celebration of eros disconnected sex from stable social bonds and stripped away its mystery and passion, was voiced by the former apostle of sexual liberation, George Leonard, in the bestselling *The End of Sex*.[48] Leonard was not an anti-liberationist in the mode of Decter or Gilder. He applauded a more open, honest, and free intimate culture. He rejected sexual censorship; he affirmed erotic pleasure as a right; and he defended an expanded notion of sexual choice, including homosexuality. Yet, Leonard believed that in their reaction to romanticists, liberationists crafted an image of sex no less oppressive.

Drawing on the work of Michel Foucault, Leonard argued that liberationists had unconsciously taken over from Victorians a construction of sex as a separate sphere of experience and identity.[49] However, where the Victorians rendered sex a sphere to be grasped in terms of considerations of health, personal feelings, love, and social responsibility, liberationists were said to have conceived of sex as a sphere of bodies, erotogenic zones, and pleasures. For liberationists, moreover, the aim of sex was, according to Leonard, self-discovery and self-realization. Unaware of their Victorianism, liberationists perpetuated the repressive notion that sexual feelings reveal our true selves and dictate our destiny. Indeed, Leonard claimed that liberationists had extended the domination of sex over our lives by imposing upon us new imperatives to give and receive orgasmic pleasure—imperatives which carried unreal expectations of self-fulfillment.

The false idol of sexual liberation, said Leonard, had come to haunt us. It had promoted depersonalization, shallow relationships, loneliness, child abuse, violence towards women, and the commercial exploitation of sex for profit.[50]

To preserve the healthy, beneficial potential of sex, Leonard believed that sex must be reconnected to the rest of our emotional, and social lives.[51] He advocated "the end of sex" as a separate sphere and its replacement by "erotic love," his term for an ideal that united eros and romance.[52] Erotic love is person-centered; it is caring and responsible; it involves individuals responding to individuals in all their humanity; in erotic love one responds to the whole person. In this regard, Leonard advised an ideal of "High Monogamy:" a quest for a deep intimate, honest, integrated, and sexually exclusive relationship.[53]

The liberationist ideology had come under critical scrutiny not only by liberals but by the Left. In his claim to be charting the unravelling of liberal America, Christopher Lasch saw in the liberationist rhetoric of choice and self-fulfillment little more than a disguise for a debased, narcissistic intimate culture.[54] Like Epstein and Leonard, Lasch interpreted the liberationists as promoting the separation of sex from emotionally dense and committed intimate bonds. With their ideology of the joys of eros, Lasch claimed, liberationists had helped to sunder the ties that link sex to love, marriage and the family.

Liberationists had promoted a narrow hedonism in the name of freedom. "Men and women now pursue sexual pleasure as an end in itself, unmediated even by the conventional trappings of romance."[55] The celebration of eros was said to mask a flight from feelings and intimacy. "Sexual separatism [lesbian-feminism] is only one of many strategies for . . . escaping from strong feeling. Many prefer the escape of drugs. . . . Others simply undertake to live alone. . . . The rising rate of suicide among young people can be attributed, in part, to the same flight from emotional entanglements. . . . The most prevalent form of escape from emotional complexity is promiscuity: the attempt to achieve a strict separation between sex and feeling. Here again, escape masquerades as liberation, regression as progress."[56]

Lasch's *Culture of Narcissism* contributed to the arguments of post-New Left social critics whose critique of American culture revolved around the concept of narcissism.[57] They maintained that the consolidation of a corporate capitalist bureaucratic society had destroyed those intermediary structures (e.g., family, church, voluntary associations) that functioned in the past to create private space within which the individual could nurture a strong, critical ego. With the destabilization of these protective spaces, the individual is thrown into the whirlwind of the market and mass consumerism without a stable and coherent inner personality. Responding to the ever-changing shifts in identity-models and lifestyle messages issuing from mass culture, the individual is said to be left fragmented and insecure, a mere shell of an autonomous self.

Critics of the culture of narcissism have argued that by legitimating the uncoupling of sex from relationships of closeness and commitment, the liberationist ideology reinforces the dissolution of those stable structures that make it possible for the individual to be an autonomous agent. Thus, these Left critics find themselves somewhat aligned with their conservative counterparts who criticize sexual liberation movements for promoting the destruction of the inner-directed self. Like conservatives, these Left critics call for the reintegration of eros and romance. However, unlike the former, for whom this reintegration is often explicitly tied to a restrictive sexual politic, the latter have typically not addressed the relationship between their restrictive sexual values and their broader progressive social agenda.

The Marxian left has often adopted a critical standpoint toward sexual liberation movements, which some have connected to the commercialization of sexuality and to broader strategies of social control. Corporate capitalism is said to have penetrated into the private realm subverting the distinction between work and home. Individual needs and activities previously untouched by commercialization have been integrated into the cash nexus of capitalism, especially with the rise of leisure, recreational, entertainment and sex industries. Moreover, it is argued that intimate desires and behavior have been transformed to reflect the behavioral and value code of capitalism. The commercialization of sex is said to entail its uncoupling from a person-centered and intimate social setting. Sex is being recast in an economizing pattern, sex becoming, according to these Marxian critics, a mere pleasure or sensual release. Sex partners become interchangeable, anonymous others, differentiated only by their performances. The subsuming of sex under categories of subject-object relations, performance standards, technical expertise, and competence symbolizes the colonization of the private intimate sphere by a capitalist economizing rationality. Writes one Marxist student of American sexuality: "In American culture, the 'new sexuality' is . . . a means whereby people create themselves as abstractions. . . . For sex to be a matter of technique, [a] form of work, an arena of competence, the partner . . . must be rendered a thing, rather than a person. . . . This represents the economization of domestic (home) relations and an alienation from one's body. . . ."[58]

Drawing from Herbert Marcuse's critique of "repressive desublimation" in *One-Dimensional Man*, some Marxists in the 1970s had little sympathy for the so-called liberation of sex they saw exhibited in the widening tolerance for homosexuality, pornography, and S/M, in the rise of sex clubs and single bars, in the celebration of swinging, open marriage, or the joys of eroticism. This "liberated sex" was described as little more than a projection of capitalist needs or values which, with its performance principle and fetishism of technique, alienates the individual from his or her true sexuality. Writes a young Marcusean, "Advanced industrial society, paradoxically, has increased its control over the individual by extending the boundaries of freedom in regard to sexual behavior through prescribed channels of institutionalized desublimation, the integration of sexuality into commerce. . . . The commercialization . . . of sex meant . . . the contraction of libido from erotic to mere sexual gratification without the sublimated bonds of friendship and tenderness."[59] Indeed, as the "brainchild" of capitalism, the sexual revolution is said to have extended capitalist hegemony by generating new markets, by integrating the individual at a deep biological and psychic level into capitalist culture, by binding needs to commodification, and by further eroding the individual's critical resistance to the manipulative control of mass culture and consumerism.

The American Left in the 1970s, or at least its Laschean and Marcusean strains, shared with many liberals of the period similar sexual and intimate values. They disputed the identification of liberation with expanded opportunities for sexual expression or with the reconfiguring of sex into erotic pleasure. In particular, liberals and leftists alike believed that the liberationist celebration of an eroticism isolated from broader personal and social feelings and relationships was misplaced. They wished to reconnect sex to the rest of our lives. Liberals framed an integrated sexuality in terms of a fairly conventional romantic ideology that connected sex to love, intimacy and family commitments. The Left shifted back and forth between a basically liberal ideal and a sex-radical vision whose ideal was less a nuclearized, family-centered intimacy than a highly individualistic, polymorphous ideal revolving around the eroticization of everyday life.

The Feminist Challenge to Sexual Liberation

The liberationist effort to loosen the tie between eros and romance and to frame sex as a separate realm of pleasure and self-expression was also challenged by feminists. Like many male liberals and leftists, some feminists thought that too much emphasis on erotic pleasure encouraged one-dimensional, body-centered, instrumental sexual values. In the name of liberation the party of eros has unwittingly undermined loving intimate bonds. Yet, feminists agreed with liberals and leftists that binding sex too tightly with romance and intimacy may drive out eroticism and unduly restrict sexual choice. While feminists sought a balance between eros and romance, some were pulled towards a restrictive sexual politic.

Women's liberation paralleled movements advocating sexual liberation. Many feminists were supportive of the sexual rebellions in the counterculture and the gay movement. Indeed, some feminists considered the women's movement the feminist wing of the sexual revolution. Yet most feminists approached the movements of sexual liberation with great ambivalence, criticizing the liberationist ideology for promoting primarily men's sexual and social interests.

In general, feminists endorsed social trends that expanded sexual choice and affirmed sex as a medium of erotic pleasure.[60] "A sexual revolution would require," declared Kate Millet, "an end of traditional sexual inhibitions and taboos, particularly those that most threaten patriarchal monogamous marriage: homosexuality, 'illegitimacy,' adolescent, pre-and extra-marital sexuality. The negative aura with which sexual activities have generally been surrounded would necessarily be eliminated, together with the double standard and prostitution. The goal of revolution would be a permissive single standard of sexual freedom."[61] Similarly, Shulamith Firestone, in her radical feminist manifesto, *The Dialectic of Sex*, defended a vision of a liberated polymorphous sexuality. Sex would cease to be a separate function; instead it would be infused in all interpersonal relations as a diffuse, life-affirming eros.[62] Many feminists struggled to legitimate women's right to define sex as a domain of pleasure. *Our Bodies, Ourselves* celebrated the female body and sexuality as a medium of pleasure and self-expression: "It [sex] is a vital physical expression of attachments to other human beings. It is communication that is fun and playful, serious and passionate."[63] In the course of the 1970s, feminist hymns to erotic pleasure and diversity were echoed in the popular writings of Nancy Friday, Lonnie Barbach, Eva Margolies and Erica Jong, among others.[64]

The feminist critique of the sexual liberationist ideology hinged on a chief insight of feminism: sex, no less than work, literature, and science, is gendered. Feminism, especially radical feminism, framed sex as a site of gender politics. What is defined as sex, who does what to whom, was said to reflect primarily gender interests and power relations.

Many feminists held that the liberationist ideology is basically an effort to impose upon women a sexual ideology that empowers men. In her explication of male literary representations of sexuality, Kate Millet sought to show that these literary portraits of heterosexuality revealed a politics of male dominance. She argued that the way the dynamics of sexual expression is framed by Henry Miller and Norman Mailer discloses a construction that not only defines female sexuality according to male wishes but dramatizes a male will to dominate women.[65] This feminist critique was targeted as well at the celebration of vaginal intercourse and orgasm that was said to be central to much liberationist discourse. For example, in "The Myth of Vaginal Orgasm," Anne Koedt proposed that the norm of vaginal orgasm was a ideological, not biologically driven, norm. The claim that there is only one orgasmic experience which is biologically based provided a warrant for a genital-centered heterosexual sexual ethic.[66] With the popularization of the centrality of clitoral orgasm by Masters and Johnson and others, the norm of vaginal orgasm was interpreted by many feminists as a male political strategy to maintain gender dominance by controlling women's sexuality. Indeed, the very norm of heterosexual coitus was viewed by some radical feminists as a political tactic by men to dominate women through defining and regulating their sexuality. Writing in *Ms*, Andrea Dworkin made this point in her typically graphic manner. "Fucking is the means by which the male colonizes the female . . . Fucking . . . in or out of marriage . . . is . . . an act of possession. The possessor is the one with a phallus."[67] The influential radical feminist theorist, Ti-Grace Atkinson, made the critique of heterosexuality the cornerstone of her critique of male dominance. "The institution of sexual intercourse is anti-feminist, first, because the source of women's arousal and pleasure is in the clitoris, not in the vagina. And, second, it is anti-feminist, because sexual intercourse is the link between the wife and the mother roles."[68]

As some feminists interpreted concepts like vaginal coitus, orgasm, and, indeed, heterosexuality itself as tied to men's gender dominance, it was a short step to viewing all sexual desire and behavior as gendered. Thus, Dana Densmore, in an important statement of radical feminism, criticized male liberationist sexual ideology for promoting men's sexual values.

> Intercourse, in the sense of the physical act . . . is not necessarily the thing we [women] are longing for. . . . Physically, there is a certain objective tension and release, at least for a man, when excitation proceeds to orgasm. With a woman even this physical issue is much less clear. . . . I think we might all agree *that* isn't why we go to bed with a man. . . . The release we feel . . . therefore is psychological. . . . We then enjoy the pleasures of closeness.[69]

Densmore connected female sexual values with intimacy, not erotic pleasure. "Without denying that sex can be pleasurable, I suggest that the real thing we [women] seek is closeness, merging, perhaps a kind of oblivion of self that dissolves the terrible isolation of individualism."[70]

By the early 1970s, many radical feminists were arguing that male and female sexuality, at least in contemporary America, was fundamentally different.[71] Male sexuality was described as genital-and-body-centered, instrumental and promiscuous; sex for men was oriented to erotic pleasure and dominance. "The emphasis on genital sexuality, objectification, promiscuity, emotional noninvolvement . . . [is] the male style, and . . . we, as women, placed greater trust in love, sensuality, humor, tenderness, commitment," stated Robin Morgan.[72] Women were more person-centered; female sexual pleasures were diffused throughout the body, not genitally focused. Women were motivated by affection and intimacy. From this radical feminist standpoint, the liberationist sexual ideology, with its emphasis on a body-and-genital-centered eroticism, exhibits men's sexual and social interests. "I would argue," said Firestone, "that . . . a relaxing of the mores concerning female sexual behavior was to his advantage; it increased the sexual supply and lowered the cost."[73] Far from liberating women, the liberationist agenda was seen as dangerous to women. It reduces women to sex objects; women are made more sexually available for men with fewer expectations of reponsibilities and commitment; women find it harder to refuse sex; and the dangers of unwanted pregnancy and violence against them escalate.

In contrast to "the fake sexual revolution of the sixties," genuine sexual freedom for women would not be a matter of sexual release or reconfiguring sex as pleasure.[74] Rather, in a male dominated society, women's sexual liberation would involve an expansion of the right of women to control and define their own bodies and sexuality. "As women, we want our own sexuality under our control."[75] Being sexually self-defining includes the right to refuse sex without bearing a stigma; to choose celibacy or a lesbian alternative; to control the consequences of sex, e.g., access to abortion and birth control strategies; and to choose when to have sex and with whom. The aim of a female sexual revolution would be to "change from sexual objects to sexual subjects. . . . We must define our sexual experiences in our own terms. . . . We must be guided by our own feelings, and learn sensitivity to our own bodies. We must respect our own needs and desires."[76]

By the mid-1970s, a strain of radical feminism had evolved—cultural feminism—that assumed a fundamental difference between women's and men's sexuality, and that the politics of female and male sexual liberation would diverge.[77] For cultural feminists, female sexual fulfillment was joined to a separatist gender politic. Only in decolonized "womanspaces" could women rediscover their true female sexual nature by stripping away the layers of alienated desire imposed by men. The cultural feminist claim that the (male) liberationist ideology masked a reactionary gender politic was a major challenge to liberationist discourses and movements.

The Mainstreaming of Post-Liberationist Discourses

There was no abrupt shift from a liberationist celebration of eros to a post-liberationist reconfiguring of eros and romance. The party of eros continued to be heard from through the 1980s, even if in a less boisterous and imperial way. Despite herpes and AIDS, articles like "The Secret of Sexual Satisfaction," "The Erotic Art of Undressing," "How to Find Your Body Map to Sexual Pleasure," and "Vibrators—Turning On to Pleasure" regularly appeared in mainstream magazines such as *Glamour, Madmoiselle,* and *Redbook*.[78] Contemporary Americans have not abandoned eros. Men and women continue to join erotic pleasure to self-fulfillment and to a satisfactorily intimate, loving bond.

A shift in the American intimate culture is, however, discernible from the mid-1970s through the 1980s. The liberationist celebration of eros as a medium of individualism, pleasure, and intimacy has lost some cultural credibility. Liberationist discourses promising an era of sexual fulfillment are being held responsible for a range of social ills. The challenge to a liberationist ideology is multivocal, although common themes have surfaced in these discourses. The construction of sex as an autonomous sphere valued for its pleasurable and expressive qualities alone is increasingly viewed in the cultural mainstream as containing dangers unforeseen by the party of eros. Post-liberationists have urged a reconnection of sex to the spiritual and social aspects of our intimate lives.

By the mid-1980s this challenge to a liberationist sexual ideology passed from highbrow to popular culture. In the course of its mainstreaming, the multivocal character of post-liberationist discourses gradually narrowed into a more univocal ideological orthodoxy. In particular, the broader social agenda of these critics of sexual liberation, especially those of the Left and feminism, were either silenced or marginalized. For example, the radical feminist project which linked the intention to effect changes in sexual mores to a broad gender politic either dropped out of popular discourses or figured as a isolated problem of male abuse or violence. In the cultural mainstream, changing sexual values and behavior was to be achieved through altering individual beliefs, not through broad institutional change.

The mainstreaming of a post-liberationist sex discourse and politic was enhanced by the AIDS epidemic. By the end of the 1980s, tens of thousands of Americans, especially gay men, had died from AIDS, many more had been HIV-infected. Moreover, the exchange of bodily fluids through sexual behavior was identified as a principal means of transmission of the virus. Sex was implicated in an epidemic of disease and death. Furthermore, the lack of consensus in the medical-scientific community about the cause of AIDS, especially betweeen 1981 and 1985, and the mixed messages sent to the public regarding heterosexual transmission in the United States, prompted public confusion and fear surrounding sex. This national anxiety was seized upon by many public figures and organizations as part of a campaign of sexual reform. AIDS made plausible an appeal to public health concerns as a rationale for changing sexual mores. For critics of a libertarian hedonistic sexual ideology, AIDS was interpreted as a symbol of the failure of the movements for sexual liberation.[79] An editorial in the conservative *National Review* seized upon AIDS as proof of the failure of a sexual liberationist agenda. "AIDS remains a prominent skeleton at the feast of sexual liberation."[80] Writing in the liberal magazine, *Rolling Stone*, B.D. Colon connected the sexual revolution, promiscuity and AIDS. "A lifestyle that involves hundreds of sexual contacts a year . . . appears to be as much a phenomenon of the modern 'sexual revolution' as is AIDS."[81] Conservatives and liberals alike interpreted AIDS as containing a clear moral message: the celebration of sexual freedom and eros was a mistake we are paying for dearly. The liberationist dream was said to have come crashing down upon us with an epidemic of disease, disorder, and death.

To make this moral case against sexual liberation, critics were not able, at least through the late 1980s, to point to an unambiguous empirical connection between AIDS, promiscuity, and heterosexuality. Despite continuous fears that the epidemic would spread into the broader heterosexual population, this did not occur.[82] The sexual transmission of the HIV virus has remained a major risk factor primarily for gay men, although partners of IV drug users also run considerable risk. Thus, to make their moral tale of the dangers of sexual expression compelling, sex reformers have had to rely upon the dynamics of the AIDS epidemic among gay men, and insist that this pattern anticipates the future for all Americans unless we change our sexual conventions. Indeed, commentators in the straight media, at least through the mid-1980s, almost uniformly focused on the connection between the sexual freedom enjoyed by gay men and AIDS. Typical is the comment by Vincent Coppola in a *Newsweek* feature story. "Ironically, the freedom, the promiscuity . . . that many gays declared an integral part of their culture have come to haunt them."[83] By highlighting the connection between AIDS and promiscuity among gay men, and by appealing to medical statements that announced the coming spread of the AIDS epidemic to heterosexuals, sex reformers were able to give a public urgency to their campaign.

Many in the media promulgated the idea that America was entering a new era of sexual restraint and responsibility. For example, a 1984 cover story in *Time* was entitled "The Sexual Revolution is Over."[84] Despite the reporter's acknowledgement that we "know very little about what is really going on," it is confidently announced that the quest for sexual pleasure and freedom is giving way to a renewal of romance, marriage, and monogamy.[85] "Veterans of the revolution, some wounded, some merely bored, are reinventing courtship and romance. . . . Many individuals are even rediscovering the traditional values of fidelity, obligation and marriage. . . ."[86] If the liberationist rhetoric of the 1960s and 1970s revolved around notions of sexual freedom, pleasure, variety, and adventure, these reporters asserted that now "the buzz words these days are 'commitment,' 'intimacy' and 'working at relationships.' "[87] In the spirit of competition, a 1986

Newsweek feature story went beyond announcing the "end of the sexual revolution" to declaring Americans' "Fear of Sex."[88] Relying upon a few random interviews with lay persons and experts, the reporters declared that "the days of carefree, casual sex are over."[89] AIDS, they say, marks the end of an era; Americans are "rewriting their code of sexual behavior."[90] For example, citing one therapist working with gay men in New York City, these reporters confidently stated, despite evidence of the spread of phone sex and private sex clubs among gay men, that "practically gone are the days of anonymous sex. . . ."[91] Indeed, in response to AIDS many Americans were said to be turning to a renewed commitment to responsible, long-term intimate relationships. "Monogamy is making a comeback. With all the experts advising limiting the number of sexual partners, gay and straight couples talk about working through the rough times and staying together. Fear of AIDS may be the ultimate tie that binds."[92] Not wishing *Newsweek* to edge them out in prophesying the dawning of a new era of sexual restraint and responsibility, *Time* followed up on its 1984 cover story with a 1987 feature, "The Big Chill: Fear of AIDS."[93] Though acknowledging that the "numbers as yet are small," the reporters assured us that "AIDS is a growing threat to the heterosexual population. . . . Barring the development of a vaccine, swingers of all persuasions may sooner or later be faced with the reality of a new era of sexual caution and restraint."[94] Citing only so-called authorities—therapists and medical experts—who are convinced that AIDS demands "tough new rules of the game,"[95] the *Time* story was part of a campaign aimed at changing American intimate culture.

In magazine articles with titles such as "Cheating Ain't Cheap: The High Cost of Infidelity," "With AIDS About, Heterosexuals are Rethinking Casual Sex," "I Don't Get Around Much Anymore," "Stop! In the Name of Love," "The Delight of Sexual Mystery," "Warning: Passionate Sex May Be Hazardous to Your Love Life," and "Farewell, Sexual Revolution, Hello, New Victorianism,"[96] and in advice texts such as *Lifemates, Intimate Play, The Lifelong Lover, How to Put the Love Back into Making Love, and How to Make Love to the Same Person for the Rest of Your Life and Still Love It!,*[97] we are witnessing a shift in our sexual culture. The concept of sex as a medium of erotic pleasure, self-expression, and a basis of intimate bonds which has been integral to American culture since the early decades of the twentieth century is now under suspicion. The expressive-hedonistic construction of sexuality is now often viewed in the cultural mainstream as a threat to our personal and social well-being. It is, says its critics, a false and destructive idol. Instead of promoting self-fulfillment, it has resulted in the expanded ranks of lonely middle-aged men and women with few prospects of intimate bonding,[98] an emotional shallowness in our relationships as our sexual focus has left us numb to feelings,[99] a pervasive boredom with sex as the quest for pleasure has had diminishing returns,[100] the absence of romance and mystery in our sexual and intimate lives as the emphasis has been on technique and performance,[101] and a virtual epidemic of sexually transmitted diseases, illegitimacy, teen pregnancies, divorce, and domestic violence.[102]

The new ethic of sexual restraint and responsibility advocated by current reformers entails its own set of sexual meanings and values. Sex is constructed less as a sphere of erotic pleasure and self-expression than as a medium of emotional, social, and spiritual bonding. To recover the mystery and joy of sex, reformers advise reconnecting sex to the dense emotional and social ties of a loving, intimate bond. Sex should be a way to explore and express loving feelings between two individuals whose commitment to the relationship overrides their individual desire for erotic gratification. Sexual practices should exhibit the gentle, tender qualities of loving intimacy rather than the body-centered, orgiastic eroticism favored by the advocates of sexual liberation. Thus, Pepper Schwartz, sociologist and popular commentator on intimate matters, recommends substituting "cozy sex" for "passionate sex."[103] The latter fetishizes organs and body parts and is "fed by anger . . . and the risk of loss, betrayal or rejection."[104] By contrast, cozy sex is gentle; the logic of technique and performance is replaced by the pleasures of "being stroked, reassured or listened to. . . . Cozy sex is an expression of . . . harmony, friendship and confidence. The certainty of commitment and reciprocal love eclipses the need to feverishly seize the moment; . . . Ultimately, cozy sex is the certification that a relationship has a stable future."[105] Similarly, in *Lifemates: The Love Fitness Program for a Lasting Relationship,* Drs. Harold Bloomfield and Sirah Vettese urge a spiritual approach to sex and love. "Liberated sex has bred sexual exploitation, performance fears . . . unwanted pregnancies, boredom . . . spiritual malaise [and] AIDS."[106] They propose a new intimate ideal called "lifemates." Lifemates projects the ideal of a lifetime heterosexual love bond in which sex functions as a medium of spiritual union. "Intimate sex is a spiritual joining to discover how open, sensitive, caring and loving you and your lifemate can be."[107]

Reformers believe that the healthy and joyous capacities of sex lie in its serving as a vehicle of social and spiritual intimate bonding. Constructing sex as a separate sphere of pleasure and self-expression is thought to set in motion a logic of individual and social destruction. Moreover, reformers believe that there are genuinely sustaining joys to sex only when it is socially and spiritually embedded. In his enormously popular advice text, *Super Marital Sex: Loving for Life*, Paul Pearsall celebrates the joys of joining spiritual and sexual intimacy. "Super marital sex is the most erotic, intense, fulfilling experience any human being can have. Anonymous sex with multiple partners ... [is] an empty imitation of the fulfillment of a sexuality of intimacy and commitment to one person for life."[108] Pearsall insists that super marital sex is less an "eroticized, genitalized sex" than sex that builds and sustains a committed intimate bond by serving as a vehicle of spiritual union.

For many post-liberationist reformers, sexual expression should always be connected to intimate, committed relationships. Moreover, they believe that sexual expression should exhibit its essentially social and spiritual meaning by being gentle, tender and caring. Sex that is focused on body parts, that involves objectification, that aims to augment individual sensual pleasures is regarded as dehumanizing and degrading. "When human sexuality is expressed as pure appetite independent of the nature of the partner," writes the psychiatrist and popular author Willard Gaylin, "we tend to label it as pathological and perverse."[109] Valuing sex for its nonerotic role as a medium of social and spiritual intimacy indicates a shift in the cultural mainstream. Indicative of this reform agenda, Mr. Gaylin wishes to frame love as "beyond pleasure." "Love, beyond pleasure, is a dedication of the self through trust and commitment to an expanded experience. ... It is a willing and conscious utilization of all our capacities for generosity, altruism, empathy, service, self-sacrifice, and devotion— transcending a narrow concern for self and survival."[110] To be sure, erotic pleasure continues to be valued as a part of love and intimacy in popular discourses. Yet reformers intend to reconfigure sex, so as to marginalize its carnal and performance-oriented aspects while featuring its social and spiritual meaning.

Conclusion

Liberationists and their critics envelop their sexual ideologies in social narratives. The former favor Whiggish stories portraying the present as a period of liberation from a repressive past. They lean towards a millennialism as they project an emancipated sexuality into the future. By contrast, many post-liberationists wrap their agenda in tales of lament. They often describe a society that has succumbed to false prophets and idols. They lean towards apocalyptic images of the future, as the present seems mired in chaos and decline.

Both hardcore advocates of eros and their critics greatly simplify the past and present. Thus, liberationists tend to grossly exaggerate the repressiveness of the past and are typically insensitive to the disciplinary constraints and normative orders implied in their own visions of an emancipated sexuality. They view all detractors of their program as repressive or sexual counterrevolutionaries.

Post-liberationists tend to see in sexual liberationist ideologies little more than the lifting of restraints on sexual expression. This, in turn, is seen as contributing to, if not causing, the spread of a hedonistic, promiscuous sexual regime which accounts for a range of current psychic and social disorders. In fact, liberationists did not advocate disconnecting sex from intimacy; instead they defended a concept of the multiple meanings of sex. In their discourses, sex functions as both a medium of erotic pleasure, self-expression, and intimate romantic bonding. Moreover, this liberationist construction contributed to expanding sexual and lifestyle choice, promoting tolerance, and proliferating sensual pleasures, identities, and social bonds. By reducing the liberationist agenda to advocating mere sexual release, post-liberationists neglect its positive, valuable aspects. This weakens their own standpoint and fosters a polarization around sexual politics and ethics.

Of course, the aim of these discourses is not to arrive at historical or sociological truths. Their agenda is moral and political: to discredit a liberationist sexual regime and to authorize an alternative. Post-liberationists have, to varying degrees, been successful, as is evidenced by the mainstreaming of their ideas. Moreover, they have successfully mobilized constituencies to endorse, and sometimes enact, aspects of their agenda.

Post-liberationists have succeeded, in part, because they are addressing serious social problems, e.g., divorce, domestic violence, AIDS, and teen pregnancies. Moreover, their attempt to link these events to liberationist movements has proved compelling to many Americans. Although this linkage strikes me as mostly wrong, post-liberationists have raised serious moral questions about the celebration of choice, eros, and diversity by underscoring some of its undesirable consequences. They have, for example, raised concerns about the link between choice and the instability of intimate bonds, the objectifying and dehumanizing aspects of hedonism, the emotional and social costs of legitimating sex apart from intimate bonds, about whether eroticism pushes romance and mystery out of sex and love, about the excessive sexualization of love and intimacy and about the underlying gender politics of movements of sexual liberation. Post-liberationists have seized on the absences and weaknesses of the liberationist ideology and have forced us to think more seriously about issues of sexual morality.

Yet, post-liberationists have, in my view, proposed a narrowing of choice and tolerance for difference that is unnecessarily limiting. As we have seen, many conservative, liberal and Left post-liberationists authorize a narrowly heterosexual, romantic, marital, monogamous norm or, as in the case of many radical feminists, one that includes same-sex intimacies insofar as they mirror this pattern. For many of them, sex is legitimate only as an expression of an intimate loving bond. Sexual expression is supposed to preserve the wholeness of each individual and exhibit personal, intimate, loving qualities. Thus, sex should be tender, caring, gentle, nurturing and always recognize and respect the whole person. The intimate bond should be long-term, and commitment ought to be symbolized by marriage or its analogue for homosexuals, the "gay union." Sexual monogamy should be normative since sex is tied to commitment, fidelity and trust. Any sexual and intimate lifestyle that departs significantly from this ideal is suspect. Thus, nonromantic sex or sex for erotic pleasure and intimate lifestyles that combine love and sexual nonmonogamy would be devalued, if not considered deviant, by many post-liberationists.

The moral rationales to which post-liberationists have appealed in order to justify this narrowing of sexual choice are hardly intellectually compelling today. Appealing to absolutes such as the "survival of the species," "the past," God's will, the Judeo-Christian tradition or natural law to legitimate a sexual ethic cannot withstand serious scrutiny. For example, "the past" or "nature" do not carry a fixed, unambiguous meaning, but are subject to interpretive conflicts that mirror current social divisions. Appeal to the Judeo-Christian tradition is no less mired in current social and interpretive conflicts and can simply be played off against secular liberal or radical traditions. The more restrictionist ethic of post-liberationists, moreover, loses normative force in the face of empirical patterns. It is hardly credible to defend a strict heterosexual norm when there is overwhelming evidence that homosexuality is, if not socially accepted, at least socially entrenched, and when it is well-documented that lesbians and gay men have evolved their own positive identities, communities, and stable forms of intimate life. Similarly, it is hardly compelling to give exclusive legitimacy to marital sex when research over the last several generations documents the widespread acceptance and prevalence of premarital sex and cohabitation.

In short, post-liberationists have offered a social narrative that is, for many Americans, much more persuasive today than a tale of liberation. However, at the level of a sexual ethic, it is deficient both because of its moral rationales (e.g., its absolutist appeals to nature, God, or the past) and its neglect of well-established social patterns.

Yet, many Americans are reluctant today to defend a liberationist ideology in light of a public perception which connects sexual freedom with disorders in our intimate affairs. America seems to be at an impasse with respect to assessing the meaning and proper role of sex in our personal and public lives.

In Part Two, my focus shifts to a more exclusive concern with sexual ethics. I will review the feminist debate over female sexuality and the debate over homosexuality in the era of AIDS as key sites in the American conflict over sexual ethics. My aim, ultimately, is to outline a sexual ethic that can preserve what I take to be the advantages of both a liberationist or libertarian ideology and its romantic alternative.

Notes

1.   Commission on Obscenity and Pornography, *The Report of the Commission on Obscenity and Pornography* (New York: Random House, 1970).

2.   Ibid., p. 24.

3.   Ibid., pp. 32, 58.

4.   Ibid., pp. 29, 53–54.

5.   Ibid., p. 85.

6.   Attorney General's Commission on Pornography, *Final Report* (Washington: GPO, 1986).

7.   Ibid, pp. 172–173.   See Carole Vance, "Porn in the U.S.A.: The Meese Commission on the Road," *The Nation* August 2/9, 1986.

8.   Ibid.

9.   On the collapse of the liberal consensus in the 1960s and 1970s, see Godfrey Hodgson, *America in our Time* (New York: Doubleday, 1976);Allen Matuson, *The Unraveling of America: A History of Liberalism in the 1960s* (New York: Harper & Row, 1984);

10.   See, for example, Kevin Phillips, *Post-Conservative America* (New York: Vintage Press, 1983).

11.   My discussion of economic trends is drawn from the following works: Robert Reich, *The Next American Frontier* (New York: Penguin, 1983); Paul Blumberg, *Inequality in an Age of Decline* (New York: Oxford University Press,

1980); Emma Rochschild, "Reagan and the Real America," *New York Review of Books* Feb. 5, 1981.

12.   Kevin Phillips, *Post-Conservative America*; Christopher Lasch, *The Culture of Narcissism* (New York: W.W. Norton & Co., 1976); Robert Heilbroner, *Business Civilization in Decline* (New York: W.W. Norton & Co., 1976); George Gilder, *Sexual Suicide* (New York: Quadrangle, 1973); Daniel Bell, *The Cultural Contradictions of Capitalism* (New York: Basic Books, 1976).

13.   This general diagnosis of America in the 1970s was shared more or less by the New Right, neoconservatives and some revisionist feminists. A fine overview of these currents can be found in Alan Crawford, *Thunder on the Right* (New York: Pantheon, 1980) and Zillah Eisenstein, *Feminism and Sexual Equality* (New York: Monthly Review Press, 1984).

14.   Andrew Hacker, "Farewell to the Family?" *New York Review of Books* Mar. 3–18, 1982. Andrew Cherlin, *Marriage, Divorce, Remarriage* (Cambridge, Mass.: Harvard University Press, 1981).

15.   "Is The American Family in Danger?" *U.S. News & World Report*, Apr. 16, 1973; Dr. Joyce Brothers, "Will Liberalized Sex Kill Romantic Love?" *Good Housekeeping*, June 1971.

16.   Midge Decter, *The New Chastity and Other Arguments Against Women's Liberation* (New York: Coward, McCann & Geoghegan, Inc., 1972).

17.   Ibid., p. 80.

18.   Ibid.

19.   Ibid., p. 83.

20.   Ibid.

21.   Ibid.

22.   Ibid., p. 90.

23.   Ibid., p. 89.

24.   Ibid., p. 124.

25.   Ibid.

26.   George Gilder, *Sexual Suicide* (New York: Quadrangle, 1973).

27.   Ibid., p. 2.

28.   Ibid.

29.   Ibid., p. 40.

30.   Ibid., p. 33.

31.   Ibid., p. 5.

32.   Ibid., p. 4.

33.   Ibid.

34.   Ibid., p. 5.

35.   Ibid., p. 21.

36.   Ibid., p. 23.

37.   My discussion of the New Right is drawn from the following studies: Pamela Johnston Conover and Virginia Gray, *Feminism and the New Right* (New York: Praeger, 1983); Rhonda Brown, "Blueprint for a Moral America," *The Nation*, May 23, 1981; Allen Hunter and Linda Gordon, " Sex, Family and the New Right," *Radical America* 11–12, (Nov. 1977–Feb. 1978); Alan Crawford, *Thunder on the Right*; Zillah Eisenstein, *Feminism and Sexual Equality*; Rosiland Petchesky, "Antiabortion, Antifeminism, and the Rise of the New Right, " *Feminist Studies* 7 (Summer 1981); Scott Tucker, "The Counterrevolution," *Gay Community News* Feb. 21, 1981; Deirdre English, "The War on Choice," *Mother Jones* Feb./Mar. 1981; Andrew Kopkind, "America's New Right," *New Times*, Sept. 30, 1977; Allen Hunter, "In the Wings: New Right Ideology and Organization," *Radical America* 15 (Spring 1981).

38.   On New Right antiabortion politics, see Rosiland Petchesky, *Abortion and Woman's Choice* (Boston: Northeastern University Press,.1985).

39.   Ibid., pp. 263–264

40.   Ibid., p. 265.

41.   See Brown, "Blueprint for a Moral America"; Barry Adams, "The Roots of Homophobia," *Christopher Street* 103 (1986); Larry Bush and Richard Goldstein,"The Anti-Gay Backlash, *"The Village Voice*, Apr. 8–14, 1981; Larry Bush, "Homosexuality and the New Right," *The Village Voice* Apr. 20, 1982.

42.   See Petchesky, *Abortion and Women's Choice*.

43.   Hacker, "Farewell to the Family?" and Cherlin, *Marriage, Divorce, Remarriage*.

44.   See Steven Seidman, *Romantic Longings* (New York: Routledge, 1991); Cf. Ehrenreich et. al. *Re-Making Love* (New York: Doubleday, 1986) and Dennis Altman, *The Homosexualization of America* (Boston: Beacon, 1983).

45.   Joseph Epstein, "Report from the Sexual Revolution," *Readers Digest* Mar. 1975. See his *Divorce in America* (New York: E.P. Dutton, 1974).

46.   Ibid., p. 74.

47.   Ibid., p. 75.

48.   George Leonard, *The End of Sex* (New York: Bantam, 1983).

49.   Ibid., ch. 8.

50.   Ibid., pp. 107, 181.

51.   Ibid., p. 13.

52.   Ibid., ch. 14.

53.   Ibid., pp. 153–159.

54.   Christopher Lasch, *The Culture of Narcissism* (New York: W.W. Norton & Co., 1979).

55.   Ibid., p.

56.   Ibid., p.

57.   See the "Symposium on Narcissism" in *Telos* 44 (Summer 1980) and the conference on the "Crisis of the Left" in *Telos* 26 (Winter 1980–1981).

58.   David Kemnitzer, "Sexuality as a Social Form: Performance and Anxiety in America," in *Symbolic Anthroplogy*, eds. Janet Dolgin et al. (New York: Columbia University Press, 1977), p. 308.

59.   David Ober, "On Sexuality and Politics in the Work of Herbert Marcuse," in *Critical Interruptions*, Paul Breines, ed. (New York: Herder and Herder, 1972), p. 119.

60.   See Ellen Willis, "Radical Feminism and Feminist Radicalism," in *The 60s Without Apology*, eds. Sohnya Sayres et. al. eds., (Minneapolis: University of Minnesota, 1984).

61.   Kate Millet, *Sexual Politics* (New York: Ballantine, 1978 [1969]), p. 86.

62.   Shulamith Firestone, *The Dialectic of Sex* (New York: William Morrow and Co., 1970).

63.   The Boston Women's Health Book Collective, *Our Bodies, Ourselves* (New York: Simon and Schuster, 1971).

64.   See Steven Seidman, *Romantic Longings* (New York: Routledge, 1991), chap. 5.

65.   Millet, *Sexual Politics*.

66.   Anne Koedt, "The Myth of the Vaginal Orgasm," in *Radical Feminism*, eds. Anne Koedt, Ellen Levine and Anita Rapone, (New York: Quadrangle, 1973).

67.   Andrea Dworkin, "Phallic Imperialism: Why Economic Recovery Will Not Work For Us," *Ms* 5 (Dec. 1976), p. 101.

68.   Ti-Grace Atkinson, *Amazon Odeyssy* (New York: Links Books, 1974), p. 86.

69.   Dana Densmore, "Independence from the Sexual Revolution," in *Radical Feminism*, pp. 113–114.

70.   Ibid.

71.   See Alice Echols, *Daring to be Bad* (Minneapolis: University of Minnesota Press, 1990).

72.   Robin Morgan, *Going Too Far* (New York: Random House, 1977), p. 181.

73.   Shulamith Firestone, "The Women's Rights Movement in the U.S.: New View," in *Voices From Women's Liberation*, ed. Leslie Tanner (New York: New American Library, 1971), p. 442.

74.   Sandra Coyner, "Women's Liberation and Sexual Liberation," in *Marriage and Alternatives*, eds. Roger Libby and Robert Whitehurst (Glenview, Ill.: Scott, Foresman and Co., 1977), p. 277.

75.   Ibid.

76.   Ibid., p. 221.

77.   See chap. 3.

78.   R. Richards, "The Secret Side to Sexual Satisfaction," *Redbook*, Jan. 1987; J.P. Davis, "The Erotic Art of Undressing," *Glamour*, Dec. 1987; S. Cohen, "How to Find your Body Map to Sexual Pleasure," *Glamour*, Apr. 1987; M.B. Rosenbaum, "Vibrators—Turning On to Pleasure," *Mademoiselle*, Jan. 1981.

79.   Cf. Susan Sontag, *AIDS and Its Metaphors* (New York: Farrar, Straus and Giroux, 1988), pp. 76–79. See ch. 4 of this book.

80.   Editorial, "AIDS and Public Policy," *National Review*, July 8, 1983, p, 796.

81.   B.D. Colen, "The Gay Plague," *Rolling Stone*, Feb. 18, 1983, p. 52.

82.   See Michael Fumento, *The Myth of Heterosexual AIDS* (New York: Basic Books, 1990). Fumento may be in error in claiming that from a world-wide vantage point AIDS is primarily confined to narrow risk groups, but his point seems valid applied to the United States at least through the 1980s. Cf. Edward Brecher, "Straight Sex, AIDS, and the Mixed-Up Press," *Columbia Journalism Review*, March/April 1988 and John Langone, "AIDS," *Discover*, Dec. 1985.

83.   Vincent Coppola, "The Change in Gay Life Style," *Newsweek*, Apr. 18, 1983, p. 80. Cf. John Fuller, "AIDS: Legacy of the '60s," *Science Digest*, Dec. 1983. See Chap. 4.

84.   John Leo, "The Revolution is Over," *Time*, Apr. 9, 1984.

85.   Ibid., p. 74.

86.   Ibid.

87.   Ibid.

88.   Barbara Kantrowitz et al, "Fear of Sex," *Newsweek*, Nov. 24, 1986, p. 41.

89.   Ibid., p. 42.

90.   Ibid.

91.   Ibid.

92.   Ibid.

93.   Martha Smilgis, "The Big Chill: Fear of AIDS," *Time*, Feb. 16, 1987.

94.   Ibid., p. 50.

95.   Ibid.

96.   Dalma Heyn, "Cheating Ain't Cheap: The High Cost of Infidelity," *Mademoiselle*, Nov. 1987, p. 202; Jan Hoffman, "Stop! In the Name of Love," *Mademoiselle*, Apr. 1988; Audrey Edwards, "Don't Get Around Much Any-more," *Essence*, Sept. 1987; Kevin Doyle, "An Epidemic of Fear," *Maclean's*, Jan. 12, 1987; Mark Jacobson, "Brave New World," *Esquire*, Sept. 1987; John Barber, "Sex in the Eighties," *Maclean's*, Jan. 12, 1987; Daava Sobel, "Sex Grows Up," *Health*, Oct. 1989; Lynn Darlaing, "Never Love a Stranger," *Made-*

moiselle, Sept. 1987; Edward Cornish, "Farewell, Sexual Revolution. Hello, New Victorianism," *The Futurist*, Jan.–Feb. 1986.

97.   William Betcher, *Intimate Play: Creating Romance in Everyday Life* (New York: Viking, 1987); Dagmar O'Connor, *How to Make Love to the Same Person for the Rest of Your Life and Still Love It!* (New York: Doubleday, 1985); Paul Pearsall, *Super Marital Sex: Loving For Life* (New York: Doubleday, 1987); David Viscott, *I Love You, Let's Work it Out* (New York: Simon and Schuster, 1987); Harold Bloomfield and Sirah Vettese with Robert Kory, *Lifemates, the Love Fitness Program for a Lasting Relationship* (New York: New American Library, 1989). I discuss the shift to a spiritualized concept of intimacy in the sex advice literature of the 1980s in the Epilogue to *Romantic Longings*.

98.   See, for example, Barbara Creaturo, "Sketches from the Single Life," *Cosmopolitan*, Mar. 1984; Patricia Morrisroe, "Forever Single," *New York*, Aug. 20, 1984.

99.   See, for example, Bruce Weber, " Sex From Now On? *Glamour*, July 1988.

100.   Willard Gaylin, *Rediscovering Love* (New York: Viking, 1986), p. 22.

101. Ellen Kessner, "The Delights of Sexual Mystery," *Cosmopolitan*, Sept. 1984.

102.   Willard Gaylin, *Rediscovering Love*, p. 11.

103.   Pepper Schwartz, "Warning: Passionate Sex May Be Hazardous to Your Love Life," *Glamour*, Nov. 1988.

104.   Ibid., p. 108.

105.   Ibid.

106.   Bloomfield and Vettese, *Lifemates*, p. 111.

107.   Ibid., p. 118.

108.   Pearsall, *Super Marital Sex*, p. xvi.

109.   E.g., Gaylin, *Rediscovering Love*; also see the advice texts I cited in n. 121.

110.   Ibid.

Part Two
SEXUAL ETHICS

3

Defining the Moral Boundaries of Eros: The Feminist Sexuality Debates

In chapter 2, I commented on the ambivalent feminist response to trends in American sexual culture. At one extreme there were feminist perspectives that described the women's movement as a sexual liberation movement; the joys of eros were celebrated as an integral part of women's coming of age. Opposing them were viewpoints which described the ideology of sexual liberation as little more than a thinly veiled maneuver by men to keep women socially subordinate by beguiling them with the false promise of sexual fulfillment. The dominant strain of feminism from the late 1960s through the early 1970s endorsed the general trend toward expanding intimate lifestyle choice and valuing erotic pleasure as a legitimate sexual function. Yet most feminists criticized the particular sexual values and meanings that accompanied the sexual liberation ideology as reflecting a male bias. For example, expanding lifestyle choice to include nonmarital, even nonromantic sex was defended by most feminists but they criticized sexual liberationists for ignoring the equally legitimate choice of refusing sex and choosing celibacy. Moreover, they took issue with the ideology of choice to the extent that it did not acknowledge that nonromantic, nonmarital sex often carried unique risks for women. Similarly, while most feminists valued eroticism—the giving and receiving of sensual pleasure—they criticized the framing of sexual pleasure as centered on vaginal intercourse and orgasm. In addition, many feminists criticized a pleasure-centered sexual exchange to the extent that it promoted instrumental, objectifying, and exploitative values. In short, it was, at best, an incomplete sexual revolution for many feminists; it either marginalized or neglected the interests and sexual values of women.

Feminists continued to advance multiple stances towards postwar sexual trends. From the mid-1970s through the mid-1980s, however, a strain of radical feminism that was critical of these trends assumed a prominent ideological role in the women's movement. The first wave of sixties radical feminists who often set out the terms of social and political debate in the women's movement, women such as Gloria Steinem, Shulamith Firestone, Kate Millet, Ann Koedt, and Ellen Willis, gave way to a second wave of theorists such as Andrea Dworkin, Adrienne Rich, Kathleen Barry, Susan Griffin, Mary Daly, and Catharine MacKinnon. These latter radical feminists achieved an authority within the women's movement that often allowed them to control ideological discussion through the 1980s, even if liberal feminists captured the political agenda of the women's movement. These second-generation radical feminists have been called "cultural feminists," since they have emphasized resisting male hostility by building a womansculture based on "female" values.

Cultural feminists have shaped the terms of the debate over sexuality from the mid-1970s through the late 1980s. By the early 1980s, however, their defense of a sexual ethic that joins a romantic sexual ideology to a separatist gender politic came under attack by feminists of a variety of ideological stripes. Heated exchanges occurred in conferences, journals, and books between cultural feminists and their critics. The result of this conflict was a far-reaching discussion over sexual ethics. This debate affords us a good opportunity to examine one site of conflict between a romantic and libertarian sexual ethic.

I begin by sketching the social setting of this debate. In particular, I outline some of the social and intellectual sources of cultural feminism. I proceed to review the debates over pornography and S/M, which have served as the primary sites in the battle over sexuality. In the concluding section, I relate the debate over sexual ethics to the theme of gender difference. This allows us to assess the strengths and limits of sexual romanticism and a libertarian alternative from the vantage point of (mostly white, middle-class) women in contemporary America.

The Rise of Cultural Feminism: Circling Sex as Romance and Eros

From the vantage point of the early 1970s, there were good reasons for feminists to feel confident about the prospects for social change beneficial to women. When NOW was created in 1966 women lacked basic individual rights, equal social opportunities and autonomous institutional bases of power. There were no active movements of legislative reform, nor was there a national policy on the status of women. By 1972, many of the demands in NOW's Bill of Rights had been partially attained, including the Congressional passage of the ERA. Between 1972–1974 Congress passed women's rights legislation covering employment, education, property and marriage rights. In 1973 the Supreme Court, in effect, legalized abortion.[1] Moreover, as NOW and other liberal feminist organizations integrated radical feminist concerns of sexuality and health, the women's movement gained a level of ideological unity that has eluded it ever since.

Beginning in the mid-1970s the situation began to change considerably. In the context of a backlash against the democratic and cultural modernist politics of the preceding decade, the women's movement encountered resistance and counter-mobilization; it suffered some serious defeats.[2] While the reforms protecting women's basic formal rights were not seriously threatened there were legislative efforts to refurbish a crumbling male privileged order. The Family Protection Act, introduced into Congress initially in 1979 and, in a revised version, in 1981, aimed at reinstating men's dominance. Abolishing abortion rights assumed a key place in the agenda of the New Right. The passage of the Hyde Amendment in 1977 cut off Medicaid funds for abortion. With the rise of a liberal and Left anti-abortionist position, and mounting lobbying efforts by the New Right, the possibility that a conservative Supreme Court could reverse the Wade v. Roe decision began to loom large. Perhaps most telling of all, the ERA which had become the political and symbolic centerpiece of the women's movement, failed to attain the 38 state ratification needed to effect a constitutional amendment. Along with these political and legislative setbacks, the stalled efforts to achieve broader social changes (e.g., the placing of childcare on the national political agenda), and the continued economic discrimination against women put the movement on the defensive.

From the present vantage point we can see that the reaction against the women's movement reflected, in part, its very successes. Its achievements were considerable—for example, civil rights legislation, the proliferation of women's studies courses and departments in universities, the appearance of health and rape crisis centers, often supported by state and federal funds, and the incorporation of feminist concerns into public policy and debate. Nevertheless, the continuing discrimination and violence toward women which left many of them socially disempowered, and the rise of an organized antifeminist politics, seemed to many feminists to challenge the future of the movement. Furthermore, at the very moment when the women's movement seemed to need unity to defend its agenda, the bonds of sisterhood seemed to be strained, if not breaking down. Social and ideological divisions surfaced within the movement that for many women posed an internal threat to the movement just as serious as the external one. To be sure, the women's movement had never been without its ideological differences. From the very beginnings of the postwar movement, there were conflicts between liberal, radical, and socialist feminists, as well as within these various ideological currents. Moreover, feminists were acutely aware of differences among women stemming from class, race and sexual orientation. Yet, it was not until the early 1970s that these differences attained strong ideological articulation in a way that seemed to threaten to unravel the fragile bonds of solidarity. From within the movement, women of color, working-class women, and lesbians contested the narrow focus of the movement's social and political agenda and began to voice concerns that their experiences and interests were not being represented. The women's movement was becoming decentered and fractured into heterogeneous conflicting groups. In a setting of a perceived antifeminist backlash, this internal fragmentation threatened to render feminism ineffective. For many feminists, the movement that had provided them with an affirmative identity and community seemed in jeopardy.

Cultural feminism emerged in a context when the effectiveness of the women's movement was thought to be threatened by a rising tide of male hostility and by internal division. Cultural feminism offered both an account of persisting male resistance to feminism and a potentially unifying agenda that could renew sisterly solidarity. The notion, advanced in many different versions by cultural feminists, that there is a deep-seated male impulse to dominate women seemed to account for men's unyielding resistance to gender equality. This claim resonated with feminists' heightened awareness of the pervasiveness of male violence toward women. In feminist consciousness-raising groups, the experiences of incest, rape, harrassment and physical assault by men were recounted. Powerful public statements like Susan Brownmiller's *Against Our Will*, Millet's *Sexual Politics*, Susan Griffin's *Rape* and Andrea Dworkin's *Our Blood* narrated stories of a male will seemingly programmed to do violence to women. The focus on a dangerous male desire that needed to exercise mastery over women to affirm masculine power provided a fresh avenue for feminist social criticism and political mobilization. Framing the body and sexuality as the site of male domination and women's struggle for autonomy defined an ideological agenda that could potentially unify the women's movement.[3]

Cultural feminism had at least one additional social appeal. Its emphasis on a culturalist and separatist agenda appealed to many feminists who were disillusioned at the prospects for significant social change and uncomfortable with the relentless in-fighting within the movement. Cultural feminism's separatist strains appealed especially to lesbians, many of whom were uncomfortable with a male-controlled gay movement, yet, who had been marginalized within the women's movement. Cultural feminism offered lesbians not only a promise of social inclusion, but a privileged social status as a kind of vanguard pioneering a woman-centered life.

The link between lesbianism and feminism is critical for understanding the formation of cultural feminism. Indeed, as we will see, lesbianism is a central, if not always acknowledged, presence in the sexuality debates. The effort to accommodate lesbianism to the women's movement was an underlying impulse of cultural feminism. Similarly, lesbians who claim to be both feminists and aligned with the gay movement have played a prominent role in criticizing cultural feminists and defending an alternative libertarian sexual ethic. This is not the place to review the broader topic of lesbianism and feminism, but it is necessary to at least sketch the role of lesbianism in shaping cultural feminism.

The lesbian issue loomed large in the women's movement through the 1970s.[4] Antifeminists sought to discredit the movement by linking it to a lesbian sexual rights agenda. Furthermore, a public image of lesbians as unconventional was threatening to many feminists. Nevertheless, lesbians played a prominent role in the movement and by the late 1960s demanded that their issues be placed on the feminist agenda. Lesbianism emerged early on, then, as a divisive topic which, along with issues of class and race, contributed to dividing feminists at a time when solidarity was needed to both press their agenda and defend it against surging antifeminist forces.

From the beginning, many in the movement resisted viewing lesbianism as a women's issue. Some feminists viewed homosexuality as a individual concern, if not psychological problem. Other feminists, more accepting of homosexuality, preferred to view lesbianism as a issue of homosexual rights. Liberal feminists were at times openly hostile. Betty Friedan labeled the lesbian issue a "lavender menace" which threatened to undermine the credibility of the movement. Under Friedan's leadership the National Organization of Women sought to silence those who voiced the position that lesbianism is a feminist issue. Friedan's discomfort with homosexuality and sexual pluralism in general was fairly typical of many liberal feminist leaders. Between 1969–1971 NOW purged its ranks of lesbians.

Radical feminists were often no less inhospitable towards lesbians. In her history of radical feminism, Alice Echols observes: "Many radical feminists . . . were often skittish if not hostile toward lesbianism.

Most commonly, they dismissed lesbianism as sexual rather than political."[5] However, the fact that many radical feminists were unconventional in their lifestyles and politics, and placed women's control of their own bodies high on the feminist agenda, facilitated a rapprochement between radical feminism and lesbianism.

Accommodation between heterosexual feminists and lesbians hinged on finding a common ideological ground. In fact, the early radical feminist focus on the politics of the personal pointed to a shared ideological space. Radical feminists had already theorized sexuality as a pivotal domain of gender politics. Men's social and ideological control over women's bodies was said to be basic to male domination. Many radical feminists proceeded, quite logically, to define heterosexuality and the whole configuration of heterosexual romance, marriage, and the family as the principal site of women's oppression and struggle. The entire institution of heterosexuality, which included the ideology of romantic love, the celebration of vaginal intercourse and orgasm, marriage and the family, was described by radical feminists as a political one: it disclosed men's will to subjugate women.[6]

This radical feminist perspective spawned a lesbian-feminist ideology. In a key early text of lesbian-feminism, "The Woman Identified Woman," heterosexuality is targeted as the pivotal domain of women's oppression and struggle for liberation. "As long as women's liberation tries to free women without facing the basic heterosexual structure that binds us in one-to-one relationships with our oppressors, tremendous energies will continue to flow into trying to straighten up each particular relationship with a man, into finding how to get better sex, how to turn his head around—into trying to make the 'new man' out of him . . . This . . . splits our energies and commitments, leaving us unable to be committed to the construction of the new patterns which will liberate us."[7] The institution of heterosexuality was said to underpin male domination by consigning women to sexual and domestic functions; by binding women's psychological and social well-being to their roles as wives and mothers; and by defining women's needs and identity in terms of their relationships to men. In a word, a female self was said to be constructed in terms of the imperative of a heterosexual norm that empowers men. Women's struggles, the lesbian feminists argued, could not be confined to the enacting of social, economic or legal reforms; women had to free themselves from male-imposed identities and roles and struggle against the institution of heterosexuality, since this kept them powerless. Women were urged to center their lives in relation to other women. "It is the primacy of women relating to women, of women creating a new consciousness of and with each other, which is at the heart of women's liberation."[8] This lesbian-feminist ideology proposed that the primary agenda for the women's movement ought to be the building of a womansculture that preserves women's integrity by cultivating female values and lifestyles.

Within this lesbian-feminist analysis, lesbianism was reconceived as "woman-identification." Lesbian-feminists argued that the conventional view of lesbianism as a sexual preference was a male viewpoint reflecting their disposition to sexualize feelings and relationships. Moreover, framing lesbianism as a deviant sexuality subject to various sanctions was said to be a way men exercise control over women who reject a patriarchal heterosexual norm.[9] Lesbian-feminists redefined lesbianism as a political and social act: political because it is an act of resistance to patriarchy and social as it entails a commitment to identify and to bond primarily with women. "Lesbianism is not a matter of sexual preference, but rather one of political choice which every women must make if she is to become women-identified and thereby to end male supremacy."[10] Becoming women-identified does not, in principle, require sexual involvement with other women, only a primary commitment to their values and interests.[11]

The effort to reconceive lesbianism as woman-identification was a key strategic move. Desexualizing lesbianism was supposed to make it more acceptable to heterosexual feminists. The message of "Woman Identified Woman" was not only that lesbians are just like other women, but that lesbians were women whose life choice it was to bond with women against male domination. In fact, this concept of lesbianism blurred the line between being a lesbian and being a feminist. All feminists, by definition, are thought to be women-identified regardless of their sexual orientation. Lesbians differ only by making their woman-identification a comprehensive commitment. All women, to use Adrienne Rich's terms, are situated somewhere along the "lesbian continuum;" women whose lives are centered entirely on other women live a "lesbian existence."[12] By collapsing lesbianism and feminism, lesbian-feminists step forward as the very prototype of the new liberated woman. They exemplify women's independence from male imposed identities; they live without men, and, indeed, outside traditional female roles; it is lesbians who are said to have pioneered the building of an autonomous womansculture. In their effort to be accepted in the women's movement and to, in fact, remake it in their own image, lesbian-feminists effected a remarkable transformation in the concept of lesbianism. From a stigmatized deviant sexuality, the lesbian now appeared as a vanguard social and political figure in the women's movement.

Lesbian-feminism as an organized movement spans the years between 1969 and 1973. Alice Echols dates the beginnings of lesbian-feminism in 1969. "Beginning in late 1969, [Rita Mae] Brown set about organizing a lesbian-feminist movement."[13] By 1972, with the dissolution of the Furies, a Washington, D.C., based lesbian-feminist collective, lesbian-feminism had lost much of its organizational force in the broader women's movement. Nevertheless, many of its basic ideas, in particular, its centering on a critique of heterosexuality, its dichotomy between female and male values, and its shifting of the political agenda from social structural reform to lifestyle change and building a womansculture, persisted and have been pivotal in the appearance of what some feminists have come to call cultural feminism.

Cultural feminism [henceforth C-F] is the term coined by Alice Echols to describe the highly influential social and ideological current within the women's movement that achieved prominence between the late 1970s and the mid-1980s. C-F was not advanced as a unified ideological agenda; there was no manifesto nor was there one organizational vehicle. C-F is a loose set of related themes and perspectives that draws heavily on the legacy of lesbian-feminism. Indeed, many of those identified as its ideological vanguard have strong ties to lesbian-feminism, e.g., Andrea Dworkin, Kathleen Barry, Mary Daly, Susan Griffin, Catharine MacKinnon, Robin Morgan, and Adrienne Rich.[14] Yet, as will become clear in the course of this chapter, C-F describes ideological and social trends within the women's movement that are broader than those of lesbian-feminism. I wish to briefly outline some of its principal ideas; in the subsequent sections I will provide somewhat detailed elaborations of C-F.

C-F projects an ideal of personal and social life for women that is centered in what are defined as female values and ways of being. This perspective assumes that female values are available in only a partial and distorted way under conditions of male dominance. The current ideal of femininity is said to construct women as men desire them—as passive, sex objects, subservient, self-sacrificing, intuitive, irrational, and maternal. Shorn of its patriarchal distortions, however, true femininity is a life-giving, spiritually elevating, personally empowering force. Cultural feminists often speak of a unique female nature that promotes empathetic and nurturing values, closeness to nature, egalitarian relationships, the acceptance of bodily functions, the valuing of sensuality and a striving towards personal wholeness, organic social bonds, and an ecological balance. C-F assumes an antithesis between female and male values and ways of being. "Maleness" often stands for a violent, destructive energy emanating from the male impulse to self-control, dominance over others, and world mastery. Male culture is said to promote a lean intellectualism and formalism that suppresses the dense richness and organic wholeness of experience. Men's disposition to frame life in terms of the abstractions and hierarchies of the rational intellect encourages a general disdain for emotions, intuition, the body as a medium of sensuality and joy, and nature as wildness and wonder. At the core of male culture is said to be a contempt and devaluation of the feminine which is identified with the "lower" orders of life (e.g., the body, nature, feelings, and the domestic sphere).

Cultural feminists subscribe to an ideology of gender difference. This difference is said to be manifested in two antithetical sexual values and intimate styles. Reflecting women's basic orientation to organic, empathetic, and nurturing values, female sexuality is characterized by a diffuse body eroticism, gentleness, romance, and monogamy; sex is seen as an expression of relational intimacy, and is person-centered. Male sexuality, in contrast, is genital and body-centered, objectifying, instrumental and promiscuous; sex for men is said to be oriented to physical pleasure and control. Writes Robin Morgan: "The emphasis on genital sexuality, objectification, promiscuity, emotional noninvolvement, and coarse invulnerability, was the male style, and that we, as women, placed greater trust in love, sensuality, humor, tenderness, commitment."[15] Although many cultural feminists explain female values in terms of women's history and social location in the domestic sphere, others describe it as natural. Sally Gearhart speaks of the "redemption of female values . . . [and the] return to the fundamental female nature of the race."[16] Even cultural feminists who insist upon a historical account of female and male culture often fall into essentialist accounts in the absence of analyses of the different and changing forms and meanings of masculinity and femininity within and across societies.

C-F is connected to a distinctive sexual politic. With its antinomy of female and male sexuality—and its tendency to celebrate the former and demonize the latter—a cultural feminist sexual politic advocates strategies to censor and inhibit a lustful, dangerous male sexuality. In addition, cultural feminists promote efforts to build an autonomous womansculture that can protect and nurture a woman-centered sexuality and life. This womansculture is often imagined as the institutional basis for the transformation—and feminization—of society.

C-F advances a unique feminist sexual ethic, which fills the space vacated by male-controlled constructions of female sexual desire. Cultural feminists are part of the on-going struggle within the women's movement to define and regulate the body and mind of women. The romantic sexual ethic of C-F states that only sex that is an expression of an intimate, loving bond is legitimate. The sex act itself should exhibit intimate qualities by being gentle, nurturing, tender and person-oriented. Sex that occurs outside a intimate setting or sex that occurs within a loving relationship but that is centered on bodily, sensual pleasure is morally degrading and unacceptable.

Cultural feminists claim that because their sexual ethic and politic articulates true female values, it is empowering for women. This contention that C-F gives voice to the authentic female experience has been contested by at least four general currents within the women's movement. First, many lesbians whose chief affiliation is with a prefeminist dyke culture, have criticized C-F for devaluing and contributing to the suppression of this culture. Second, lesbians affiliated with the gay movement have taken C-F to task for promulgating a restrictive sexual ethic that reinforces a politic of sexual repression. Third, heterosexual feminists who affirm the value of sexual pleasure and lifestyle diversity have criticized cultural feminists for imposing a narrow sexual orthodoxy. Finally, some women of color and working-class women see in C-F another effort by the white middle class to colonize and control them.

By the beginning of the 1980s there was widespread discontent in the women's movement concerning C-F. Sex became a chief battleground in the struggle over defining and directing the women's movement. A far-reaching debate ensued between cultural feminist defenders of sexual romanticism and their critics, many of whom edged toward a libertarian ethic. Two issues have galvanized and focused the debate. First, the cultural feminist campaign against pornography was met with a response by feminists who mounted a counter-offensive in the form of "women against censorship." Second, the debate over S/M provoked by the rise of a lesbian S/M movement has proven to be a key site for feminists struggle over sexual meanings. In the two sections to follow, I give a critical overview of a debate featuring a cultural feminist discourse that wishes to erect elaborate institutional and ideological boundaries around sex and a libertarian discourse that emphasizes the self-fulfilling aspects of an unbounded, prolific sexuality.

Cultural Feminism and Its Critics I: The Porn Debate

By the mid-1970s, cultural feminists developed an impressive critique of pornography. Unlike liberal critics, who objected only to the excesses of pornography or to the public's involuntary exposure to it, cultural feminists disputed the liberal presumption that pornography has an enlightening social role. While cultural feminists saw in pornography little or no redeeming value, they distinguished their critique from that of conservatives, who were said to object to its sexually explicit character regardless of its content and context. Cultural feminists insisted that their critique was not directed at its nudity, eroticism, or even the public display of sexuality.[17]

Cultural feminists maintain that pornography is not, in fact, primarily about sex, which was merely the medium for relating a message about gender norms and roles. Specifically, pornography discloses a drama of male domination. "Pornography is primarily a medium for expressing norms about male power and domination, thereby functioning as a social control mechanism for keeping women in a subordinate status."[18] Pornography is said to rationalize male power by fostering a contempt for women. "Pornography functions to perpetuate male supremacy and crimes of violence gainst women because it conditions, trains, educates, and inspires men to despise women, and men despise women in part because pornography exists."[19] In short, cultural feminists define pornography as a site of gender politics.

Cultural feminists argue that pornography depicts women in a way that reflects men's wishes and fantasies, revealing their impulse to control and do violence to women. "The true subject of pornography is not sex or eros but objectification, which increasingly includes cruelty, violence against women. . . ."[20] Violence need not take the form of men inflicting physical pain. Pornography is said to display a symbolic violence in obliterating women as autonomous sexual and social agents, and rendering them mere objects of desire. Susan Brownmiller protests that pornography projects women as "anonymous, panting . . . playthings, adult toys, dehumanized objects to be used, abused, broken and discarded."[21] Pornography, it is argued, does not represent women as subjects. Women are never shown as initiating action, or directing their own or men's behavior. They simply react to male wishes and take pleasure in being subject to male control. "Women are presented as passive and as slavishly dependent upon men. [Their] role . . . is limited to the provision of sexual services to men. . . . Women's sexual pleasure . . . is subordinated to that of men and is never an end in itself. . . . What pleases women is the use of their bodies to satisfy male desires."[22] Women exist in the male pornographic gaze merely as eroticized body parts. "Pornography propagates a view of women as nothing but 'tits' and 'ass'—silly creatures who exist to be fucked, sexually used, and forgotten."[23] In short, pornography dehumanizes women, by depicting them as passive sex objects whose primary value lie in the pleasure they give men.

Cultural feminists press the additional claim that pornography denies women their autonomy by suppressing their unique sexual desires and values. This criticism assumes that women's sexuality is different from men's. "Men are turned on by what they see, remember, or anticipate; sex has a more central place in the male psyche where sexuality tends to be impersonal and abstract; sex is centered on the genitals; and it is closely related to aggression. . . . All told, male sexuality is performance-oriented. Women respond to diffuse touching; their sexuality is more personal, intimate, and emotional—unlike the reified male style, women's sexuality is imbued with nurturance, women's sexual style is process-oriented."[24] Pornography is said to disregard these gender differences by depicting women's sexuality in ways that reflect how men wish them to be. Women's sexuality is represented as body-centered (rather than person-centered), genitally-focused (rather than diffusely erotic), oriented toward sexual intercourse (rather than clitoral pleasures) and motivated by carnal pleasures (rather than affection and intimacy). Pornography, writes Laura Lederer, "is almost totally penis-centered, often devoid of foreplay, tenderness or caring, to say nothing of love and romance."[25] Susan Lurie remarks that in pornography "the male fantasy . . . represses the true nature of female sexuality."[26]

Central to this cultural feminist critique is the objection to the value pornography places on sex as a separate site of pleasure and play. This is said to entail a level of sexual objectification, depersonalization and instrumentalism that is morally objectionable. Thus, Kathleen Barry protests all attempts to separate sex from intimate ties. "In my view, where there is any attempt to separate the sexual experience from the total person, that first act of objectification is perverse."[27] Barry endorses a sexual ethic that legitimates sex only as an expression of the whole person in an intimate relationship. She holds, moreover, that this ethic is grounded in women's unique sexual values. "We are really going back to the values that women have always attached to sexuality, values that have been robbed from us [by a male dominated culture]."[28] These female sexual values "are the values and needs that connect sex with warmth, affection, loving, caring."[29] Indeed, Barry views these female sexual values as representing the essential positive meaning of human sexuality itself. "Sexual experience involves the most personal, primitive, erotic, sensitive parts of our physical and psychic being—it is intimate in fact."[30] The implication is that male sexuality, especially to the extent that it values eroticism as an end in itself, is unnatural and debasing.

Cultural feminists contend that pornography permeates our culture.[31] It is a multi-billion dollar business; pornographic representations are said to pervade the mass media. Its global cultural presence makes it a formative force influencing our attitudes and behavior. Pornography shapes male sexual fantasy and desire and eroticizes men's exercise of power over women. Furthermore, by constructing men as motivated by a violent sexual lust incited by women who are aroused by their passivity and victimization, pornography is said to make acceptable men's use of force to control women. Rape, women-beating, and the various kinds of harassment and intimidation that maintain male domination are considered the direct effects of pornography.

Cultural feminists offer a "situational" explanation of pornography and, at times, a more transhistorical thesis. The former explains the recent spread of pornography, and its supposedly more violent nature as part of a male backlash against the women's movement. Threatened by women's demands for greater autonomy, men have reacted defensively and, in response to the magnitude of the perceived threat, sometimes violently. Men wish to reestablish an arrangement ensuring their own uncontested supremacy. From this perspective, both pornography and the alleged rise in violence towards women are manifestations of the same antifeminist backlash.[32] This backlash is made possible because woman-hatred is a general feature of American culture. Cultural feminists argue that pornography is simply the ideological nucleus of a misogynist culture that values women only if they perform caretaking, domestic or sexual functions for men.[33] If pressed, most feminists explain widespread misogyny in terms of a "social control" paradigm that defines men as a privileged gender-class whose rule is maintained by their institutional and ideological hegemony. However, some cultural feminists formulate a more transhistorical argument. Pornography and the broader culture of sexism and misogyny is traced to an ahistorical notion of male nature. Andrea Dworkin continually pushes beyond a sociological to a transhistorical thesis that locates woman-hatred in male nature. "Pornography reveals that male sexual pleasure is inextricably tied to victimizing, hurting, exploiting; that sexual fun and pleasure in the . . . male imagination are inseparable from . . . brutality."[34] Male violence is traced by Dworkin to a biological source. "Violence is male; the male is the penis; violence is the penis."[35]

Feminist critics of antipornography feminists are not entirely unsympathetic to their arguments, nor are they of one ideological stripe.[36] They acknowledge the sexist aspects of pornography, and criticize the exploitation of workers in pornography and the images of women being abused. At one level, their disagreement is one of degree. Feminist critics see pornography as less sexist, less violent, less degrading, and less exploitative than their opponents. Empirical disputes between cultural feminists and their critics revolve around how pervasive pornography is, its causal link with male dominance and violence, and its sources. There are, as well, disagreements over political strategy. Many feminist critics who concede the misogynist character of pornography oppose augmenting a patriarchal state's regulatory authority over public representations, since this power could easily be turned against feminists and lesbians.

The dispute between cultural feminists and their critics turns ultimately on the basic meaning of pornography. Critics defend the more conventional view that pornography is primarily about sex.[37] They argue that the cultural feminist critique of pornography, ostensibly advanced against male domination, masks a more dubious sexual political agenda. It is this hidden sexual politic that the critics of the antiporn feminists aim to disclose and discredit.

Despite the cultural feminist claim to be criticizing pornography for perpetuating male dominance, feminist critics accuse them of disguising a deep ambivalence towards eroticism.[38] Critics contend that opponents of pornography are, in fact, reacting to its expressive-hedonistic construction of sex. Cultural feminists are said to be uncomfortable with pornography's aggressive, genital-and-body-centered eroticism. By attributing these sexual values to men, and by featuring their violent, instrumental aspects, cultural feminists presumably have a strategy to both manage whatever personal distress is evoked by these sexual images and to mobilize women against a different and dangerous male desire.

Cultural feminists are criticized for promulgating a sexual ideology that denies to women a range of sexual and lifestyle choices, thus reinforcing lingering prohibitions against women who are sexually aggressive, lustful, and nonconventional.[39] Paralleling conventional liberal perspectives, moreover, these feminist critics defend pornography from a sexual political standpoint: it affirms sexual pleasure for both men *and* women; it promotes diverse sexual styles; it gives a voice to oppressed sexualities.[40] In short, feminist critics claim that the cultural feminist gender critique of pornography masks a fear of its erotic representations.[41]

These criticisms miss the more subtle reasoning of the feminists opposed to pornography. They do not deny that they are responding to pornography's sexual ideology. They insist, however, that these sexual meanings are not gender-neutral. Rather, insofar as the sex in pornography emphasizes anonymous encounters, genital pleasures, performance concerns, and sheer physical release, pornography exhibits a male-styled sexuality. To the extent that women's sexuality is portrayed in male-identified terms, their own sexual desires and their right to define their own sexuality are denied. Hence, cultural feminists conclude that the defense of pornography as promoting a sex-positive and pluralistic culture is misplaced. They argue that, in fact, pornography extends men's power by defining women's sexuality in a way that leaves them powerless.

Cultural feminists insist that it is not eros that they are criticizing but the universalization of male eroticism. This is a plausible rejoinder to their critics, who view the framing of pornography as a gender dynamic as masking a retreat from eros. Accordingly, feminist critics have had to challenge the cultural feminist construction of male and female sexualities as fixed bipolar opposites.

The cultural feminist critique of pornography leans heavily on a belief in a polarized gender order that produces two distinct sexualities.[42] Male sexuality is described as visual, performance-oriented, aggressive, genital-and-body centered and promiscuous; female sexuality is understood as tactile, process-and-person-centered, intimate and monogamous. Critics do not deny existing behavioral and value differences between female and male sexuality, but argue that antipornographers greatly simplify them, and accuse their opponents of suppressing significant differences among women and important similarities between the sexes. They are censured for exaggerating and reifying whatever differences currently exist between men and women. Ultimately, many antipornography feminists are said to subscribe to an essentialism which posits a female sexuality that is constant across women's diverse social and historical circumstances.[43] Critics underscore the telling point that women's sexuality is far more varied and multifaceted then this argument allows.[44]

If, as critics have suggested, sexuality cannot be so neatly gender-typed, the cultural feminist effort to specify a unique female erotic life, or to ground a sexual ethic in women's common gender experience, loses credibility. It gives currency, moreover, to the critic's claim that the gender-typing of aggressive, body-centered, pleasure-centered, orgiastic sexuality as male by cultural feminists represents, in part, a retreat from eroticism or at least certain forms of eroticism, whose gendered status is ambiguous.[45]

Feminist critics are correct, in my view, in uncovering an ambivalence toward eroticism in the cultural feminist critique of pornography. Antipornography feminists are critically responding to pornography, in part, because it features an aggressive, body-centered, pleasure-centered sexuality as a legitimate medium of individualism and social bonding. Pornography does abstract the sex act as a mere erotic experience. Every conceivable organ and orifice is explored using every possible stimulant, for the sole purpose of maximizing erotic pleasure. Individuals are typified in one-dimensional sexual ways with an exclusive focus on their body parts, erotic gestures, positions, and movements. Pornography intends to narrow the social exchange to a bounded erotic one.[46] It is pornography's expressive-hedonistic construction of sex, a construction that splits eros off from romance and differentiates the self as a erotic subject, to which cultural feminists, in part, are reacting critically.

The antipornography feminists are, in my view, mistaken to gender type all sexuality and thereby render the sphere of sexuality simply an extension of gender politics. Gender meanings inform sexual practices but they are not comprehended by them. The relationship between gender and sexuality is complex and multidimensional; there are slippages and disjunctions between gender and sexuality. For example, coitus is not in itself an act expressing solely a male desire, nor is it necessarily an act of male dominance. Research indicates that heterosexual women in postwar America routinely report valuing coitus as both a medium of intimacy and erotic joy.[47] Whether sexual intercourse is a political act of men subjugating women depends upon its interpersonal context which determines, say, a woman's possibilities for initiating, negotiating, and refusing the act, as well as her ability to define the place of vaginal intercourse in the entire sexual and social exchange.

Cultural feminists may reluctantly concede this point, but will insist that the gendered nature of sex is revealed when one considers its interpersonal context. If vaginal intercourse per se is not exclusively male-identified, it is to the extent that it is motivated primarily by erotic pleasure or is the center and climax of sex, or when it occurs in an impersonal or casual encounter. Let us assume for the sake of argument that these practices reflect men's sexual values. It still does not necessarily follow that depictions of female sexuality in male terms will be repressive. Whether women experience such representations as oppressive depends upon the extent to which they already have sexual dispositions in these directions; whether women are presented as active autonomous subjects; and whether they can selectively draw upon these sexual meanings in ways that affirm and enhance their own sexual autonomy. From this perspective, pornographic images of women's sexuality may, depending upon the way the gendered interpersonal context is characterized, be defended as making available to women a range of sexual desires, styles, and scripts that expand rather than restrict their sexual autonomy.

Feminists opposed to pornography are wrong to hold to an overdetermined gender analysis of sex. In doing so they reify sexuality in quite conventional middle class gender terms. Yet, they are not mistaken in underscoring continued differences in contemporary America between female and male sexual styles. Sex frequently carries unique meanings and social implications for women. This must be considered in any analysis of pornography.

The need to frame sexuality within a gender context is not adequately dealt with by feminist defenders of pornography who at times approach sex as if it were entirely genderless. An abstract defense of pornography as affirming sexual pleasure and a plurality of sexual lifestyle choices without considering that under present social conditions sex often carries unique dangers for women, weakens their case. Risks of disease, physical assault, pregnancy, and the stigma of a "loose woman" are still issues that surround sex for many women. These dangers are heightened with the acceptance of expressive-hedonistic sex. Similarly, the defense of pornography as a medium of erotic values raises serious questions about the meaning and morality of sexual objectification. Pornographic sex typifies men and women as sexual beings. In pornography every gesture, pose, motivation, and aspect of the context are directed to heightening erotic pleasure. Inevitably, this entails a focus on the body or specific organs and orifices, and a concern with techniques of sensory stimulation in abstraction from the nonerotic features of the individual. In other words, while pornography does *not* reduce men and women to "objects," it does focus on their sexual self-presentation. This sexual typification is defended by many feminists insofar as it occurs in an interpersonal context of consent and mutuality of pleasure and respect. This position does not, however, sufficiently consider that in our society men and women experience sexual typification differently.[48] The depiction of men as "sex objects" is typically self-enhancing, insofar as sexual desirability and potency affirms masculinity. Furthermore, this depiction does not threaten to reduce them to a sexual role to the extent that men represent socially powerful figures.[49] On the contrary, it may contribute to men's experience of themselves as powerful. For a woman to be rendered a sex object is often to be burdened with a demeaning resonance. Lacking social positions of privilege and power, identified with subservient and servicing roles, women's depiction as sex objects frequently accompanies reduction to a sexual function and subordinate status. Women's sexualization has been a primary strategy by which they have been denied full individuality and autonomy. Such considerations of gender must be addressed in any analysis of pornography or any cultural representation or discourse on sex.

The pornography debate bears witness to a struggle among feminists to define the current ideological agenda of the women's movement. Moreover, feminists have moved into the space opened by the partial evacuation of male controlled legal, medical, and scientific discourses of female sexuality. The pornography debates may be seen, in part, as a struggle to define and regulate women's sexual lives.

C-F frames pornography in terms of a discourse of the dangers of male sexuality. Unlike Victorian women who were placed in the role of domesticating a dangerous male desire, cultural feminists counsel women to purge themselves of male-imposed sexual concepts and embrace female values. Affirming female sexual values means defining sex as an act of sharing and nurturing to be confined to an intimate, committed relationship. This more or less conventional middle-class romantic sexual ethic is given a feminist twist when it is wedded to the cultural feminist project of building a separate womansculture.

Critics of C-F highlight its restrictive sexual ethic. They argue that the discourse of the dangers of pornography masks a deep ambivalence towards eroticism that passes into an unnecessarily restrictive sexual politic. Feminist critics often frame pornography within a discourse of the sensual and expressive pleasures of sex. Pornography is said, moreover, to affirm women as autonomous sexual subjects with the same sexual options as men. Social equality, they insist, must extend to equal rights and opportunities to pursue sexual pleasure and a sexual lifestyle of one's own choice. This discourse of the pleasures of sex edges toward a libertarian sexual ideology, holding that sex has multiple meanings and is legitimate in diverse social settings. Given an interpersonal context of consent and mutual respect, sex can be defended not only as an expression of intimacy or love, but also as a form of pleasure, play or communication in a variety of types of social exchanges. These libertarian feminists are critical of the sexist and exploitative aspects of pornography but defend it for affirming eroticism and lifestyle choice.

An important issue in the debate between cultural feminists and their critics is the relationship between the women's movement and sexual liberation movements. Twentieth-century feminists have frequently exhibited great ambivalence towards sexual liberation movements and ideology. This ambivalence, as we have seen in chapter 2, intensified during the 1970s. Feminists affiliated with the counterculture or the gay movement defined the women's movement as a contributor to sexual liberation movements. Many feminists who were uncovering the multiple layers of male domination, frequently firsthand in these liberation movements, resisted linking women's struggle to male-controlled movements. Cultural feminists oppose any identification of the women's movement with a sexual liberationist movement. The social prominence of C-F in the 1970s and 1980s, side by side with the continued presence of a sex-radical wing of the women's movement, has sparked a far-reaching discussion over the relationship of feminism to sexual liberation movements—a discussion which touches on key issues in sexual ethics. This debate has occurred in various contexts but none more important and provocative than that to which we presently turn, of feminism and lesbian S/M.

Cultural Feminism and Its Critics II: The Debate Over Lesbian S/M

Twentieth-century feminists have frequently responded with ambivalence to sexual liberation movements, with second-wave feminists divided over viewing the women's movement as a sexual liberation movement.[50] Many feminists have felt that women's struggle for gender rights and equality was inextricably linked with sexual liberation movements. Other feminists have insisted that the sexual liberationist agenda is so thoroughly male-controlled that its sexual politic remains wedded to a reactionary gender politic. These feminists insist upon differentiating the women's movement from the movements of so-called sexual liberation (e.g., the gay movement, counterculture, or the *Playboy/Joy of Sex* sexual libertarian movement); indeed, women's sexual liberation is understood as different and, for some feminists, in opposition to a male defined sexual liberation agenda.

From the mid-1970s, cultural feminists have been in the forefront of the feminist critique of sexual liberation movements. They have interpreted these movements as promoting male domination by conflating the agenda of sexual freedom with male-identified sexual values. These male-controlled movements aim to universalize male sexual values and perpetuate their gender dominance in the name of human sexual freedom. Some cultural feminists argue, for example, that the sexual libertinism of many New Left men masked their hostility to their female counterparts who were making demands for social equality. Threatened by women's rising expectations for autonomy and leadership roles, many New Left men advocated free love in order to keep women socially subordinate by sexually objectifying them.[51] Similarly, many cultural feminists criticize the male-dominated gay liberation movement for promoting a male agenda. Drawing on a common stereotype of gay men, cultural feminists object to the prevalence among gay men of genitally-fixated, performance-oriented, and promiscuous sexual values. Adrienne Rich assails gay male life for its "prevalence of anonymous sex and the justification of pederasty among male homosexuals, the pronounced ageism in male homosexual standards of sexual attraction, and so forth."[52] Highlighting the differences between gay men and lesbians, Robin Morgan underscores the former's advocacy of sexual objectification, casual sex, and the promotion of man-boy love which, in her view, "is an euphemism for rape."[53] Cultural feminists are among the most vocal of those demanding the disassociation of lesbians and feminists from a gay male-controlled homosexual liberation movement. Judith Pasternak is emphatic that "there is no place within lesbian-feminism for the oppressive, coercive, women-hating imagery in gay culture."[54]

The discussion of the link between feminism and sexual liberation movements has been focused, through the 1970s and 1980s, on the relationship between the women's movement and the gay/lesbian movement. This issue assumed center stage as cultural feminism was challenged by women who were not lesbian-feminists, but identified with a lesbian/gay movement. In particular, the rise of a lesbian S/M movement which claimed both a lesbian and a feminist affiliation occasioned a major challenge to C-F. Moreover, lesbian S/M advocates defended perhaps the most radical version of a feminist libertarian sexual ethic. In the conflict over lesbian S/M, we can further examine the merits and limits of sexual romanticism versus a libertarian sexual ethic.

Role-playing and the eroticizing of power was not a recent innovation of S/M lesbians. Prior to the postwar women's movement, lesbians had evolved a subcultural life that frequently revolved around the polarized roles of the butch and the fem. Contrary to the conventional feminist position, which criticizes butch/fem role-playing as mimicking the worst features of a male supremacist order, some recent perspectives hold that its significance within at least the pre-gay-and-women's liberation era was often both politically and erotically subversive. Adopting masculine styles of self-presentation challenged traditional sex-role stereotypes; it was—and some say still is—one way in which women could claim the privileges and power of men, including the right to be sexually potent. Joan Nestle remarks that "Butch-fem relationships, as I experienced them, were complex erotic statements, not phony heterosexual replicas. They were filled with a deeply Lesbian language of stance, dress, gesture, loving, courage, and autonomy. None of the butch women I was with . . . ever presented themselves as men; they did announce themselves as tabooed women by wearing clothes that symbolized the taking of responsibility. Part of this responsibility was sexual expertise. In the 1950's this courage to feel comfortable with arousing another woman became a political act."[55]

Some contemporary lesbians, especially S/M advocates, assert that sexual role-playing has more to do with sexual style and erotic pleasure than with gender codes. In her personal history of the lesbian S/M movement in San Francisco, Pat Califia relates that it wasn't until the late 1970s that a lesbian S/M community cohered.[56] From a loose network of friends and acquaintances a lesbian S/M support group emerged which went by the name Samois, describing itself as "feminist lesbians who share a positive interest in sadomasochism. . . . We believe that S/M must be consensual, mutual, and safe. . . . We believe that sadomasochists are an oppressed sexual minority. Our struggle deserves the recognition and support of other sexual minorities and oppressed groups."[57] With the publication of *What Color is Your Handkerchief?* and *Coming to Power*, Samois moved the issue of S/M into the center of the current feminist sexuality debate.

Samois describes S/M as a sex act aimed at enhancing mutual pleasure through eroticizing social exchanges that involve power dynamics. Janet Schrim offers the following characterization and defense of lesbian S/M:

> "S/M is a consensual form of activity intended for the pleasure of all participants. S/M is not violence. Violence is non-consensual and it's intended to coerce, injure, or kill. S/M does involve power and power roles in a temporary situation. Many anti-S/M feminist have the mistaken notion that we live the roles 24 hours a day. S/M is not in itself a lifestyle. It is a sexual preference. . . . In an S/M scene . . . both top and bottom exercise power. The roles have been agreed on. (Incidentally, the roles do not correspond to male dominant-female submissive social patterns. I've seen many feminine lesbian tops and many butch lesbian bottoms.) The action has been agreed on at least in general and sometimes in great detail. Each of us in an S/M scene is concerned with her own pleasure and with her partner's pleasure. Furthermore, an active and informed concern for safety runs through it all—physical and emotional safety. Sometimes we are casual sex partners. Sometimes we are friends. Sometimes we are lovers."[58]

Advocates of S/M define it as a sex act analogous to kissing, masturbation or oral-genital sex; it does not, they say, indicate a type of person, mentality or a lifestyle. Role-playing does not, in principle, extend beyond the S/M scene, and therefore is said to carry no significant gender political implications. S/M is defended foremost as an act of pleasure; its advocates report heightened sensual, emotional, and intellectual pleasures. The essential dynamic of S/M is claimed to be the enactment of a fantasy of relational dominance or submission. By polarizing the roles of control and submission, and by employing highly ritualized dress, gestures, movements, and talk to dramatize the feelings around the experience of dominance and surrender, each partner is said to be able to explore often tabooed physical and psychological sensations.[59] Scenes involving bondage, verbal abuse, or physical restraint are not intended to inflict pain, instead, in a social context of consent and trust, these acts function as the means by which the fantasy of dominance and submission is enacted. S/M is defended as a consensual sex act whose aim is primarily to enhance mutual pleasure in a safe and respectful social exchange.

Pat Califia tells of the repeated efforts by cultural feminists in particular to silence S/M lesbians.[60] For example, WAVPM (Women Against Violence in Pornography and the Media) refused Samois' request to hold a workshop on S/M for a national conference on feminist perspectives on pornography. Califia reports that Samois members were even barred from attending the conference. The group's publications were met with similar strategies of repression, when harsh attacks on their writings appeared in major feminist and lesbian publications. Some feminist bookstores refused to carry pro-S/M material. Many magazines or journals refused to provide space for S/M lesbians to rebut their critics or to print letters protesting this censorship. As these strategies of repression through censorship proved less effective and credible, critics mounted their own ideological offensive. Their major publication to date is the anthology *Against Sadomasochism*.[61]

This hostility towards S/M lesbians by cultural feminists was to be expected. Cultural feminists argue that S/M is an invention of male-dominant heterosexual culture; that S/M exhibits dehumanizing and violent male values; and that it mirrors and reinforces dominant gender roles that perpetuate male dominance.

Cultural feminists argue that in a male-dominant society men have institutional and ideological power. Their dominance means that masculine traits and male roles are valued more than feminine ones. Lacking institutional power, women lack control over their lives. As a subordinate group, women and feminine-typed gender traits and roles are said to be culturally devalued. In other words, a male dominant society assumes a gender hierarchy that privileges masculinity and the control of women by men. S/M, it is argued, is a product of and reproduces this hierarchical gender order. S/M expresses men's contempt of women and their need to repress feminine values as a condition of maintaining masculine power. Viewed sociologically, S/M is said to reveal the realities of a sex-role system where men and masculinity are privileged and women and femininity are disempowered and devalued. To say it differently, S/M reproduces in the sexual sphere the core structural dynamic of a male dominant society—

namely, men's power to control women through physical force, psychological intimidation, and social privilege.

Cultural feminists interpret the appearance of lesbian S/M as a case of women who are male-identified. S/M lesbians are said to have internalized male values and behavioral patterns. They have adopted patriarchal heterosexual models of behavior with their dichotomous roles, gender hierarchy, relations of dominance and submission, and masculine privilege.[62] Cultural feminists assail S/M lesbians for unwittingly legitimating male supremacism. By eroticizing the power imbalances between men and women, they sanction conventional sex-role stereotypes and a gender order that empowers men. By eroticizing the masculine will to power, S/M is said to create in women a subconscious emotional attachment to a hierarchical gender system that oppresses them. Reflecting the broader culture of male dominance, S/M lesbians are accused of idealizing masculine power and privilege. The power the top exercises over the bottom through humiliation, restraint, abuse, or intimidation in a S/M scene is said to replicate the everyday reality of male control through similar strategies of victimization and subordination. By taking over the patriarchal moral hierarchy, S/M lesbians promote such male values and orientations as aggression, hierarchy, instrumentalism, objectification, and a body-centered hedonistic and promiscuous sexuality. Finally, these critics maintain that because women are socialized and positioned to accept "masochistic" traits (e.g., passivity, submission, victimization) while simultaneously taught to idealize the power of men, women can no more be said to consent to do S/M than to choose being heterosexual. Women cannot consent to do S/M so long as they have been socialized to identify power as a male privilege experienced by women only as its object or victim. Consent is said to be precluded by women's condition of psychological and social dependency.

In the end, these feminist critics view S/M, like pornography, as a backlash reaction against the women's movement. Cultural feminists maintain that the S/M movement's rhetoric of sexual liberation, idealizing both male power and a masculine culture, masks a misogynist ideology and reactionary gender politic. Its spread among women represents a danger to the women's movement, for the presence of S/M lesbians divides feminists. It threatens to undermine the feminist project of building a womansculture based on female values. Thus, S/M is deemed incompatible with feminism.

The debate over S/M bears witness to a basic division among feminists regarding the meaning of sexuality and its relation to gender dynamics. Differences in the descriptions and judgements of S/M reflect divergent conceptual frameworks, values, and social agendas.

What S/M advocates define as a legitimate sex act involving mutual pleasure and trust, their critics describe as a dramatization of a hierachical gender order. Whereas its advocates see nothing intrinsically male-identified in a woman issuing commands or directives in a S/M scene, their critics see only the enactment of male power. Similarly, whereas supporters interpret S/M as challenging conventional sexual and gender arrangements, their critics see a mirroring process. Finally, whereas advocates see in S/M an issue of sexual identity politics akin to lesbian and gay politics, critics see it as an issue of gender politics. S/M liberation, says feminist critics, is another instance of a sexual liberation movement masking a reactionary gender politic.

Although critics of S/M are correct to insist on analyzing its gendered aspects, they err in reducing this practice to a gender dynamic. To the extent that S/M practitioners describe this act as sexual, as involving experiences of genital-and-bodily expression which Americans today would recognize as sexual, such practices need to be comprehended in the language of sexuality, i.e. the language of bodily desire, sensual pleasure, sex act and technique, erotogenic zones, etc. Native accounts of S/M leave little doubt that, whatever other meanings this practice may have, it can legitimately be described as a sex act. At the core of S/M is a transfigurational process: tabooed acts and symbols are appropriated for their erotically expressive and hedonistic qualities.[63] Its status as a nonconventional practice, like (say) homosexuality or nonmonogamy, should caution us against denying S/M the status of a legitimate sex act, notwithstanding compelling evidence of its harmful personal and social effects. The struggle to legitimate S/M as an acceptable sex act, sexual identity, and basis of community formation should be understood, at least in part, as a issue of sexual politics akin to the struggles around homosexuality.

As in the case of the pornography debate, however, libertarian feminists tend to commit themselves to an equally reductionist view of S/M as only a sexual practice. S/M can no more be completely abstracted from its gender context and meanings than can pornography. A social exchange that revolves around role-playing, aggressive/submissive feelings, and power imbalances is going to carry gender significance. Libertarian feminists cannot both claim, as feminists, that gender is a master category implicating our experiences in gender meanings and power dynamics and that, as libertarians, sex acts can be immune from gender implications.

Cultural feminists do, moreover, raise serious moral questions about S/M as a sexual practice. The focus in S/M, as described by its advocates, is on maximizing sensual pleasure through role-playing. It necessarily involves sexual objectification and a centering on erotic gratification that heightens the importance of sexual performance considerations. S/M would seem to inevitably promote instrumental, aggressive, and objectifying orientations. Do not these values contradict feminist values (e.g., nurturance, person-centeredness, tenderness, sharing, nonhierarchical relationships)? Would not most feminists find these values especially undesirable in the sexual domain?[64]

Defenders of S/M counter that all sex but especially sex oriented to pleasure and self-expression, involves an instrumental and objectifying dimension, since it focuses on the erotic aspects of individuals and their interaction. Similarly, sex is said to necessarily incite a range of physical and emotional sensations, including aggressive impulses towards control and submission. Sexual partners who are aware of these feelings and use them to augment mutual pleasures can do so legitimately to the extent that the exchange is one of consent and mutuality of respect and pleasure. S/M advocates argue that the sexual romanticism of C-F unnecessarily suppresses the possibilities for pleasure and self-expression. This reveals, they suggest, their own anxieties over the carnal and aggressive aspects of sex. Critics of S/M are accused of rehabilitating an almost Victorian view of women and intimacy.[65]

This defense of S/M, however, only begins to address the moral issues raised by the cultural feminist critique. One does not need to endorse the romanticism of C-F to see as compelling their general point that the quality of sexual experience needs to be addressed in a more complete way than is done by libertarians. Thus, even if sex and, in particular, sex as a form of erotic pleasure, does involve an instrumentalist and aggressive dimension, as libertarians argue, it does not follow that these behavioral characteristics and values should be encouraged. If a concentrated emphasis on sensual pleasure implies a degree of depersonalization or instrumental behavior which is considered to be morally suspect, then our assessment of sex for pleasure must become at least equivocal, even if the sex occurs in a social exchange of consent and mutuality. There is, in general, a reluctance on the part of sexual libertarians to seriously consider the qualitative emotional and relational aspects and social ramifications of sex. A sexual ethic that abstracts from the qualitative aspects of sex by defending *all* sex where the formal conditions of consent and mutuality are present is hardly defensible in the face of both Marxist and feminist analyses of the social and political structuring of sex. The incorporation of a moral reflection on the quality of sex into a sexual ethic is, it seems to me, essential today in light of the explicit politicizing of sex.

The clash between cultural feminists and their critics over pornography and S/M is one of sexual ethics, although it is implicated in broader conflicts over the feminist project today. Each side frames female sexuality in terms of a sexual ideology that advances claims about the nature of sex, its preferred qualities, and the link between sex, gender and politics. Moreover, each side advances empirical claims about women's sexuality to support its moral position. Thus, cultural feminists insist that their sexual ethic is not simply a regulative ideal, but reflects women's experiences. Their critics repeatedly appeal to personal observations to challenge C-F and to defend their own libertarian sexual ideology. To be sure, cultural feminists can respond to critics by arguing that their sexual ethic articulates authentic female values and ways of being that are only partially realized today due to a male-dominated culture that has colonized and deformed women's sexuality. Nevertheless, cultural feminists cannot ignore or discount women's sexual practices without being vulnerable to charges of utopianism or colonization. In the final section I consider how recent empirical studies bear on the feminist debate over women's sexuality.

Gender Difference and the Question of Sexual Ethics

The ideology of gender difference has frequently been used to legitimate gender inequality. The notion that women are different has been associated, at least within the middle class since the mid-nineteenth century, with their image as spiritual-moral beings whose proper sphere is the household and whose chief function is to care for men and their productions. Women have been defined in relation to domestic roles which have often left them subordinate to men who were assigned powerful public roles.

The women's movement in the postwar period initially challenged this ideology of difference. Second-wave feminists emphasized the similarities in physical and psychological abilities of men and women as integral to a defense of women's equality. Thus, feminists criticized lingering Victorian images of women as less carnal and less genitally responsive than men, images which reinforced a double standard that denied women their sexual autonomy. They drew upon the research of sexologists (notably Kinsey and Masters and Johnson) that asserted the similar capacities of men and women for sexual arousal and pleasure. By the late 1970s, however, the ideology of difference had reappeared among feminists. To be sure, feminists who stressed gender difference simultaneously insisted upon women's equality. Nevertheless, this feminist discourse of difference carried complicated moral resonances. For example, feminist representations linking women with emotional nurturance, moral guardianship or spiritual healing can easily be accommodated to concepts of women in support and servicing roles. Cultural feminism is perhaps the most prominent ideological expression of this rehabilitated discourse of gender difference among contemporary feminists. To some extent, however, its credibility rests upon a range of feminist-inspired research and theorizing which asserts gender difference. I wish to consider some of this research on gender difference and relate it to the question of a feminist sexual ethic.

Feminist social research in the 1970s frequently underscored the persistance of divergent gender patterns. Studies of psychological development contrasted a "feminine personality" whose self is more continuous with others, or relational, to a "masculine personality" characterized by a more rigidly bounded, separate self. Drawing on object-relations psychoanalytic thinking, Nancy Chodorow, for example, concluded that "growing girls come to define and experience themselves as continuous with others; their experience of self contains more flexible or permeable ego boundaries. Boys come to define themselves as more separate and distinct, with a greater sense of rigid ego boundaries and differentiation. The basic feminine sense of self is connected to the world, the basic masculine sense of self is separate."[66] Much research on early childhood development by feminists sought to show that the primary agents of socialization construct identities according to rather conventional concepts of gender difference. Bipolar gender typing was said to begin at birth, extend into adulthood, and encompass every aspect of the self, from the individual's name to his or her dress, toys, play, attitudes towards self, relationships, work, and love.[67] Carol Gilligan's highly influential research featured the gendered character of moral reasoning. Reflecting women's more relational psychic structures and a socialization process that values women's caretaking roles, Gilligan described a so-called feminine morality that emphasizes empathy or being responsive to and taking responsibility for others. This feminine "ethic of care" was contrasted to a "masculine morality" that stresses abstract rights, principles of fairness, and formal procedures and rules.[68] Finally, feminist social researchers claimed to have demonstrated how these basic gender differences are manifested in divergent intimate patterns. In general, they argued that women develop longer-lasting, more emotionally expressive and intimate types of relationships. Their friendships, for example, were said to revolve around intimate personal knowledge, shared feelings and problems, and sustained emotional support. Men's friendships instead cohered around a shared activity or interest; their relation-

ships were said to be characteristically bounded or compartmentalized, so that the sharing of personal feelings and intimate knowledge
is quite limited. "Generally," commented Lillian Rubin, "women's
friendships with each other rest on shared intimacies, self-revelation,
nurturance and emotional support. In contrast, men's relationships
are marked by shared activities. Talk usually centers around work,
sports, sharing expertise. . . . But, most of the time, their interactions
are emotionally contained and controlled. . . ."[69] Similarly, men and
women were said to diverge in their approach to love, women adopting a more expressive style emphasizing emotional and verbal intimacy, personal disclosures, and sharing personal problems, while
men were said to favor instrumental patterns in which love entails
common activities, providing for and protecting a loved one, and
practical, financial or technical-mechanical aid.[70]

These psychosocial gender differences were said to extend into the
domain of sex in complex ways. A major thesis advanced by feminist
researchers was that women approach sex as part of their overall
relational involvement. Sex is a way women emotionally invest themselves in a relationship, and presumably experienced by women as
meaningless, if not degrading, except as a way to establish, extend,
deepen, or confirm a relationship. Because sex has this relational
meaning for women, it is said to lack a compulsive, performance-and
genital-oriented character. Women's sexuality is described as person-
centered, erotically diffuse, nurturing and monogamous.

To the extent that men experience themselves as rigidly bounded,
separate individuals who must incessantly produce, achieve, succeed,
and control as a condition of masculine self-affirmation, sex is said to
become another arena for confirming this separateness and power.
Emotional detachment during sex, or its instrumentalization, serves
to maintain men's rigid ego boundaries and masculine identity, both
of which are threatened by the feelings of dependency and vulnerability evoked during sexual intimacy. Hence, central to male sexuality
is a disposition to neutralize the emotional aspects of sex and identify
sex as a form of pleasure or play, a mode of control, or a performance
through which masculinity is confirmed. Male sexuality is thought to
be more compulsive, body and genital-centered, performance-oriented, and promiscuous.[71]

These differences between female and male sexuality are said to be
evident in behavior. Consider, for example, adolescent sexual behavior.[72] Studies by feminist researchers of the period claim to show
the persistence of traditional gender patterns. Teenage boys are still
expected to be the active agents in the sexual exchange; they are
expected to initiate sex, and push for sex earlier in relationships and

as a condition of the relationship. Boys approach sex as genitally centered and construct it in terms of pleasure, adventure, and masculine performance criteria. They consider sex in various relational contexts, including casual encounters, to be legitimate. Girls are described in this research as less sexually active and motivated. Teenage girls continue to adopt the traditional role of controlling male desire and setting limits. They identify sex as a more diffuse activity and place a high value on hugging, kissing, and touching. Sex is said to be approached by teenage girls as a means to build or sustain a relationship, adolescent girls value sex only if it is coupled to romance and love. In short, feminist researchers believed they had established that gender differences characterize teenage sexual patterns.

This research, which very clearly dovetails with the cultural feminist construction of gender difference, is seriously flawed. Much of this research frames the discussion of female and male sexuality in such abstract and global antithetical terms that it ignores important differences among women and among men as well as important continuities between the two genders. This empirical literature is not innocent of ideological bias.

This feminist empirical construction of contrasting sexual values and orientations promotes stereotyped and reified notions of gender. This bias is at times quite explicit. For example, Angela Hamblin speaks of "our own authentic female sexuality/sensuality . . . which genuinely springs from and expresses our own female nature."[73] Beatrice Faust explains gender difference in biological terms. "Women's need for intimacy in sexual relationships originates in the balance of hormones to which they were exposed in utero. Men's tolerance of impersonal sex derives from a different balance of the same hormones."[74] Statements which generalize to all women at all times betray an essentialist bias. For example, Lillian Rubin remarks that "for a woman, there's no satisfactory sex without an emotional connection."[75] In a more complex manner, arguments for difference that are framed within universal developmental schemes or make transhistorical claims about gender are equally prone to reification. For example, Chodorow's claim that the general condition of mothering by women produces different psychic structures in boys and girls which underpin gender and sexuality differences, *regardless* of sociocultural context and without considering variant configurations of mother-presence and father-absence, runs the risk of universalizing context-specific dynamics.[76]

These feminist discourses reify gender differences in stereotyped ways. Concepts of female and male sexuality appear as uniform, contrasting natural facts. Male sexuality is caricatured by featuring its instrumental aspects. Statements like "for men, the erotic [rather than the emotional] aspect of any relationship remains forever the most compelling"[77] or "[male sexuality] is centered on the genitals and it is closely related to aggression . . . All told, male sexuality is performance oriented,"[78] are indicative of this instrumentalist stereotype. These discourses distort by omitting key features of male sexuality and by flattening the concept of male sexuality into a one-dimensional mode.

A nation wide survey of male sexuality done in the late 1970s challenges this feminist stereotype.[79] The men surveyed overwhelmingly favored marriage over an arrangement that allowed for more sexual variety. Half the respondents identified a monogamous marital relationship as their ideal; only 6.3 percent chose "many casual partners" as their preference.[80] Moreover, these men reported that they married primarily for reasons of companionship, home life, children and love—not just for sex or domestic servicing. Their ideal sexual partner was a sexually active woman who initiated sex and was sexually active.[81] Contrary to the image of male sexuality as compulsively genital, 59 percent of the respondents indicated that hugging, kissing, and touching without vaginal intercourse was enjoyable.[82] The survey made it clear, moreover, that by a sexually active and responsive woman these men did not mean a woman who merely serviced their needs. Reciprocity was identified as essential to satisfactory sex. Almost all the men said that it was important for their female partner to have an orgasm, most men saying that they delayed their own until their partner had an orgasmic experience. More than 66 percent of these men report that their partner's satisfaction was the chief criterion for ending sex.[83] Asked what made a good lover, most men answered that it was understanding a woman's sexual needs and making her feel loved.[84] Although most men surveyed felt that love was not necessary for good sex, they insisted that sex was better in a loving relationship. Almost one-half of the respondents indicated that love was the most important thing in their lives.[85] Numerous studies confirmed the point that, though men can and do detach sex from emotions, they also infuse sex with intensely romantic significance.[86] Furthermore, many men of this period did not conceive of these different sexual meanings as contradictory. In other words, sex carried multiple meanings for many postwar men. It was used to affirm their masculinity and to confirm or dramatize their dominance, but also to give and receive pleasure and love. Finally, sex has been experienced by many men in postwar America as a way to explore and show feelings of dependency, vulnerability, and affection that cannot be easily displayed in other spheres. My point is that male sexuality in postwar America is much too complex, diverse, multifaceted, and changing to be reduced to an instrumentalist stereotype.

Women's sexuality is constructed by feminists of the time in an equally one-sided, even if more positive, way. For example, Ethel Persons' claim that "penile penetration is not essential for women," or her assertion that "whether or not a woman is orgasmic has few implications for [her] personality organization" hardly reflects what women of the time reported in surveys or expressed in a range of public documents.[87] Similarly, Lillian Rubin's flat statement that "for a woman there's no satisfactory sex without an emotional connection" is contradicted by much survey data which documents a trend among both men and women in the postwar period towards accepting hedonistic-expressive sexual constructions.[88] For example, *The Hite Report*, which betrays a clear feminist bias, documents in women's comments the importance of the emotional context of sex. Yet, this survey also discloses a salient genital and orgasmic character to women's sexuality. Women overwhelmingly reported that they liked vaginal intercourse. An orgasmic experience is often described as among their greatest sexual pleasures, and its absence was said to be a great source of personal displeasure.[89] The findings of *The Cosmo Report* further contradict the stereotype that women always imbue sex with deep emotional and romantic significance. Almost 75 percent of the women respondents indicated that good sex is possible without love.[90] Almost 30 percent of the single women said they feel free to have sex outside an ongoing relationship.[91] In fact, one-quarter of the *Cosmo* women acknowledged having between 11–25 sex partners over the course of their lives.[92]

These findings strongly suggest that despite the image of women as person-oriented, monogamous, and romantic, there are many women who approve of and enjoy casual sex. Further evidence that women in postwar America are accepting of pleasure-oriented sex is given in the finding that 73.6 percent of those surveyed said they have participated in an orgy, sex club, or partner-swapping party.[93] Both the *Cosmo Report* and the *Redbook Report* document that many women at times use porn, sex toys (vibrators, feathers, oils, dildos), dress and sex talk to enhance sexual pleasure.[94] The surveys dating from the mid-1970s depict women with sexual values quite similar to men's, at least with respect to being sexually active, accepting a wide spectrum of sex acts and positions, demanding sensual gratification, and being willing to use various techniques and stimuli to enhance pleasure. In general, these women approach sex as having multiple meanings and legitimate social contexts.

The findings of these surveys is supported by research in two unexpected areas: teenage sex and extramarital sex. We have already alluded to research that points to the persistence of traditional sex patterns for adolescent girls. However, researchers are divided over postwar patterns. Some researchers highlight, for example, the decline of the "double standard" which permitted only boys to be sexually active, initiate and direct sex, demand gratification, and be sexually pluralistic. Along several key dimensions (e.g., acceptance of adolescent sex, right to sexual satisfaction, tolerance of sexual pluralism) girls appear to be men's sexual equals, even if some differences and inequalities persist.[95] Furthermore, although girls continue to insist more than boys that sex be tied to romance or love, researchers point out that girls often use the word "love" in a way that lacks its traditional connotation of a long-term relationship involving extended commitments and responsibilities. Frequently, love indicates little more than feelings of attraction or affection with minimal relational involvement. As one researcher put it, "in the absence of notions like commitment and responsibility, horniness can look an awful lot like 'love.'"[96] In other words, some girls have sex for reasons of physical attraction or pleasure but to avoid guilt and disapproval frame sex in the culturally approved language and symbolism of romantic love. This interpretation is further supported when we consider that though teenagers approve of sex as part of a relational commitment, teen romances are notoriously short-lived. In one study, about one-fifth of the boys and one-tenth of the girls said that their most recent sexual affair lasted a week or less; only 14 percent of all teen sexual relationships in this study endured for more than a year.[97] Apparently, the appeal to a relationship as a culturally approved justification for sex is being invoked to allow girls to act on sexual desires for pleasure or adventure they cannot otherwise act upon while remaining a "good girl."

Extramarital sex is another domain in which women's sexuality has been considered to diverge sharply from men's. Yet, some research points towards a convergence in rates of extramarital sex. The studies by Kinsey, Hunt, and Pietropinto and Simenauer suggest a more or less steady rate of extramarital sex by men at about 50 percent.[98] Kinsey reported the rate for women at less than half of that. Hunt found that although there was a dramatic rise in extramarital sex among younger women, the overall rate didn't change much since Kinsey. However, the *Redbook* study reported that by age 30 almost one-third of the wives tried it, by age 40 the figure was 40 percent.[99] The *Cosmo Report* put the figure at 53.7 percent—virtually identical with men.[100] Even more telling is that women, like men, are likely to have extramarital sex *regardless* of whether they are happy in their marriage. Women appear to be involved in extramarital sex for similar reasons as men: sexual freedom, variety, adventure, and the need to feel attractive and desirable. In her study of young adult feminist-oriented women, Lynn Atwater found that extramarital affairs were not traditional romantic involvements; often they were casual and short-termed. Women sought erotic fulfillment, but also an emotionally satisfying relationship where they insisted on being treated as equal partners. Atwater reports that these women typically enjoyed these affairs and benefitted by heightened feelings of autonomy. She emphasizes the extent to which these women departed from traditional romantic patterns: "There was virtually no evidence of the traditional model of female sexuality in the descriptions women gave of their extramarital sexual activity. Rather, women demonstrated an evolving script of female sexual expression with a common theme of female-centered sexuality, of enjoyment for oneself, of not living vicariously through one's partner. Women emphasized the gratification that could be obtained through variety in partners. This variety was defined by relations with younger partners (for both physical and expressive reasons), sexual involvement based primarily on erotic attraction to the male body, and, especially, an emphasis on particular sexual activities like cunnilingus, extensive body contact, and kissing."[101] This research suggests, once again, that at least some women conceive of sexual autonomy in terms of expanding erotic options, styles, and relational possibilities in ways typically associated with men.[102]

I do not wish to deny that there are differences in the way contemporary men and women approach sex. Rather, I want to underscore the point that the image of female and male sexuality as contrasting types ignores meaningful continuities between men and women and heterogeneity among them. Stereotyping female and male sexuality in rigid antithetical ways may be an expression of the pessimistic mood of many feminists in the face of what they perceived as an antifeminist backlash. A discourse of gender difference that celebrates the uniqueness of women's sexuality may enhance feminist pride and help to mobilize women to build woman-centered spaces. This discourse will, however, create tensions within the women's movement, because a celebration of women's unique sexuality may stigmatize those women whose sexual longings deviate from that norm. As we have seen, many women do not experience their sexuality as person-centered, diffusely erotic, or necessarily imbued with nurturing, romantic longings. For these women the ideology of gender difference may function to censor or devalue their desire. Moreover, as a flat, one-dimensional concept of female sexuality is elaborated into a feminist

*Was this a result of traditional patterns in their marital sexual activity?

sexual ethic, as in the case of cultural feminism, many women will react against it as too restrictive in light of social developments offering expanded possiblities for their sexual autonomy.

The ideology of gender difference, especially as it has been tied to a restrictive sexual ethic, appears somewhat at odds with social trends that promise more gender equality, at least with respect to intimate affairs. To the extent that more women are achieving social positions that enhance their autonomy and equality, they are able to assume *more* control over their sexuality. These women are *less* compelled to approach sex as a domain of danger. Unlike their parents and grandparents, many women reaching maturity in the 1980s are less controlled by their family, men, and by one-dimensional media representations. More women than in the recent past have expanded opportunities for economic independence, political empowerment and lifestyle choice. Women today have relatively easy access to reliable and safe birth control methods. They are socialized into a culture far more sex-positive and with far more heterogeneous sexual images and lifestyle choices than were their predecessors.[103] The 1970s witnessed the appearance of women-centered constructions of female sexuality in womans magazines,[104] in erotica or pornography produced by and for women,[105] in sex manuals that promote a libertarian sexual ethic,[106] in writing and art by women affiliated with the gay culture,[107] and in the cultural productions of major female literary figures and artists.[108] These representations have typically framed femininity as including erotic desire, assertive sexual styles, and intimate lifestyle choice. In these circumstances many women will, and indeed have, repudiated a sexual ideology that stipulates that sex is legitimate only as an expression of love, only as enacted in acts of personal tenderness, and only if confined to long-term relationships.

The persistence of ambivalence among feminists, as is illustrated by the social prominence of cultural feminism, relates, in part, to the fact that sex continues to carry unique dangers for women in a male-dominated society. For example, the risks of unwanted pregnancy and the likelihood of raising a child as a single mother with little or no support from the father makes sex potentially fateful for women in a way it is not for men. The susceptibility of women to sex-related violence, from rape to sexual abuse, gives to sex an edge of peril from which most men feel free. The persistence, even if it is less credible today, of a double standard that renders sexual assertiveness and eroticism self-affirming for men but potentially demeaning, even stigmatizing for women imbues sexual expression that deviates from conventional, romantic, monogamous sexuality with resonances of danger for women. To the extent that some women feel that their socioeconomic insecurity requires them to use their sexuality as a resource to influence men and achieve male social and economic support and protection, these women will perceive a more open, free-wheeling, eroticized sexual ethic as threatening their prospects for a secure, respectable social status. Not only will some women associate certain dangers with sexual expression that men will not, but to the extent that there are elements of a unique women's culture that revolves around the concept of the "good girl" and a culture of romance, some women may feel that only sex that is tied to romance, intimacy, and long-term commitment affirms their feminine self-identity.[109] For these women only sex that sublimates carnal desire into a quest for romance and perhaps maternal longings is experienced as truly self-fulfilling. They may perceive the uncoupling of sex from romantic, intimate and perhaps maternal or domestic longings as both dangerous and alienating.

My point is that the division between sexual romantics and libertarians among feminists reflects, in part, the different ways women are socially positioned to experience the dangers and pleasures of sex. Given women's vulnerability to sexually-related violence, abuse, and harassment; given their continued socially subordinate status; and given aspects of a women's culture that continues to tie femininity to expectations of feminine virtue, some women will accentuate the dangers of sex that is carnal, erotic or casual. Many women will feel pressure to erect rigid controls and place severe restrictions on sex. A sexual romantic ethic will appeal to these women because it builds in protections for women in binding sex to commitment, caring, and respect.

Given social developments that empower more and more women both economically and politically, and given alternative hedonistic-expressive mainstream constructions of female sexuality, many women will feel as much constricted as protected by a romantic sexual ethic. Undoubtedly, the appearance of libertarian sexual ideologies with mass support among women reflects women's changing social condition. At a minimum, it is indicative of the opportunities women perceive today for enhanced sexual autonomy.

Sexual libertarians defend the notion that sex can have multiple meanings and be legitimate in diverse relational contexts. Given an interpersonal context of consent and mutual respect, sex can be legitimate not only as an expression of intimacy or love, but also as a form of play, pleasure, adventure, and communication in relationships as varied as one-time casual encounters and long-term romantic unions. Libertarians do not take issue with the importance of joining sex to romance, love, intimacy, and monogamy. Rather, they object to the position that locates sex only within a unidimensional moral framework, and to the claim that sex has or should have only one legitimate meaning and proper relational context. Libertarians contend instead that a narrowly conceived feminist sexual orthodoxy, such as cultural feminism, reinforces a patriarchal order that has traditionally limited women's sexual autonomy.

In the early 1980s, a libertarian sexual ideology stepped forward as the major feminist alternative to this sexual romanticism. Its unequivocal defense of sexual tolerance stemming from its minimalist formal ethic appealed to feminists' growing awareness of social and sexual differences among women. Furthermore, the libertarian effort to theorize sex as an analytically autonomous domain irreducible to gender dynamics contributed to freeing sex from the feminist drift into a rigid sexual political orthodoxy. Libertarians force us to approach sex as an order dealing with bodies, desires, pleasures and sexual identities (e.g., gay, lesbian, S/M, leather) that are not collapsible into the terms of gender. Libertarians stand in the way of the hardening of sexual orthodoxies and rigid hierarchies. Yet, in their effort to free sex from a narrow feminist political morality, libertarians have underestimated the extent to which gender remains a pivotal category for analyzing sexual behavior. In particular, they have neglected the persistence of gender differences and the continued dangers of sex for women in a male-privileged society. Similarly, I have argued that a defense of sexual autonomy and pluralism is troublesome when it rests upon a formalistic ethic that cannot further morally discriminate. A sexual ethic that endorses the proliferation of sexualities without considering their qualitative features virtually relinquishes a critical role.[110] Libertarian feminists show an unwillingness to discriminate between sexualities, or endorse restrictions other than on particular acts that are not consensual and reciprocal. This radical retreat from a substantive ethic stems, at least in part, from the fact that the principal proponents of libertarianism among feminists are identified with sexual minority groups, in particular a lesbian or S/M culture. These are groups that are oppressed precisely by a substantive sexual ethic.

By the mid-1980s, cultural feminism lost what ideological hegemony it had achieved through the 1970s. The conference held at Barnard College in 1982, which eventuated in the publication of *Pleasure and Danger*, was a major ideological assault upon cultural feminism. The *Heresies* "Sex Issue," *Powers of Desire* and a series of critiques of the antipornography movement culminating in the book *Women Against Censorship* put C-F on the defensive. Indeed, as we move into the 1990s, cultural feminism is giving way to a postmodern feminism that explodes the category of "women" into a multiplicity of desires, identities and lifestyles that render problematic a concept of sisterhood as anything more than a convenient political fiction.[111]

Yet, women will continue to find C-F, or some variant of sexual romanticism, pertinent, because gender differences persist, in large part because male dominance persists. In this sociocultural and political setting, sex for women will continue to bear an edge of risk and danger. A discourse of sex that focuses on the restrictions and moral limits placed upon it will be perceived by many women to be self-enhancing and empowering. Beyond this continuing relevance to women, the sexual ideology of C-F has broader implications for sexual politics and ethics. Its insistence that a sexual ethic must include a concern with the qualitative dimensions of sex is essential to an analysis and critique of socioerotic behavior. Similarly, this emphasis provides an important standpoint for critical analysis of the contemporary history of sex and current emancipatory ideals. To be more precise, C-F provides a vantage point from which to criticize the identification of sexual liberation with the mere release and increase of sexual desire and behavior. It resists the expectation that sex will satisfy a range of non-sexual needs, and the temptation to burden sex with unrealistic expectations and meanings. Unfortunately, the cultural feminist critique of this narrow ideology of sexual liberation has, all too often, been joined to an equally one-dimensional sexual norm. It needlessly circumscribes the opportunities for sensual and psychic pleasures in sex. It suppresses the possibility that sex can become a basis for the affirmative construction of diverse individual and collective identities. In short, C-F fails to see the progressive openings in recent movements of sexual affirmation and pluralism.

Conclusion

Cultural feminism's romantic sexual ethic, coupled, as it is, to an ideology of gender difference, seems driven by a separatist feminist agenda. In defining female sexuality as nurturing and person-centered in contrast to male sexuality described as pleasure-centered and violence-prone, cultural feminists not only mark out clear boundaries between the two genders, but render men a threat to women. Similarly, by attributing lustful, aggressive sexual drives to men and associating this drive with violence against women, cultural feminists stake out a gender politic of separatism on the grounds of basic sexual and psychic needs.

Its critics have rightly pointed out that C-F overburdens sex with gender significance. By rigidly gender-typing sexual desires and acts, cultural feminists may promote a gender politic that is separatist, but a sexual politic that is restrictive. Moreover, by endorsing as authentically female only sex that is intimate, bonding and person-centered, C-F censors and stigmatizes a wide range of sexual and intimate choices. C-F finds itself, ironically, in the position of backing a conservative sexual politic.

Libertarians have underscored some of these limitations of C-F but have themselves fallen prey to the reductionism and absences they deplore. Libertarians seem driven by their own project to promote sexual choice and the proliferation of sexual pleasures and identities. Their strategy entails degendering sex. Libertarians wish to unburden sex of the layers of moral meanings that serve to restrict choice and marginalize nonconventional sexualities. They appeal to a minimalist sexual ethic which invokes mutual consent and respect as the governing sexual norms.

Libertarians encounter two sorts of problems. First, their project leads them to underestimate the gender structuring of sexual dynamics, therefore pushing them into a weak, if not completely untenable, position, from a feminist standpoint. For example, the libertarian defense of pornography or S/M on hedonistic grounds virtually neglects the different implications for men and women of a pleasure-centered eroticism entailing a high level of objectification, instrumentalism and aggression. Libertarian feminists cannot assume gender inequality while denying its impact on the formation of sexuality. This limitation is related to a more general concern: the sexual ethic libertarians propose does not include any moral reflection on the qualitative aspects of sexuality. They are, accordingly, unable to provide any moral judgements beyond merely formal ones (i.e. consent) regarding sexual desires and acts. Libertarianism presupposes a liberal individualistic standpoint that does not allow for critical analyses of how structural factors (e.g., gender or class inequalities) impact on sexual choice or dynamics.

The debate between cultural feminists and libertarian critics has a significance beyond a narrow ideological struggle within the women's movement. This debate articulates conflicting feelings women have about sexuality—feelings that reflect their social status in contemporary America. Many women continue to be ambivalent toward sex and especially eroticism that is linked to their unique vulnerability to violence, unwanted pregnancy, and social stigma. Accordingly, many women are favorably disposed to a sexual ethic that emphasizes both restraint and the social and spiritual aspects of sex. Sexual romanticism, with its focus on intimate bonding and fidelity as well as the tender, nurturing and person-centered aspects of sex, appeals to many women for its enhancement of their security and respect. Yet, many women today find themselves in a social position that allows them more sexual choice and permits an approach to sex that features its erotic and expressive aspects without exposing them to the dangers discussed above. Many women will, accordingly, find some version of sexual libertarianism appealing. Thus, despite the specific political motivations of cultural feminists and their libertarian critics, this conflict over sexual ethics gives expression to more general divisions among women in contemporary America. It relates, as I have suggested, to the fact that women are subject both to gender inequalities and to trends of empowerment.

I am not saying that this debate has no relevance to other groups in the United States. The way that it will play out among other groups will depend on the social position of these groups. To further explore the contextualizing aspects of a sexual ethic, I turn to the gay male sexuality debates. The same debate between romanticism and libertarianism is played out here, but in reverse. From the late 1960s through the early 1980s, at least in the urban gay subculture, the libertarian ethic has been dominant. Romantic critics have been heard, but they have been marginal. The AIDS epidemic, however, has served to push the romantics from the periphery to the center. Libertarianism has been subject to perhaps its most critical scrutiny by a population for whom the question of sexual ethics has become a matter of life and death.

Notes

1. See Jo Freeman, *The Politics of Women's Liberation* (New York: Longman, 1975); Olive Banks, *Faces of Feminism* (Oxford: Martin Robertson, 1981); Ethel Klein, *Gender Politics* (Cambridge, Mass.: Harvard University Press, 1984); and Sara Evans, *Born To Liberty* (New York: The Free Press, 1989).

2. On the antifeminist backlash, see Zillah Eisenstein, *Feminism and Sexual Equality* (New York: Monthly Review Press, 1984); Linda Gordon and Allen Hunter, "Sex, Family and the New Left: Anti-Feminism as a Political Force," *Radical America*, 11 (6) and 12 (1) Nov. 1977–Feb. 1978; Pamela Johnston Conover and Virginia Gray, *Feminism and the New Right* (New York:

Praeger, 1983); Rosiland Pollack Petchesky, "Sexual Politics in the 1980s," in *Abortion and Women's Choice* (Boston: Northeastern University Press, 1985); Kathleen Frankovic, "Sex and Politics—New Alignments, Old Issues," *PS* 15 (Summer 1982).

3. Cf. Ann Snitow, "Retrenchment versus Transformation: The Politics of the Antipornography Movement," in *Women Against Censorship*, ed. Varda Burstyn (Toronto: Douglas & McIntyre, 1985). Also Shane Phelan, *Identity Politics: Lesbian Feminism and the Limits of Community* (Philadelphia.: Temple University Press, 1989), p. 40.

4. See Jo Freeman, *The Politics of Women's Liberation* and Alice Echols, *Daring to be Bad* (Minneapolis: University of Minnesota Press, 1990).

5. Echols, *Daring to be Bad*, p. 211.

6. Typical of the radical feminist critique of the sexual revolution is Firestone, *The Dialectic of Sex*; Lynne Segal, "Sensual Uncertainty or Why the Clitoris is not Enough," in *Sex and Love*, ed. Sue Cartledge and Joanna Ryan (London: Women's Press, 1983); Beatrix Campbell, "A Feminist Sexual Politics: Now You See It, Now You Don't," *Feminist Review*, Vol. 5, (1981); Dana Densmore, "Independence from the Sexual Revolution," in *Radical Feminism*; Kate Millet, *Sexual Politics* (New York: Ballantine Books, 1969); Sheila Cronan, "Marriage," in *Radical Feminism*; The Feminists, "A Political Organization to Annihilate Sex Roles," in *Radical Feminism*; New York Radical Feminists, "Politics of the Ego Manifesto, in *Radical Feminism*; and see the remarks by Alison Jaggar, *Feminist Politics and Human Nature* (Totowa, New Jersey: Rowman & Allanfeld, 1983) and Anne Koedt, "The Myth of the Vaginal Orgasm," in *Radical Feminism*. Also see the following anthologies: *Voices From Women's Liberation*, ed. Leslie Tanner (New York: New American Library, 1971); *Women in a Sexist Society*, eds. Vivian Gornick and Barbara Moran (New York: Basic Books, 1971); *Sisterhood is Powerful*, ed. Robin Morgan (New York: Random House, 1970). A useful overview of radical feminism is provided by Ellen Willis, "Radical Feminism and Feminist Radicalism," in *The 60s Without Apology*, ed. Sohnya Sayres et al. (Minneapolis: University of Minnesota Press, 1984).

7. Radicalesbians, "The Woman Identified Woman," in *Radical Feminism*, p. 245.

8. Ibid.

9. Charlotte Bunch, "Lesbians in Revolt," in *Lesbianism and the Women's Movement*, eds. Nancy Myron and Charlotte Bunch (Baltimore, Md.: Diana Press, 1975).

10. Ginny Berson, "The Furies," in *Lesbianism and the Women's Movement*, p. 18. Also, Lillian Faderman, *Surpassing the Love of Men* (New York: William Morrow, 1981), p. 413. Cf. Shane Phelan, *Identity Politics*.

11. In fact, many early lesbian feminists insisted that woman-identification included erotic bonding with women. See, for example, Rita Mae Brown,

"The Shape of Things to Come," or Charlotte Bunch, "Lesbian in Revolt," in *Lesbianism and the Women's Movement.*

12. Adrienne Rich, "Compulsory Heterosexuality and Lesbian Existence," in *Powers of Desire.* See the critical remarks by Ann Ferguson, "Patriarchy, Sexual Identity and the Sexual Revolution," *Signs* 7, (Autumn 1981).

13. Insightful comments on cultural feminism are provided by Alice Echols, "The New Feminism of Yin and Yang," in *Powers of Desire* and "The Taming of the Id: Feminist Sexual Politics, 1968–83," *Pleasure and Danger*, ed. Carole Vance (Boston: Routledge & Kegan Paul, 1984).

14. Kathleen Barry, *Female Sexual Slavery* (New York: New York University Press, 1984); Mary Daly, *Gyn/Ecology* (Boston: Beacon Press, 1978); Andrea Dworkin, *Our Blood* (New York: Harper & Row, 1976); Susan Griffin, *Woman and Nature* (New York: Harper & Row, 1978); Adrienne Rich, *Of Woman Born* (New York: Bantam Books, 1977); Robin Morgan, *Going Too Far* (New York: Random House, 1977).

15. Robin Morgan, "Lesbianism and Feminism: Synonymous or Contradictions?" in *Going Too Far*, p. 181.

16. Quoted in Echols, "The New Feminism of Yin and Yang," p. 445.

17. Major statements of the antipornography movement are collected in the anthology *Take Back the Night*, ed. Laura Lederer (New York: William Morrow, 1980). Henceforth cited as *TBTN*.

18. Irene Diamond, "Pornography and Repression: A Reconsideration of 'Who' and 'What,'" in *TBTN*, p. 188.

19. Diana Russell, "Pornography and the Women's Liberation Movement," in *TBTN*, p. 304.

20. Ibid., p. 314.

21. Susan Brownmiller, "Excerpt on Pornography" from *Against Our Will: Men, Women and Rape*, in *TBTN*, pp. 19–20.

22. Helen Longino, "Pornography, Oppression, and Freedom: A Closer Look," in *TBTN*, p. 42.

23. Beverly LaBell, "The Propaganda of Misogyny," in *TBTN*, p. 176.

24. Beatrice Faust, *Women, Sex and Pornography* (New York: MacMillan, 1980), p. 80.

25. Diana Russell with Laura Lederer, "Questions We Get Asked Most Often," in *TBTN*, p. 27.

26. Susan Lurie, "Pornography and the Dread of Women: The Male Sexual Dilemma," in *TBTN*, p. 160.

27. Kathleen Barry, *Female Sexual Slavery* (New York: New York University Press, 1984), p. 266.

28. Barry, *Female Sexual Slavery*, p. 267.

29. Ibid.

30. Ibid.

31. See, for example, Barry, *Female Sexual Slavery*, p. 214 and Adrienne Rich, "Afterword," in *TBTN*.

32. See, for example, Andrea Dworkin, *Pornography* (New York: Perigee, 1979) and "Why So-called Radical Men Love and Need Pornography," in *TBTN*.

33. See Andrea Dworkin, *Right-Wing Women* (New York: Perigee Books, 1979), pp. 221–223.

34. Andrea Dworkin, *Pornography*, p. 69.

35. Ibid., p. 57. Cf. Susan Griffin, *Pornography and Silence* (New York: Harper & Row, 1981), pp. 91–92.

36. An important collection of critical pieces is to be found in *Women Against Censorship*, ed. Varda Burstyn (Toronto: Douglas & McIntyre, 1985). Also see the collection by the Feminist Anti-Censorship Task Force, *Caught Looking: Feminism, Pornography & Censorship* (Seattle, Wash.: The Real Comet Press, 1986). Ann Ferguson, "Pleasure, Power, and the Porn Wars," *The Women's Review of Books* 3 (May 1986) and Deirdre English, "The Politics of Porn," *Mother Jones*, April 1980.

37. Cf. Paula Webster, "Pornography and Pleasure," *Heresies*, "Sex Issue," 3 no. 4 (May 1981), pp. 49–50; Donna Turley, "The Feminist Debate on Pornography: An Unorthodox Interpretation," *Socialist Review* 87 (May–Aug. 1986), p. 89; Daphne Read, "(De)Constructing Pornography: Feminisms in Conflict" in *Passion and Power*, eds. Kathy Peiss and Christina Simmons (Phil.: Temple University Press, 1989); Pat Califia, "The New Puritans," *The Advocate*, April 17, 1980; Kate Ellis, "Pornography and the Feminist Imagination," *Socialist Review*, 75/76 (Summer 1984).

38. See, for example, Ellen Willis, "Feminism, Moralism and Pornography," in *Beginning to See the Light* (New York: Alfred A. Knopf, 1981), p. 224.

39. Ellen Willis, "Toward a Feminist Sexual Revolution," *Social Text* 2 (Fall 1981), p. 8.

40. For example, Ann Snitow, "Retrenchment versus Transformation," p. 115; Pat Califia, *Sapphistry: The Book of Lesbian Sexuality*. 2d ed. (Tallahasee, Florida: Naiad Press, 1983), pp. 15–16. In addition, some feminists argue that most pornography is not violent. Gayle Rubin estimates that "ninety percent of [porn] . . . is frontal nudity, intercourse, and oral sex with no hint of violence or coercion." See Deirdre English, Amber Hollibaugh and Gayle Rubin, "Talking Sex: A Conversation on Sexuality and Feminism," *Socialist Review* 11 (July–Aug. 1981), p. 57. Also see Alan Soble, *Pornography* (New Haven: Yale University Press, 1986).

41. Cf. Joanna Russ, *Magic Mommas, Trembling Sisters, Puritans & Perverts* (New York: The Crossing Press, 1985); Amber Hollibaugh, "The Erotophobic Voice of Women," *New York Native*, Sept. 26–Oct. 9, 1983, pp. 32–34; Dorothy Allison, "Lesbian Politics in the '80s," *New York Native*, Dec. 7–20, 1981.

42. See, for example, Andrea Dworkin, *Our Blood*, p. 108.

43. Cf. Ann Snitow, "Retrenchment versus Transformation," p. 112.

44. See Sharon McDonald, "The Oy? of Lesbian Sex," *The Advocate*, Dec. 9, 1982; Susie Bright, "Year of the Lustful Lesbian," *New York Native*, July 30–Aug. 12, 1984; Pat Califia, "What is Gay Liberation," *The Advocate*, June 25, 1981. See n. 105–108.

45. The cultural feminist critique of eroticism, or at least a "male"-styled aggressive, pluralistic eroticism, is tied to a separatist political agenda. By claiming that male and female sexualities are different, and that the former is demeaning and dangerous whereas the latter is spiritually elevating and bonding, cultural feminists rationalize female bonding and the building of a womansculture as the central feminist project.

46. See Susan Sontag, *Styles of Radical Will* (New York: Farrar, Straus and Giroux, 1969) p. 66; Angela Carter, *The Sadeian Woman* (New York: Harper & Row, 1978), pp. 12–16; Beatrice Faust, *Women, Sex and Pornography* (New York: MacMillan, 1980).

47. See, for example, Shere Hite, *The Hite Report: A Nationwide Study of Female Sexuality* (New York: Dell, 1976), p. 620, and Morton Hunt, *Sexual Behavior in the 1970s* (Chicago, Ill.: Playboy Press, 1974), p. 215.

48. Cf. Linda LeMoncheck, *Dehumanizing Women* (Totowa, New Jersey: Rowman & Allenheld, 1985); Gregg Blachford, "Looking at Pornography: Erotica and the Socialist Morality," in *Pink Triangles: Radical Perspectives in Gay Liberation*, ed. Pam Mitchell (Boston: Alyson Publications, 1980); Robin Tolmach Lakoff and Raguel L. Scherr, *Face Value: The Politics of Beauty* (Boston: Routledge, 1984). My intention is only to underscore some general differences in the way men and women in the contemporary United States experience sexual objectification. For other purposes, it might be appropriate to further differentiate this experience along the dimensions of class, sexual orientation or race. For example, I would imagine that a women who is sexually objectified by another women in an affirmative lesbian context might experience this as erotically empowering, whereas the same women in a heterosexual context might very well feel that this is a reductive, disempowering gender experience. Some African American gay men have recently challenged the view held by many (white) gay men that the gay experience of pornography is erotically affirmative because it occurs in a context of gender equality. Critics argue that when it is black gay men who are sexually objectified by white gay men it is a reductive, disempowering racial experience. Thus, while many white gay men saw the attack on the Mapplethorpe exhibit as an attack on them, at least some African American gay men and women have criticized Mapplethorpe for projecting dehumanizing, stereotypical images of African Americans. See Isaac Julien and Kobena Mercer, "True Confessions: A Discourse on Images of Black Male Sexuality," in *Brother to Brother*, ed. Essex Hemphill (Boston: Alyson 1991) and Jackie Goldsby, "What It Means To be Colored Me," *Outlook* 9 (Summer 1990).

49. See Gayle Rubin, "Thinking Sex," in *Pleasure and Danger*.

50. Ellen Willis, "Towards a Feminist Sexual Revolution," p.51. Cf. the following statement by Ti-Grace Atkinson: "By no stretch of the imagination is the women's movement a movement for sexual liberation." "Why I'm Against S/M Liberation" in *Against Sadomasochism* ed. Robin Ruth Linden et al. (East Palo Alto, Ca.: From Frog in the Wall, 1982). Alison Jagger has argued that the women's movement criticized the "prevailing conception of sexual liberation" for exhibiting a male, heterosexist bias; yet its call for women to control their own bodies contained an agenda of sexual emancipation for women. Alison Jagger, *Feminist Politics and Human Nature* (Totowa, New Jersey: Rowman & Allanheld, 1983), pp.322–323. Along the same lines, see Ellen Willis, "Radical Feminism and Feminist Radicalism," in *The 60's Without Apology*.

51. Perhaps the classic analysis is Andrea Dworkin, "Why So Called Radical Men Love and Need Pornography," in *TBTN* and Dworkin, *Right-Wing Women*.

52. Adrienne Rich, "Compulsory Heterosexuality and Lesbian Existence," in *Powers of Desire*, p. 193.

53. Jill Clark, "Interview: Robin Morgan," *Gay Community News*, Jan. 20, 1979. Cf. Kathleen Barry, "Sadomasochism: The New Backlash to Feminism," *Trivia* 1 (Fall 1982), p. 80.

54. Judith Pasternak, "The Strange Bedfellows: Lesbian Feminism and the Sexual Revolution," *Womannews*, Oct. 1983, p. 11.

55. Joan Nestle, "Butch-Fem Relationships," *Heresies* "Sex Issue," p. 21. Also see Nestle's "The Fem Question," in *Pleasure and Danger*; Wendy Clark, "The Dyke, The Feminist, and the Devil," *Feminist Review* 11 (Summer 1982).

56. Pat Califia, "A Personal View of the History of the Lesbian S/M Community and Movement in San Francisco," in Samois, *Coming to Power* (Boston: Alyson, 1982).

57. Samois, "Who We Are," in *Coming to Power*.

58. Janet Schrim, "S/M for Feminists," *Gay Community News*, May 9, 1981, p. 8. Also see Pat Califia, "Feminism and Sadomasochism," *Heresies*, "Sex Issue"; Gayle Rubin and Pat Califia, "Talking about Sadomasochism: Fears, Facts, Fantasies," *Gay Community News*, Aug. 15, 1981.

59. See Edmund White, "Sado Machismo," *New Times*, Jan. 8, 1979; Susan Sontag, "Fascinating Fascism," *New York Review of Books*, Feb. 6, 1975; Geoffrey Mains, *Urban Aboriginals* (San Francisco: Gay Sunshine Press, 1984); Arnie Kantrowitz, "From the Shadows: Gay Male S/M Activists," *The Advocate* May 29, 1984.

60. See Califia, "A Personal View of the History of the Lesbian S/M Community and Movement in San Francisco," in *Coming to Power*. Cf. Jill Clark, "Women's Center Votes to Exclude S&M Group," *Gay Community News*, Dec. 25, 1982.

61. *Against Sadomasochism*, ed. Robin Ruth Linden et al.

62. See, for example, Sally Roesch Wagner, "Pornography and the Sexual Revolution: The Backlash of Sadomasochism," Robin Morgan, "The Politics of Sado-masochistic Fantasies," and Jeanette-Nichols, Darlene Pagano and Margaret Rossoff, "Is Sadomasochism Feminist? A Critique of the Samois Position," in *Against Sadomasochism*.

63. Pat Califia, "Unraveling the Sexual Fringe: A Secret Side of Lesbian Sexuality," *The Advocate*, Dec. 27, 1979, p. 19.

64. Barry, *Female Sexual Slavery*, p. 267.

65. See, for example, J. Lee Lehman, "Lust is Just a Four-Letter Word," *Heresies*, "Sex Issue;" Pat Califia, "Feminism and Sadomasochism," *Heresies*, "Sex Issue;" "A Statement from the Boston Lesbian Sadomasochist Group," *Gay Community News* Nov. 27, 1982; Gayle Rubin, "The Leather Menace: Comments on Politics and S/M" in *Coming to Power*.

66. Nancy Chodorow, *The Reproduction of Mothering* (Berkeley University of California Press, 1978). Cf.Dorothy Dinnerstein, *The Mermaid and the Minotaur* (New York: Harper & Row, 1976).

67. For example, Judith Long Laws and Pepper Schwartz, *Sexual Scripts*, (Hinsdale, Ill.: Dryden Press, 1977).

68. Carol Gilligan, *In a Different Voice* (Cambridge: Harvard University Press, 1982).

69. Lillian Rubin, *Intimate Strangers* (New York: Harper & Row, 1983), p. 130. Cf. Michael McGill, *The McGill Report on Male Intimacy* (New York: Harper & Row, 1985).

70. Francesca Cancian, "The Feminization of Love," *Signs* 11 (Summer 1986).

71. Typical of this research explaining sexuality by gender is Judith Laws and Pepper Schwartz, *Sexual Scripts*, pp. 55–58.

72. See G. Zellman and J. Goodshreds, "Becoming Sexual in Adolescence," in *Changing Boundaries*; S. Radlove, "Sexual Response and Gender" in *Changing Boundaries*; Letitia Anne Peplau, Zick Rubin, and Charles Hill, "Sexual Intimacy in Dating Relationships," *The Journal of Social Issues* 33:2 (1977).

73. Angela Hamblin, "Is a Feminist Heterosexuality Possible?" in *Sex and Love*, p. 107.

74. Beatrice Faust, *Women, Sex, and Pornography*, p. 112.

75. Lillian Rubin, *Intimate Strangers*, p. 103.

76. See the critique by Nancy Fraser and Linda Nicholson, "Social Criticism without Philosophy," in *Feminism/Postmodernism*, ed. Linda Nicholson (New York: Routledge, 1990). More generally, see the excellent critique of essentializing, universalistic feminist social theories by Elizabeth Spelman, *Inessential Woman* (Boston: Beacon Press, 1988).

77. Lillian Rubin, *Intimate Strangers*, p. 103.

78. Faust, *Women, Sex, and Pornography*, p. 90.

79.   Anthony Pietropinto and Jacqueline Simenauer, *Beyond the Male Myth* (New York: Times Books, 1977).

80.   Ibid., p. 88.

81.   Ibid., pp. 33, 243.

82.   Ibid., pp. 35–36, 201, 231.

83.   Ibid., pp. 154, 159, 163–164.

84.   Ibid., p. 120.

85.   Ibid., p. 208.

86.   See for example, Linda Levin and Lonnie Barbach, *The Intimate Male* (New York: Anchor Press, 1983); Zick Rubin, *Liking and Loving* (New York: Holt, Rinehart, and Winston, Inc., 1973).

87.   Ethel Persons, "Sexuality as a Mainstay of Identity: Psychoanalytic Perspectives," in *Women: Sex and Society*, eds. Catherine Stimpson and Ethel Person (Chicago: University of Chicago Press, 1980).

88.   Rubin, *Intimate Strangers*, p. 101.

89.   Shere Hite, *The Hite Report: A Nationwide Study of Female Sexuality* (New York: Dell, 1976), pp. 630–631.

90.   Linda Wolfe, *The Cosmo Report* (New York: Arbor House, 1981), p. 390. Also see Pat Califia, "Lesbian Sexuality," *Journal of Homosexuality* 4 (Spring 1979), p. 261.

91.   Ibid., p. 392.

92.   Ibid., p. 333.

93.   Ibid., p. 386.

94.   Carol Travis and Susan Sadd, *The Redbook Report on Female Sexuality* (New York: Delacorte Press, 1977), p. 83.

95.   Robert Coles and Geoffrey Stokes, *Sex and the American Teenager* (New York: Harper & Row, 1985), pp. 44–49.

96.   Ibid., pp. 49, 197–198.

97.   Ibid., p. 101.

98.   See Morton Hunt, *Sexual Behavior in the 1970s* (Chicago, Ill.: Playboy Press, 1974), pp. 256–269; Pietropinto and Simenauer, *Beyond the Male Myth*, p. 278.

99.   *The Redbook Report*, p.166.

100.   *The Cosmo Report*, p. 394.

101.   Lynn Atwater, *The Extramarital Connection* (New York: Irvington, 1982), pp. 140–141.

102.   See Seidman, *Romantic Longings* (New York: Routledge, 1991), chap. 5.

103.   Cf. Barbara Ehrenreich, Elizabeth Hess, and Gloria Jacobs, *Re-Making Love: The Feminization of Sex* (New York: Doubleday, 1986).

104. For example, *Viva, Ms.* or *Cosmopolitan.* See Seidman, *Romantic Longings*, chap. 5.

105. See, for example, *Pleasures: Women Write Erotica*, ed. Lonnie Barbach (New York: Harper & Row, 1984). Regarding the spread of women's pornography, see "Ex-Rated 'Couple Films' Finding a New A Outlet," *New York Times*, Oct. 6, 1986.

106. Califia, *Sapphistry*, Barbach, *For Yourself: The Fulfillment of Female Sexuality*; Sheila Kitzinger, *Woman's Experience of Sex* (New York: Penguin Books, 1985).

107. For example, see the artwork, poems and essays in *Heresies* "Sex Issue." The essays and stories of Dorothy Allison, Pat Califia, Rita Mae Brown, Susie Bright, and Joan Nestle, just to name a few, have been critical in providing alternative constructions of female sexuality. By the early 1980s, a lesbian culture that valued an expressive-hedonistic eroticism was in the making.

108. For example, Erica Jong, Marilyn Frye, Sarah Schulman Renata Alder, Marjorie Pierce.

109. Sharon Thompson, "Search for Tommorrow: On Feminism and the Reconstruction of Teen Romance," in *Pleasure and Danger*, pp. 354–355. Ann Barr Snitow, "Mass Market Romance: Pornography for Women is Different," in *Powers of Desire*, pp. 253–254; Paula Webster, "Pornography and Pleasure," p. 50.

110. See Ellen Willis, "Towards a Feminist Sexual Revolution;" Ann Ferguson, *Blood at the Root* (London: Pandora Press, 1989) and "The Sex Debate in the Women's Movement: A Socialist-Feminist View," *Against the Current*, Sept.–Oct. 1983.

111. On the postmodern explosion of the category of womanhood, see Judith Butler, *Gender Trouble* (New York: Routledge, 1990); Denise Riley, *Am I That Name?* (New York: MacMillan, 1988); Diana Fuss, *Essentially Speaking* (New York: Routledge, 1989); Spelman, *Inessential Woman.*

4

AIDS and the "Homosexual Question": the Gay Sexuality Debates

I have argued that the concept of sexual liberalization is useful in describing some of the changes in sexual conventions in twentieth-century America. Liberalization refers, in part, to expanded social acceptance for sexual practices that have lacked public approval. For example, researchers have found evidence of a greater public acceptance of masturbation and oral-genital sex in the course of this century. Sexual liberalization also means granting social approval to new sexual practices, e.g., anal sex, or the use of sex aids. Liberalization suggests further the expanded public tolerance of sexual expression on the part of segments of the society, such as teenagers or the elderly, whose sexuality has previously been either denied or not accepted.

Beyond expanding the range of legitimate sexual expression, sexual liberalization means expanded tolerance for a wider spectrum of sexual and intimate lifestyle choices. In particular, two aspects of this dynamic seem pivotal. First, in the course of this century a slippage between sex, love, and marriage, especially in the post-World War II period, has made possible a diversity of legitimate intimate and sexual lifestyles. The slippage between love and marriage has allowed individuals to choose a sexually intimate relationship outside of marriage. Thus, cohabitation is one lifestyle option which many Americans have chosen in the 1970s and 1980s. The slippage between sex and love, moreover, has been productive of new forms of intimate life—from casual sex, swinger groups, and transient romantic liaisons to "open marriages." As the splitting off of sex from love has achieved a measure of legitimacy, lifestyle choices have expanded for many Americans.

Finally, in the course of the twentieth century we can observe the rise of new sexual identities and communities that have sought to enlarge the moral boundaries of intimate lifestyle choice in the United States. Of special importance is the rise of a homosexual identity in the early decades of the twentieth century, which by the 1960s served as the basis for an elaborated community demanding public acceptance and social inclusion. More than, say, the dramatic rise of cohabitation in the 1970s, the appearance of a swinger network, or the formation of a leather S/M culture in the 1980s, in the post World War II period homosexuality has become a chief site of struggle around defining and regulating the limits of sexual expression and intimate lifestyle choice.

This chapter will focus on the "homosexual question" in contemporary America. This allows us to explore issues of choice and tolerance in United States sexual culture. I begin by outlining the social context of contemporary discussions of homosexuality. Movements toward mainstreaming homosexuality and a reactive antigay politic provide the context for the unprecedented public discussion of the topic that has been occasioned by AIDS. In the public response to the HIV epidemic, the meaning and social role of homosexuality is being vigorously contested. Indeed, AIDS has become a principle site for Americans to struggle over sexual ethics—to clarify the meaning and morality of sex.

Mainstreaming Homosexuality/Defending Heterosexual Privileging

Historians underscore an important distinction between homosexual behavior and homosexual identity.[1] The former is said to be universal, whereas the latter is viewed as historically unique. Indeed, some historians hold that a homosexual identity is a product of the social developments of late nineteenth-century Europe and the United States.[2] In any event, it seems fair to say that a unique construction of identity crystallized around same-sex desire between 1880 and 1920 in America.[3]

The modern western concept of the homosexual is, according to some historians, primarily a creation of late nineteenth-century medical-scientific discourses. In the context of elaborating systems of classification and descriptions of different sexualities, as part of a quest to uncover the truth about human nature, the homosexual is said to have stepped forward as a distinct human type with his/her own mental and physical nature. Foucault has been credited with originating this historicization of the homosexual identity. "As defined by the ancient civil or canonical codes, sodomy was a category of forbidden acts; their perpetrator was nothing more than the juridical subject of them. The nineteenth-century homosexual became a personage. . . .

Nothing that went into his total composition was unaffected by his sexuality. It was everywhere present in him: at the root of all his actions because it was their insidious and indefinitely active principle; . . . The sodomite had been a temporary aberration; the homosexual was a species."[4] The category of homosexuality carries a definition of the essential nature of the self. As individuals are inserted into this discursive framework through the growing authority of medicine, science, psychiatry, and law, individuals who have same-sex longings are defined as a unique, abnormal human type: the homosexual.

These discourses on homosexuality did not, however, function as a monolithic controlling power over the individual. At least through the early decades of this century, individuals were often able to construct alternative concepts of same-sex desire by either drawing on nineteenth-century "romantic friendship" symbolism and idealized images of same-sex love developed by sex radicals like Edward Carpenter, or by relying on folk images of same-sex intimacies.[5] In fact, medical-scientific discourses themselves projected ambiguous meanings. Foucault alludes to the potential for reversal within these discourses. "There is no question that the appearance in nineteenth-century psychiatry, jurisprudence, and literature of a whole series of discourses on the species . . . of homosexuality . . . made possible a strong advance of social controls. . . . But it also made possible the formation of a 'reverse' discourse: homosexuality began to speak in its own behalf, to demand that its legitimacy or 'naturality' be acknowledged, often in the same vocabulary, using the same categories by which it was medically disqualified."[6] Despite the emergence of a homosexual identity label in the early decades of the twentieth century, self-identified homosexuals did not immediately announce their legitimacy; they typically understood their homosexuality as an individual psychological condition. This is hardly surprising, given the absence of a community to mobilize behind an affirmative language of homosexuality prior to World War II.

Homosexuals began to speak for themselves in the language of civil rights and social inclusion in the post-World War II period.[7] Initially, the war spawned urban networks among homosexuals; the antihomosexual politics of the 1950s and 1960s in the midst of the the general liberalization of society and the materialization of homosexual life in urban areas provided a favorable context for movements of homosexual empowerment. By the early 1970s a self-identified, self-accepting homosexual population had swelled, and a collective homosexual life developed in the exclusively gay bars, social clubs, friendship networks, and political organizations that cropped up across the urban landscape of America. Skirmishes between a new militant, self-respecting homosexual and the guardians of heterosexual privilege broke out in bars, the courts, and in the worlds of science, literature, and art. In particular, these emerging gay subcultures gave birth to a cultural apparatus that challenged religious and scientific-medical definitions of homosexuality as an illness or sin. Discourses issued forth from the gay culture that projected new, affirmative identities: homosexuality was reconfigured as a natural human expression, as a basis for a new minority, as an alternative lifestyle, and as a political rebellion against patriarchy and heterosexism.[8] Symbolic of this change was the substitution by the homosexual community of the term "gay" for "homosexual." Whereas the latter term carried resonances of deviance, disease, and destruction, and gave the legal, medical and scientific institutions control over individuals' lives, "gay" signified dignity and personal integrity; it framed homosexuality as a social identity. Self-definition as gay symbolized a community that was intent on taking control of its own lives.

Despite a strain among homosexuals to retreat into an exclusive gay enclave in the face of homosexual oppression, the community-building successes of the 1970s motivated many to push into the mainstream. Indeed, by the late 1970s, gays could claim subtantial victories. Prominent mass-circulation magazines like *Look, Time*, and *Newsweek* ran sympathetic stories on homosexuals, often appropriating the affirmative identity language of the gay subculture.[9] Homosexual themes, often portraying homosexuals as an oppressed minority, appeared regularly in novels, the theatre, and art. Legislative victories are perhaps most indicative of this movement towards social inclusion. By the mid-1970s more than half the states had repealed their sodomy laws; dozens of cities across the country passed "gay" rights laws; the civil service commission eliminated its ban on hiring homosexuals; in some states gay couples could qualify to adopt children; gay rights was included in the 1980 Democratic platform; and in 1973 the American Psychiatric Association removed homosexuality from its list of personality disorders.[10] Some straight and gay commentators spoke of the "homosexualization of America."[11] Gays, they argued, were mainstreaming their lifestyles—from a self-styled adventurous sexual style to their codes of dress, music and dance. In a word, despite continued social intolerance towards homosexuality, homosexuals were moving from the social periphery to the center. Needless to say, this would not have been possible without considerable support from the centers of institutional power in the United States, e.g., the churches, the Democratic party, unions, women's and minority organizations, civic and professional organizations and cultural elites.

The reconfiguring of the meaning of homosexuality by its advocates into a lifestyle alternative or minority status, and the movement of lesbians and gay men into the social center parallels the transformation of the social role of African-Americans and women during the same period. The alteration of the meaning and social role of women, African-Americans and homosexuals alike signalled a glacial shift in the social physiogomy of American society. These social developments met with hostility by large segments of the society. Indeed, the status of homosexuals in the mid-1970s was akin to that of African-Americans prior to the 1960s. There was virtually no federal legislation protecting them from discrimination in housing, employment, public accommodations, real estate transactions, the military, immigration and so on. Most states opposed changes in their sodomy laws and cities resisted the enactment of gay rights laws. In towns across the country, individuals who lived an openly gay life risked job and social status, and were subject to the threat of arrest, ridicule, assault and loss of family and community. Gay men and lesbians began to mainstream in the 1970s, but social acceptance remained extremely limited and precarious. Moreover, as gays organized to speak their cause, opposition coalesced.

By the late 1970s an organized antigay politic was visible.[12] Its impetus came initially from the New Right. Anita Bryant's "Save Our Children" campaign in Dade County, Florida began a wave of highly organized antigay actions. Backed by fundamentalist religious groups, Bryant and her troops portrayed homosexuals as a major threat to the family and children. In 1977, they succeeded in repealing Dade County's gay rights ordinance. Similar antigay campaigns followed. In 1978, gay rights ordinances were repealed in St. Paul and Minneapolis, Minnesota, Wichita, Kansas, and Eugene, Oregon.[13] In the same year, California's Senator Briggs introduced Proposition 6. It would forbid the employment of teachers who were homosexual or who "advocated" homosexuality, and give schools the authority to fire these teachers. Although the Briggs initiate was defeated, a similar bill passed in Oklahoma.

The two most important antigay legislative efforts occurred at the Federal level. In 1979, Senator Paul Laxalt introduced the Family Protection Act which stipulated that "no federal funds may be made available . . . to any public individual or private . . . group . . . which presented homosexuality . . . as an alternative . . . acceptable lifestyle."[14] Gay people could be fired from all state or state-funded jobs; they could be found to be ineligible for social security, welfare, veteran's pay, and student assistance; and any organization that publicly accepted homosexuality would be ineligible for government assistance. Equally menacing from the standpoint of homosexuals and civil rights activists was Resolution 1666, introduced into Congress by Representative Larry McDonald. This Bill prohibited homosexuals from ever receiving a protected status under federal, state or local law.[15] These legislative initiatives were intended to challenge the mainstreaming of homosexuality by drawing on the still resonant cultural symbolism of the homosexual as a threat to civilization.

Although both the Family Protection Act and Resolution 1666 were defeated, they shaped an ideological context favorable to an antigay politic. By the end of the 1970s, the New Right had launched a major propaganda offensive against homosexuality. Through direct mailing strategies the New Right played on public fears of a homosexual menace to promote their pro-family agenda. For example, the Moral Majority ran a full page advertisment in major newspapers across the country which declared: "We oppose any effort by homosexuals to flaunt their perversion . . . and/or attempt to force their lifestyle upon our children."[16] Antigay themes became an integral part of New Right ideology and politics.

Support for this antigay politic spread from the New Right to mainstream conservatives. Thus, George Will defended Anita Bryant's "Save Our Children" crusade by invoking the spectre of a homosexual menace. "[Gay rights] Ordinances like Miami's are part of the moral disarmament of society. Once they establish society's official indifference to homosexuality, society will be hard put to find grounds for denying homosexuals the right to marry. . . . Homosexuals complain that such laws constitute discrimination on the basis of sex. . . . Next will come the right of homosexuals to adopt children, to have homosexuality fairly represented as an alternative life-style in every child's sex-education classes. Opposition to Miami's ordinance is a way of saying Enough! and it is eminently defensible."[17] Will's rationale for withholding civil rights from homosexuals rested upon a view of homosexuality as unnatural or abnormal. Ignoring the American Psychiatric Association's decision in 1973 to withdraw homosexuality from its list of personality disorders, Will asserts that "homosexuality is an injury to healthy functioning, a distortion of personality."[18] No clinical evidence or appeal to any relevant research was offered beyond allusions to the "well-known" promiscuity of homosexuals. Because Will believed homosexuality to be a personal choice affected by social conditions, he urged a state-backed antihomosexual agenda. Even though this contradicted his conservative libertarian principles, Will insisted that the state had a duty to promote basic moral values and "surely, healthy sexuality is one; the family, and hence much else, depends on it."[19] This defender of individualism advocated the denial of civil rights and equal social opportunities to homosexuals on the presumption that homosexuals presented a major social threat.

Two essays that appeared in *Commentary* in the late 1970s further document the spread of antigay politics into the conservative mainstream. In "Are Homosexuals Gay?" Samuel McCracken argued that behind homosexuals' quest for rights is the wish to achieve public approval.[20] Homosexual rights advocates rationalized their claim to social inclusion on the grounds that homosexuality was a natural human expression and that, barring discrimination, homosexuals were capable of living fulfilled lives. McCracken disagreed. To begin with, McCracken declared, despite evidence to the contrary, "homosexuals are not in reality the object of widespread denial of rights."[21] Moreover, McCracken continued, homosexuality was not natural. "It is, in a certain sense, unnatural. Human bodies seem more obviously designed for heterosexual intercourse. . . ."[22] Nor was homosexuality, according to McCracken, a normal lifestyle capable of bringing satisfaction and joy to the individual. In support of this claim, he alluded to the so-called fact of homosexual promiscuity which he took to be defining of homosexuality. Divorcing sex from love and limiting it to short-term unstable affairs was said to be symptomatic of the unfulfilling character of the lives of homosexuals. Finally, to the extent, that homosexuality might appeal to youth as a way to avoid adult responsibilities (marriage and family), McCracken counseled the state against according to it public legitimacy.

Whereas McCracken was somewhat cautious in linking homosexuality to a state of individual and social pathology, Midge Decter, in "The Boys on the Beach," showed no such reserve.[23] Not only did Decter apply a fairly orthodox medical model to homosexuality, but she escalated public fears by imputing to homosexuals a growing will to power. In a classic backlash strategy, she transformed an "oppressed" group into the victimizer.[24]

The defensive tone of her article was exhibited at the very outset. Decter observed that the pregay liberation male homosexual was tender, playful, girlish and discreet. Today's homosexual was aggressive and intolerant, mocking heterosexual conventions. Indeed, far from being an oppressed group, homosexuals—freed from the social reponsibilities of marriage and family— were, according to Decter, fast becoming a privileged elite in control of many institutions, especially in the cultural sphere.

Behind Decter's anxiety over a growing homosexual presence was her view of homosexuals as a dangerous social force able to remake America in their own image. Homosexuals project America as an extension of their own indulgent, immature adolescence. "Homosexuals of all ages present a never-ending spectacle . . . of a tender adolescence."[25] This was of course, another way of defining homosexuality as an arrested abnormal developmental state. Reflecting this medical concept, Decter insisted that homosexuality was less a choice to bond with individuals of the same sex than a flight from the obligations of adulthood, marriage and paternity for a life of what she imagined as narcissistic, promiscuous, and pleasure-seeking. Unable to face up to their adult male duties, homosexual men took refuge in a prolonged adolescence.

Decter made it clear that homosexuality was a grave social danger. A persona of youthful innocent adolescence masked a deeply felt self-hatred. Underneath what Decter took to be a lifestyle of constant pleasure-seeking, there was a desperate effort to escape the reality of who and what they are. Their outward gaeity disguised an inner self-pity. As homosexuals gained social acceptance, Decter presumed, the gay persona would give way to its true self-destructive nature. Decter alluded to the rise of S/M which is "ubiquitous in the homosexual world."[26] She imagined that S/M revealed the essential truth of the homosexual condition: "the need to brutalize and be brutalized" and "the longing for self-destruction."[27]

Homosexuality was viewed by Decter as a flight from life itself. With their promise of a life of self-indulgence and pleasure, homosexuals seduced weak-minded young men away from the responsibilities of adulthood. Homosexuals threatened to unravel the delicate structures of restraint and discipline that make civilization possible. Ultimately, the choice of homosexuality is, Decter asserted, an unconscious death wish—for homosexuals and for humanity. It followed, according to Decter, that homosexuality should not be tolerated; homosexuals were themselves intolerant and threatened society. The demand for civil rights and social inclusion was motivated by a hidden, perhaps unconscious agenda: homosexual domination and the destruction of civilization.

A common feature of this backlash literature is the absence of any historical perspective. The socially formed condition of lesbian and gay men is taken as natural and universal. There is no historical analysis of the social forces that have molded gay life in this discourse. In particular, social oppression plays no role in these accounts. Yet the realities of homosexual oppression-then and now-are undeniable. Lesbians and gay men are subject to an array of discriminatory laws, cultural stereotyping, harassment, violence and social marginalization. Similarly, this backlash literature ignores virtually all descriptions by self-identified lesbians and gay men of their own lives—

from memoirs and novels to survey research. Neither ethnographic descriptive literature nor clinical psychological data on homosexuality was consulted. These backlash accounts rely almost exclusively on personal observations which were typically guided by stereotyped preconceptions. Thus, despite the diversity of homosexual lifestyles documented in well-known studies of the time like *Homosexualities* and *The Gay Report*, this literature perpetuates the construction of "the homosexual," as if there is some essentially fixed and universal human type that does not vary by gender, class, race, region or subcultural identification.[28]

The history and sociology of homosexuality is ignored in these discourses because, as I have already suggested, this was primarily a backlash movement.[29] These critics were contesting the materialization of a gay subculture and its movement towards social mainstreaming in the 1970s. At one level, they were convinced, despite the virtual absence of evidence, that homosexuality poses a serious threat to society by disturbing gender roles, enfeebling masculinity, and destabilizing marriage and the family. As is typical of backlash movements, its writers seized on one group as a principal source of the social ills of the time. Homosexuals were targeted as scapegoats to explain such complex social changes as women's movement into the paid labor force, escalating divorce rates, declining fertility, and the enfeeblement of national will. Scapegoating entails constructing myths that portray the menacing group as a demonic power. Mythmaking, and the construction of the menacing group as having subhuman qualities, substitutes for a historical and sociological analysis that would reveal the complexities and the humanity of the scapegoated group. The antigay discourse was largely, I contend, an effort to contest affirmative constructions of same-sex desire by reinvesting the image of the homosexual as a polluted, dangerous figure with social credibility. Its aim was to withdraw moral legitimacy from a homosexual rights movement. The reverse side of de-legitimating homosexuality is the authorization of the exclusive legitimacy of a social order that privileges heterosexuality as the core of a sexual and social identity, gender order, and familial system.

AIDS: Contesting the Meaning and Social Role of Homosexuality

From the late 1970s through the early 1980s, a major public struggle ensued over homosexuality. The elaboration of a gay subculture in the 1970s, combined with a climate of social liberalization, favored a movement towards the mainstreaming of homosexuality. Gay advocates sought civil rights, cultural respectability, social integration and political empowerment. They had considerable support from liberal social elites as well as from grass-roots movements and organizations. By the late 1970s, as we have seen, an organized antigay movement challenged gay advocates' demands for social acceptance. A struggle occurred at multiple sites, but central to the conflict was the control of the definition of the meaning and social role of homosexuality. Advocates projected images of homosexuality as a natural human preference, as the basis for an alternative lifestyle or minority group. They stated that the only difference between heterosexuality and homosexuality was the social response: the former authorized as normative, the latter, stigmatized. Moreover, the stigma was said to reflect a combination of ignorance, prejudice and self-interest.

Critics appealed to a mix of religious and medical rhetorics to delegitimate same-sex intimacies. Homosexuality was viewed as a sign of a psychological and moral malady; the homosexual was said to be a distinct human type whose very nature endangers society. Homosexuality was described as a sort of pleasure principle run amok: the very antithesis of civilization, which relies upon discipline, restraint, and social responsibility.

It is misleading to describe this conflict as a simple division between advocates and opponents of homosexuality. Within these broad camps, there were internal disagreements over the meaning and social role of homosexuality. Thus, critics were divided over whether to accept homosexuality as a personal lifestyle choice while according it no public approval, whether to condemn the homosexual, or simply his or her behavior. There was division among those who placed homosexuality within a Judeo-Christian context and those that framed it within a medical-scientific discourse. Moreover, between these extremes of advocates and opponents, there were those who fell somewhere in between. Among liberal elites, for example, there was a tendency to endorse gay rights without defending the full equality of homosexuals. For example, Morton Kondracke defended gay rights against Anita Bryant's antigay campaign, but never questioned the privileging of heterosexuality.[30] Paul Robinson advised gay advocates to retreat from their activist agenda of social inclusion: "Discretion has always been a better defense of gay rights than the law will ever be."[31] Liberals were not alone in wavering on the issue of equality for homosexuals. For example, in response to gay critics of a pro-family Left agenda, John Judis defended gay rights but privileged heterosexuality: "Society does not have the same responsibility towards homosexuality . . . that it has toward the child-bearing family. As long as the family is the main institution for perpetuating our society, its members require special concern. . . . In this sense, society must do what it can to defend and preserve the family."[32] Judis's position was often echoed by other members of the Left, or simply assented to by their silence towards the antigay backlash.[33]

The contemporary struggle over homosexuality cannot be separated from broader social conflicts. The issue of homosexuality has been intertwined with conflicts around sexuality in general and around issues of gender and the family in particular. It has been connected, moreover, to societal-wide struggles between cultural libertarians, who press for an expansion of the moral boundaries of self-expression, and their opponents, who advocate a more restrictive morality as a condition of personal and social well-being.

These social conflicts over homosexuality, and the fact that homosexuality functioned as a site for broader social struggles over sexuality, gender and party politics, structured the response to the "AIDS epidemic." AIDS became a principal site for major battles over the social fate and meaning of America. To the extent that the issue of homosexuality was implicated in these diverse social and political struggles, these cultural conflicts have shaped public and personal constructions of the meaning and social role of homosexuality. Through the 1980s, AIDS was the most socially consequential site where the public discussion over the moral boundaries of sexuality transpired.

The public discourse on homosexuality occasioned by AIDS is not uniform or unidimensional. Multiple, contradictory constructions of homosexuality cluster together and intermingle in a dense tangle of meanings. These interpretations reflect not only different values and social agendas, but occur in diverse genres, rhetorical styles, and discursive languages—religious, medical, scientific, journalistic, and literary. I propose to relate AIDS discourses to fairly broad social and political agendas. My intent is to use AIDS to map out a wide range of discursive interventions with which we can specify some of the moral boundaries of desire and sexual expression in America today.

Concentrating on the public reponse to AIDS as it relates to homosexuality, especially between 1982 and 1986, I sketch three broad discursive interventions. Conservatives—both the New Right and mainstream centrist Republicans—seized on AIDS to rehabilitate the notion of "the homosexual" as a deviant, diseased or perverse human type. AIDS is seen both as revealing the truth of a universal homosexual nature, and as proof of that dangerous nature. In particular, conservatives point to the divorce of desire from love as the very root of the perverse and promiscuous nature of homosexuality, which links it to disease and death.

The reverse side of this pollution of homosexuality is the purity of heterosexuality, and the valorization of a monogamous, romantic, and marital sexual ethic. In terms of their broader agenda, conservatives link AIDS to the permissiveness of the 1960s; AIDS becomes a symbol of the very failure of social liberalization.

AIDS inevitably served as a battleground between conservatives and liberals. Major liberal segments of the heterosexual media repudiated the use of AIDS to promote an antigay politics. Indeed, liberals and the Left often highlighted the hysterical character of the conservative reaction to AIDS in order to discredit the Right. This does not mean, however, that liberals have reacted to AIDS simply as a medical fact. Liberals have used AIDS to promote a specific moral agenda. Many were prepared to describe homosexuality as falling within the moral boundaries of American society only if it approximated a middle-class romantic ideal. In this regard, they have enlisted AIDS in their campaign to construct an image of the "respectable homosexual," and to legitimate a sexual ethic of monogamy and romance where eros is justified only in this context. Liberals use AIDS to legitimate a social order that allows for choice, but only within clearly defined limits. They defend their ethic of choice and constraint against both conservative repressiveness and the New Left, countercultural and liberationist rhetorics of human emancipation. Curiously, the response on the part of the straight American Left, through at least the late 1980s, was exceedingly faint and not, in my view, a serious part of the mainstream discussion.

Interestingly, liberal themes exhibited prominently in the straight media were conspicuous in the gay male media as well. I divide this gay response into two principal camps. Some gays seized on AIDS to advance their own program of sexual and social reform. They see AIDS as marking the failure of a way of life, namely the fast-lane, freewheeling sexual lifestyle of the 1970s urban subculture. AIDS signals, like Stonewall, a critical turning point in the coming of age of gay men; for these gay reformers, AIDS is the beginning of maturity and social responsibility among homosexual men. In other words, AIDS is deployed to further an agenda of mainstreaming by assimilating to dominant straight intimate lifestyles. Taking issue with this assimilationist reform impulse are gays who see in AIDS not the failure of their lifestyle, but of society. AIDS is understood as a symbol of a homophobic society still in the grip of ignorance and backward attitudes. AIDS should occasion a renewal of social criticism and an agenda of broad social change. In particular, gay men are counseled to resist medical control and to defend subcultural lifestyles while shifting their erotic culture to safe sex practices. Many gay discourses combine a critique of the fast-lane gay lifestyle with an equally critical analysis of an intolerant, bigoted society that resists gay assimilation. Randy Shilts' bestseller, *And The Band Played On*, perhaps best illustrates this rhetorical genre.

AIDS and Heterosexual Constructions of Homosexuality

In the heterosexual media, AIDS was identified early as a gay disease and has so lingered in the public perception, despite indisputable evidence to the contrary, available as early as 1982.[34] In part, the medical establishment has been responsible for this labelling. Although CDC (Centers for Disease Control) researchers knew as early as August 1981 that homosexual men were not the only population afflicted by Kaposi's Sarcoma and a range of unusual opportunistic infections, the CDC labelled the new syndrome "Gay-related immunodeficiency"(GRID) early in 1982. Motivated, no doubt by sincere social concern, as well as by the sensationalist aspects of the story, the key national media, with virtually no critical scrutiny of the medical-scientific experts, declared the existence of a "homosexual cancer," a "gay plague" or a "gay epidemic." These terms announced an intrinsic tie between homosexuality, disease and death.

The two most prominent epidemiological theories through the mid-1980s connected GRID and as of late 1982, AIDS to homosexual behavior in an integral way.[35] Proponents of the so-called "Overload theory" held that the "gay lifestyle," by which was meant a pattern of sexual promiscuity, drug abuse, a history of sexually transmitted diseases, and poor health habits, was responsible for the collapse of the immune system. In 1983 the Human Immunodefiency Virus was discovered, which is now considered to be the primary cause of AIDS. HIV breaks down the body's resistance to disease, leaving it vulnerable to a host of infections. The virus is transmitted through blood and body fluids, including semen. The introduction of semen into the body during sex releases the virus into the blood stream. Sex is, thus, implicated in AIDS. Homosexual men who practice anal intercourse are especially vulnerable to HIV since the delicate tissue of the anus is easily torn. This allows the semen, and therefore the virus, of the infected person to pass directly into the partner's blood system.

Both the Overload theory and the viral theory underscore the association between sexual behavior and AIDS among homosexual men. Indeed, these two theories underscore the role of sexual promiscuity as the intermediary causal link to both disease and death. The Overload theory posits an ironic and insidious dynamic: the immediate sensual pleasures of promiscuous sex set in motion a hidden causality of disease and death. The very act of sexual union—with its cultural resonances of love and the production of life—is turned into an act of death. Although the viral hypothesis does not view AIDS as the very signature of homosexual desire, it asserts an indirect tie between promiscuity and AIDS among homosexual men. It is, after all, primarily through nonmonogamy that sex threatens viral infection.

Prompted by medical research, perhaps merely sanctioned by it, promiscuity became a focal point in the heterosexual media coverage, especially through 1986. The media has shown a seemingly endless fascination with the sexual aspects, and especially the quantitative aspects, of homosexual behavior. A widely reported study by a CDC task force in 1981 provided the initial medical justification for this preoccupation.[36] Assuming a connection between gay sexual patterns and the large number of male homosexual AIDS cases, CDC researchers compared their sexual patterns with a control group. They reported that the AIDS group had approximately twice as many sex partners. Although the precise nature of the connection between the number of sex partners and AIDS was unclear to the researchers, they asserted a causal tie.

Serious doubts have been raised about this study.[37] A central flaw is the study's failure to define what constitutes a sex act. When does an act between two men count as a sex act with a sexual partner? Does the number of sex partners suggest a common reference for heterosexuals and homosexual men? If gay men count behavior in which there is no exchange of semen as sex acts (e.g., mutual masturbation, body rubbing, kissing) then the number of sex partners per se is largely irrelevant to AIDS. If the key factor is the introduction of semen into the blood stream, then the relevant data concerns the number of sex partners with whom there occurred sex acts of this type. Even here, it is complicated by the fact that there is very little evidence that oral-genital sex is a high-risk practice. In fact, the comparison between the AIDS cases and the control group along the key dimension of exposure to semen revealed no statistically significant differences. Whatever the casual link between homosexual behavior and AIDS, the initial CDC study provided few credible clues.

Despite the flaws and tentativeness of much of the early research linking promiscuity to AIDS among homosexual men, the heterosexual media seized upon this as the explanation. An unintended—I hope—consequence of this symbolic figure was that a public stereotype defining and stigmatizing homosexuality as an amoral, perverse, and dangerous sexual desire was reinforced. Headlines and feature stories in virtually all the major national media dramatized a gay lifestyle that amounted to little more than a relentless quest for sexual pleasure through anonymous sex. For example, a piece in *The San*

Francisco Examiner interpreted the high percentage of homosexual men with AIDS as confirmation of the conventional wisdom that gays are "a population whose lifetyle is based on a freewheeling approach to sex."[38] John Fuller, in *Science Digest*, observed that the victimization of homosexual men by AIDS was further proof of what science has told us all along about homosexual men. "Sociologists and psychologists had long noted that the constant search for new sexual partners is a persistent pattern among many gay males."[39]

I want to underscore a key point regarding this discourse: the promiscuity of homosexual men is not considered incidental, or a historically specific property of same-sex behavior, nor a phenomenon to be grasped contextually. Rather, it is viewed as essential to homosexuality. In other words, this discourse resurrects an older notion of the male homosexual as a person with unique physical, emotional and behavioral traits. His essence is that of a hypersexual human type. Homosexual men are said to sexualize themselves and others; they reduce persons to eroticized bodies; they frame sex as a mere physical release or relentless pleasure-seeking. Promiscuity is thought to manifest the lustful, amoral nature of the homosexual. Homosexual desire symbolizes pure lust or unrestrained desire, subject only to the quantitative limitations of physical exhaustion. It is this compulsive, hyperactive, insatiable desire that is thought to compel homosexuals to eroticize the forbidden and to transgress all moral boundaries, rendering them a profound social danger. Homosexuality is constructed, especially in conservative discourses, as the very antithesis of the heterosexual intimate ideal where sex is joined to love, intimacy, and fidelity.

Conservatives have appealed to AIDS to authorize moral boundaries that de-legitimate homosexuality. The juxtaposition of the figures of the heterosexual family unit and the single, promiscuous homosexual specifies a moral order privileging the former as healthy, good, right, and socially beneficial while discrediting the latter as diseased, abnormal, wrong, perverse, and socially dangerous. In many conservative representations, AIDS is said to not only reveal the truth of homosexuality as unnatural but to be its just punishment. "The poor homosexuals—they have declared war upon nature, and now nature is exacting an awful retribution," writes the syndicated columnist Patrick Buchanan.[40] Reverend Charles Stanley, head of the 14.3 million member Southern Baptist Convention declares, "It [homosexuality] is a sinful lifestyle, according to the scripture, and I believe that AIDS is God indicating his displeasure and his attitude towards that form of lifestyle."[41] Articulating the same moral judgement within a medical-scientific discourse, Dr. James Fletcher writes in the

Southern Medical Journal: "If we act as empirical scientists can we not see the implications of the data [AIDS among homosexual men] before us? Might not these 'complications' [AIDS] be 'consequences' [of homosexuality]? Were it so a logical conclusion is that AIDS is a self-inflicted disorder. . . . Indeed from an empirical medical perspective alone current scientific observation seems to require the conclusion that homosexuality is a pathologic condition."[42]

In the above moral rhetorics, AIDS represents a just punishment for homosexuals for violating a natural order, whether legislated by God or Nature. There is, moreover, another more subtle logic of moral judgement insinuated into these conservative discourses. AIDS is seen as the homosexual's death wish turned upon himself. In postwar American culture, homosexuality has often been imagined as symbolizing an unconscious will to subvert and destroy society. Images of subversion surround the homosexual. The near-ubiquitous association of homosexuals with the corruption of children—the very symbol of social purity—is indicative of this symbolism. It is, I believe, precisely because homosexuality is often constructed as a social danger evoking resonances of decline and chaos that AIDS has been construed as the truth of homosexuality and its just punishment. AIDS symbolizes the wish for the annihilation of the "other" being turned inward, back against the homosexual himself. It is because homosexuality continues to symbolize for many Americans a threat to society and life itself that even in the face of the enormous suffering and loss of lives in the AIDS epidemic, the public reaction has often been complacent, indifferent and even vengeful. For threatening society and killing "the innocent," homosexual men are thought to have received their just deserts in AIDS.

AIDS has been used by conservatives to revive the notion of the homosexual as a dangerous and polluted figure. AIDS has been invoked as proof of the diseased, contagious and dangerous nature of homosexuality. AIDS has allowed backlash forces to claim that homosexuals are, in fact, a public health threat. It has provided a pretext to attack gay institutions and to push homosexuality back into a state of invisibility and marginality. After the defeats of many of the backlash legislative initiates of the late 1970s, AIDS stimulated renewed efforts to remedicalize and recriminalize homosexuality. For example, the Dallas Doctors Against AIDS issued the following declaration. "Such a sexual public health concern must cause the citizenry of this country to do everything in their power to smash the homosexual movement in this country to make sure these kinds of acts are criminalized."[43] The deployment of AIDS by conservatives has contributed to the social oppression of lesbians and gay men, especially persons with AIDS. The conservative response helped to legitimate a public response to gay men with AIDS which was for several years nothing short of inhumane. Persons with AIDS were refused medical and dental care; hospital staff refused to care or attend to them; funeral parlors would not bury them. Persons with AIDS were fired from their jobs, evicted from their homes, and stigmatized by society—sometimes left alone and made to feel guilty and ashamed for their illness.[44]

The heterosexual media has not been uniform in its configuring of AIDS. Many liberals interpreted AIDS less as disclosing the universal truth of homosexual desire than as revealing the failure of the sexual revolution. Instead of criticizing a hypostatized homosexual desire, liberals identify the urban gay male subculture and its libertarian sexual ideology as the key causal link between homosexuality, promiscuity, and AIDS. At times, it must be said, the line between liberal "historicism" and conservative "universalism" or essentialism, and the line between tolerance and repression, collapses. For example, after criticizing conservative attempts to enlist AIDS in a politics of repression, Charles Krauthammer alludes to a possible natural link between homosexuality and disease. "In reality no one knows whether AIDS is accidently a homosexual disease or intrinsically so."[45] Moreover, without a historical perspective on the development of the gay subculture, the liberal perspective simply shifts the reification of the promiscuous homosexual from an abstract gay desire to an equally ahistorically conceived gay subculture. Liberals have, however, consistently opposed backlash efforts to use AIDS to reinstitute a harsh regime of homosexual oppression. They have criticized the AIDS hysteria and attempts to exploit the disease to further fuel an antigay backlash.

Although the liberal media has sought to avoid politicizing AIDS, they have seized on AIDS to reaffirm a sexual ethic that binds sex to romance, love, intimacy, and monogamy, although expanding the range of legitimate intimate lifestyles to include both heterosexual and homosexual cohabitating couples. The liberal media has used AIDS to rehabilitate a pre-gay liberation ideal of the "respectable homosexual": discreet, coupled, monogamous and cohabitating, bound by love, shared reponsibilities, and property.

The *New York Times*, for example, has virtually campaigned to create and legitimate this ideal of the respectable homosexual.[46] Its coverage of AIDS has regularly included interviews with prominent figures in the gay community or so-called "experts," who uniformly criticize the immature and irresponsible lifestyles of gay men in the 1970s. Articles regularly report changes in homosexual behavior and attitudes. Key indicators of the "fast-lane" gay lifestyle (e.g., number of sex partners, STDs, bathhouse attendance) were scrutinized to detect a retreat from promiscuity. Statements by community leaders or medical experts detecting a new emphasis on dating, courting, and nonsexual socializing have been interpreted as indicating a social trend. The *Times* has done more than report these events. By enlisting select experts and community leaders to serve as spokespersons for social reform, the *Times* has become a major social force in promoting a change in models of gay intimacy and identity.

Its advocacy role became quite clear in several human interest stories featuring homosexual couples who were obviously intended to serve as role models. One such story, entitled "Homosexual Couple Finds a Quiet Pride", focuses on two white professional men who have lived together for some forty years.[47] They are, in appearance, indistinguishable from conventional professional heterosexuals. In other words, there is no trace of a more unconventional gay subcultural style to their self-presentation. There is an implied discreetness to their homosexuality and their demeanor exudes an almost exaggerated 1950s sense of staid respectability. They are described as preoccupied with such typical heterosexual middle-class concerns as career, family, domestic affairs, hobbies and anniversaries. The "success" or longevity of their relationship is summed up by the remark, "You have to work at it," as if the presumed short-lived nature of relationships among the younger generation reflects their immaturity.[48] Quite clearly, the *Times* is offering a construction of this couple that is intended to serve as a model of an ideal homosexual style. With moral codes and identity models in flux, and with homosexuality itself assailed by backlash forces, this image of a discreet, monogamous, coupled and conventional homosexual life is endorsed as an alternative to the more unconventional gay intimate lifestyles of the 1970s. In fact, the principle thesis of the article is that a "heterosexual model" is now being adopted by homosexuals. "In recent years, some homosexual couples have begun to adopt many of the traditions of heterosexual marriage. Besides having wedding and anniversary parties, couples are exchanging vows . . . in religious services known as 'gay unions.' They are drawing up contracts . . . to provide legal protections for themselves and their partners. They are adopting children. . . ."[49] Setting aside the veracity of this statement, the message is clear: despite its devastation of the gay community, AIDS is a positive catalyst encouraging homosexual men to adopt the more mature and responsible intimate patterns of heterosexuals. AIDS is said to have prompted gay men to discover the charms, civility, security, and safety of romance and monogamy. Liberals, no less than conservatives, have exploited AIDS for their own moral purpose. Whereas the latter enlist AIDS as part of their backlash politics, the former use AIDS to relate a moral tale of the virtues of romantic love and monogamy.

AIDS & Gay Constructions of Homosexuality

There is a common theme running through the liberal heterosexual and gay AIDS discourses: AIDS manifests the failure of an ideology and way of life. Indeed, AIDS takes on a redemptive significance. It has initiated a period of self-criticism and reform. AIDS is described as the principal catalyst in the rebirth of the gay community. In other words, the suffering brought on by AIDS is made meaningful by rendering it as instigating a personal and social awakening and maturation.

Gay men were among the earliest defenders of the Overload theory. This might seem odd, since the basic message of this theory is that homosexual men have brought AIDS upon themselves through their own profligate lifestyle. In a much discussed early piece in the gay press, "We Know Who We Are," Michael Callen, Richard Berkowitz and Richard Dworkin concluded, despite the prelimary and confused nature of the evidence at the time (1982), "that there is no mutant virus and there will be no vaccine. We must accept that we have overloaded our immune systems with common viruses and other sexually transmitted infections. Our lifestyle has created the present epidemic of AIDS among gay men."[51] The full moral weight of this self-incriminatory rhetoric is partially deflected by targeting the gay subculture as the source of the gay lifestyle and therefore of AIDS. Michael Callen assails the conventions of a sex-obsessed urban gay subculture. "Throughout ten years of promiscuity, I have tried to be a good gay and wear my STDs as red badges of courage in a war against a sex-negative society."[50] Callen's harsh judgement of the gay subculture is not exceptional. For example, writing in *The Village Voice*, Stephen Harvey comments: "For years, gay men have been prey to a brand of propaganda perpetrated among themselves which, in its subtle way, has been scarely less insidious than the harangues aimed at the community from without. . . . Co-ghettoists have implied . . . that there was something stunted and incomplete in the lives of any gay man who couldn't get into those obligatory Saturday nights of mass euphoria in the dark. . . . To cast doubt on any aspect of the way we habitually behave has been decided out of hand as reactionary. . . . In this town at least . . . what gay solidarity means is the high times you have with regulars of the bars, disco, bathhouse of your choice."[52] Many

gay men interpreted AIDS as signalling the failure of the gay subculture, and in particular its libertarian sexual culture.

Although the sexual conventions of the gay subculture are targeted
as the main causal tie between promiscuity and AIDS, the individual
is not absolved from all guilt, but, in many gay discourses, is implicated in his own victimization. Thus, Callen appeals to those promiscuous gays "who know who they are to acknowledge and change their
lifestyle. We have remained silent because we have been unable or
unwilling to accept responsibility for the role that our own exces-
siveness has played in our present public health crisis but, deep down,
we know who we are and we know why we're sick."[53] The late David
Goodstein, one-time owner and editor of *The Advocate*, insists that
AIDS is the responsibility of individual gay men. "As gay men, AIDS
is our responsibility. By responsibility I mean that we are the cause
of who we are, what we have and what we do."[54] The claim that gay
men must bear some of the moral burden is a constant theme in the
wave of articles on homosexual men whose stories are narrated as an
individual odyssey from promiscuity to AIDS.

Sexual promiscuity stands at the center of the gay media framing
of AIDS. It is viewed as a product of a historically unique gay subculture. A direct causal relation is posited between sexual promiscuity
and the current epidemic and the antigay backlash. For homosexual
men who hold to a more conventional middle-class romantic intimate
ideal, for older homosexuals who came of age in a milieu emphasizing
heterosexual intimate models, for men uncomfortable with their sexuality or gay liberationists whose ideals are perceived to have faded
behind a focus on self-fulfillment, AIDS has served as a symbol of the
failure of current gay life and as an occasion for gays to vocalize their
discontents.

I am suggesting that for both heterosexuals and homosexuals, AIDS
has served as a pretext to reconsider the meaning of homosexuality
and to advocate reforms of the gay subculture. I believe that many
gay men have felt that the suffering and heightened oppression they
have experienced in the AIDS crises could be somewhat neutralized
or even made self-confirming by reconceiving AIDS as a great moral
drama. AIDS has come to signify in many gay discourses the beginning
of a period of renewal and rebirth of gay life.

The notion that AIDS marks a turning point for gays is neatly
captured in the apocalyptic imagery of Larry Kramer's angry and
moving piece, "1,112 and Counting."[55] Kramer frames the AIDS epidemic as an ordeal of collective survival. "Our continued existence as
gay men . . . is at stake. . . . In the history of homosexuality we have
never been so close to death and extinction before."[56] In order for gays

to survive AIDS, Kramer advocates a shift from the current hedonistic preoccupations of gay men to a new ethic of sexual and social responsibility. Where Kramer edges toward apocalyptic symbolism, other gay men speak in an oddly upbeat, even millennial, tone of the epidemic initiating a new era of maturity and respectability. Toby Marotta observes that "most gays share my view—that [AIDS] is the most profound maturing incident for the gay community in its history."[57] David Goodstein couples a critical view of pre-AIDS gay life to the prospects for renewal and reform initiated by the disease. "During the last half of the 1970's, it wasn't chic in gay male circles to place a high value on life-companions or close friendships. Now we have another chance for progress: to acknowledge the value of intimate relationships."[58]

Central to this image of a coming era of gay maturity is the appropriation of the intimate ideals and rituals of middle-class heterosexual culture. Arthur Bell comments: "Indiscriminate sex with phantom partners in backrooms is beginning to diminish. The grudge and filth bars are losing their appeal. Fistfucking is fading. Barbarity is on the way out. Romance [is] . . . on the way in."[59] Stories abound in the gay media of homosexual men rediscovering the "quiet joys and healthy lifestyles" of romantic love and monogamy. Typically, such narratives describe a pre-AIDS period of immaturity and indulgence, with AIDS marks the great turning point where, after a protracted period of soul-searching, one is reborn, and the profligate, self-destructive ways of the past given up for the new morality of health, romance, and monogamy. Typical is the story by Arnie Kantrowitz, "Till death do us part."[60] He begins by recalling the liberating experience of sexual promiscuity. "My experiment in sexual anarchy was a rare delight, a lesson in license, an opportunity to see both flesh and spirit glaringly naked. I will never apologize to anyone for my promiscuity."[61] Yet, that is exactly what Kantrowitz does as he narrates his odyssey of personal growth. From the standpoint of the era of AIDS, his early sensual delights now appear to him as compulsive and narcissistic. The endless cycle of excitement, release, and exhaustion left him jaded and empty. "I decided to trade self-indulgence for self-respect."[62] Having personally witnessed the guilt-ridden, self-destructive ways of his pre-AIDS days, he "decided to get healthy."[63] Exercise and proper diet replaced drug abuse and late nights. With health and self-respect intact, there could be only one proper dramatic finale. "Finally, I rediscovered the difference between lust and love and began an affair."[64] The transfiguration of AIDS into a moral drama of reformation and renewal has allowed some gays to be so emotionally distanced from the enormity of suffering it has brought that the current period is defined as one of optimism. The journalist Steve Martz observes, in what has become a common motif, that "the energy formerly reserved for the sexual hunt [can now be] channeled into the community in other ways [such as] . . . the growth of gay community centers, sports clubs, choruses, and a host of other groups."[65] He concludes by remarking that "all of which I believe makes 1983 a time for optimism and joy."[66]

Criticisms of gay sexual culture are often coupled to a critique of the heterosexual social response to AIDS.[67] For example, when Randy Shilts, in his bestseller *And the Band Played On*, takes gay leaders, especially gay entrepreneurs and sex radicals, to task for trading in the high ideals of gay liberation for a sexually reductive, commercialized ideal of self-fulfillment,[68] he is equally critical of the mainstream public response to AIDS.[69] He insists that the medical, scientific, governmental and media institutions failed to respond effectively to AIDS because of their hostility to the marginal populations affected, especially homosexual men.[70]

Within at least one discursive intervention into HIV politics, the strategy involves elaborating the critique of society while dropping the critique of the gay culture. In these AIDS discourses, especially prominent among gay leftists, the framing of AIDS as a moral tale relating the failure of gay life is itself criticized. For gay leftists, AIDS symbolizes the failure of American social institutions, as evidenced in their grossly ineffective response to the epidemic, not that of the gay subculture. AIDS figures as a tale of homosexual oppression; the social response to it documents the intolerance that lurks beneath the liberal surface of a basically homophobic society.[71] AIDS provides, for these critics, an occasion to reactivate a liberationist agenda with its renewal of gay social activism.

An example of this style of discourse is the 1982 piece, "AIDing Our Guilt and Fear," by long-time gay activist and journalist Michael Bronski. He observes that in spite of the extremely provisional medical information available (1982), the straight media describes AIDS as a gay disease that threatens all Americans.[72] AIDS has prompted, moreover, the renewal of stereotypes about the promiscuous, immoral homosexual who threatens society with disease, vice, and death. AIDS has made it legitimate to publicly express antigay feelings. Unfortunately, says Bronski, this stereotyping of homosexuals by the straight media has been echoed by those gays who blame AIDS on a "fast-lane" lifestyle. Bronski cites, as examples, two leading gay newspapers which ran pieces by physicians who asserted, on the basis of the flimsiest evidence, that AIDS among homosexual men is caused by promiscuity. He quotes an anonymous gay physician: "Perhaps we've needed an situation like this to demonstrate what we've all known all along: Depravity kills!"[73] Bronski criticizes gays who accept and, indeed, promote an interpretation of AIDS which judges gay life to be a failure. This makes gay men responsible for their own victimization. It may, moreover, lead homosexuals to surrender control over their lives to those heterosexual institutions (e.g., medicine, science) which have in the past oppressed them. Bronski discerns a surfacing of guilt and internalized homophobia among gay men in their susceptibility to a view of AIDS that blames themselves.

Although Bronski takes the social response to AIDS to be indicative of social intolerance, he does not make the mainstream reaction itself a focus of social criticism. Instead, he advocates that we treat AIDS as a medical event or disease, not an occasion for moral and social commentary. Interestingly, this was the position advanced by Dennis Altman. In "AIDS: The Politicization of an Epidemic," Altman criticizes both straights and gays for using AIDS as an pretext for social criticism.[74] Sensing that AIDS is prompting an escalation of antigay sentiments, he advocates the "de-homosexualization of AIDS." "I would like to see the discussion of AIDS shift to one that sees it as a test of . . . medicine and health care, rather than a metaphysical judgement of lifestyles."[75]

It is not, I believe, possible to frame AIDS solely as a medical fact. Indeed, Altman's more elaborate statement, *AIDS and The Mind of America*, imbues AIDS with moral significance.[76] Not only does he see in the ineffective social response to AIDS in the United States a sign of homophobia, but at times he takes AIDS as entailing a judgment of sexual morality. He cautiously suggests that AIDS indicates the errors of a libertarian sexual ethic that he helped to shape and legitimate. "It is difficult in view of . . . AIDS to escape the feeling that those of us who argued for liberating sex . . . were wrong."[77]

This reluctance to seize on AIDS as an occasion for social criticism is absent in Cindy Patton's *Sex and Germs*.[78] She frames AIDS as a story of the failure of liberal America, arguing that the straight media seized upon AIDS to attack trends toward a more sexually open and pluralistic erotic culture.[79] In particular, AIDS was used as a pretext to initiate a far-reaching assault on the gay community. The public hysteria around homosexuality prompted by AIDS is taken as a sign of the enhanced social influence of the New Right and their conservative social agenda.[80] In other words, Patton describes AIDS as a major site of sexual political struggles between sex-negative, antigay forces and defenders of eros and sexual liberation. She intends to defend an indigenous gay sexual culture which celebrates eros while reconfiguring pleasures to conform to safe sex practices.[81]

The genre of AIDS interpretation represented by Patton has the advantage of shifting blame from gay men to social institutions. Although I believe that Patton is too reductive in interpreting the social response to AIDS as one of homophobia and antigay backlash in order to illustrate American illiberalism, she is right in underscoring the prejudices and parochial politics informing the United States social response. This genre of AIDS discourse does not further victimize persons with AIDS by rendering the disease a failure of the gay lifestyle. Instead, this interpretation features America's failure to live up to its liberal ideals of respecting social difference. Finally, by viewing HIV as requiring only a change in sex practices, and not a wholesale cultural shift, Patton leaves lifestyle options open to individual choice rather than mandated by hygenic, public health imperatives.

Patton's claim that AIDS does not require, on the grounds of public health alone, a wholesale break from past sexual conventions finds strong echoes in the gay culture. As we have seen, while one sector of the gay community has seized on AIDS to advocate social reform, other gays have defended their sexual culture and proposed a shift only in specific sexual practices. This position is articulated, for example, by Tim Vollmer.[82]

Vollmer does not dispute the claim that a unique gay subculture materialized in the 1970s that valued an adventurous, free-wheeling sexual style. He defends this culture for providing positive images of homosexuality and for its sheer sexual brilliance. Vollmer does not deny the seriousness of AIDS. Indeed, besides the personal tragedies it has left in its wake, it threatens, he says somewhat apocalyptically, to unravel gay communal life. Vollmer believes that sex has been a primary basis of gay male identity and community, and that AIDS threatens to make sex the bearer of disease, death, and social disintegration. In this perilous situation, Vollmer advises gay men to resist stereotypical, homophobic images of the profligate homosexual. Gays, he urges, must not relinquish control over their lives to heterosexual media or medical authorities. Vollmer counsels gay men to avoid a mindless emulation of heterosexual intimate models, and instead to innovate new models of sexual and interpersonal relationships that build upon existing gay culture. Vollmer defends a pluralistic sexual ethic that accepts self-designed and diverse sexual and intimate lifestyles so long as safe sex guidelines are followed.

As this discussion makes clear, AIDS has become a major site in the struggle over the moral boundaries of sexual desire, expression and identity in contemporary America. In particular, the "homosexual question" which is at the heart of AIDS has crystallized public feelings around the issue of sexual variation. The essentially elite public responses to AIDS that I have reviewed make it clear that there is great division in the United States regarding the meaning and social role of homosexuality.

At one level, a global division exists between those who wish to exclude homosexuality from moral legitimacy, and homosexual advocates. In the former category are some conservatives, but also some liberals, who appeal to precepts of religious or natural law or medical rhetorics. They aim to de-legitimate homosexuality by describing AIDS as evidence of its perverse or pathological character.

This latter claim has no credibility. It is now agreed upon by virtually all researchers that AIDS is caused by a virus—HIV—which has targeted both heterosexuals and homosexuals.[83] To the extent that homosexual men have been a large percentage of HIV-positive persons in the United States, this is explained by unique social and historical factors. Historians and sociologists have documented the rise of a unique gay male community in the 1970s in which sex functioned as a primary source of gay identity and community.[84] An elaborate system of sexual exchanges and liaisons materialized, along with discourses that imbued sex with meanings related to the celebration of the body, pleasure, gay identity, sexual and social rebellion, and gay brotherhood.[85] Moreover, anal sex became a central sexual practice. Indeed, it served as a symbol of a new masculine gay pride. This gay male subculture provided a favorable milieu for the rapid spread of HIV unbeknownst to the gay men who carried it. Since the mid-1980s, researchers have documented significant behavioral changes among homosexual men which explain the declining rate of HIV infection in this population.[86] If, as researchers believe, IV drug users and their largely heterosexual partners will represent a larger percentage of the HIV positive population in the 1990s, AIDS will likely lose its power as a rhetorical strategy to de-legitimate homosexuality.

Vocal and strident public opposition to homosexuality has not found a great deal of support in elite liberal discourses. Although liberals have not been outspoken homosexual advocates, they have, in the main, opposed state strategies of repression, from tatooing and quarantining HIV -infected persons to remedicalizing and recriminalizing homosexuality. Yet if liberals defend homosexuality it is in fairly narrow terms. As we have seen, some have seized on the AIDS issue to legitimate an exclusively middle-class marital intimate ideal. AIDS is said to symbolize the unhealthiness of excessive sexual freedom, in particular divorcing sex from love. Liberals tend to accept homosexuality only if it mirrors the dominant middle-class heterosexual marital model. This reform agenda, like the conservative one, ignores the social and historical character of contemporary homosexuality. Specifically, a heterosexual marital ideal will not be a realistic option for many gay men in the absence of all the social, legal and governmental supports that maintain this ideal. But liberals, by and large, have neither been willing to challenge a heterosexist order, nor to advocate the kinds of social reforms that would permit this marital ideal to serve as a viable alternative for male homosexuals. Moreover, the liberal reform agenda fails to take into account the unique gender dynamics of an all-male community in contemporary America. Many social analysts have argued, cogently, in my view, that in such a culture which exhibits fairly conventional masculine attitudes and behaviors, sexual and intimate expression will exhibit unique patterns that depart significantly from dominant heterosexual and lesbian models.[87] Defending the exclusive legitimacy of a marital intimate pattern that binds sex to love in a monogamous intimate ideal may not only stigmatize gay patterns that depart from this norm, but may prove to be an ineffective message to gay men responding to HIV. There is, in fact, a good deal of evidence that while gay men have altered their behavior in light of HIV, the turn to sexual monogamy is the choice of a small minority.[88] If reducing the risk of HIV infection among homosexual men is the goal, the more effective message would seem to be, "practice safe sex whether it's in a monogamous or nonmonogamous lifestyle."[89]

The question as to whether gay men have evolved a unique intimate culture, and whether this can stand as a legitimate alternative to the marital model, is a contested issue in the gay community. In analyzing responses to AIDS in the gay community, we have observed divergent views that reflect basic disagreements about the meaning and morality of sexual and intimate life. Does AIDS mean, as some say, a failure of a gay culture to support a healthy lifestyle? Does the pluralistic, free-wheeling sexual culture of the 1970s represent an internalized homophobic reaction? Or, as other gay men argue, is this culture a healthy expression of a gay male community which has invented its own conventions to satisfy needs for intimacy and autonomy? The dispute, moreover, between gays who take AIDS as symptomatic of the failure of the gay subculture and those who interpet it as a sign of an intolerant homophobic society in need of reform reflects a deep, long-standing division over sexual ethics within this community. I wish to briefly turn to this dispute over sexual ethics within the gay community.

The Conflict over Sexual Ethics in the Gay Community

Disagreement in the gay community regarding the significance of AIDS reflects a basic division over the meaning and morality of sex, which predates AIDS. It was present from the beginnning of the making of a gay movement and community in the late 1960s. As the 1970s came to an end, this conflict intensified. In gay newspapers, conferences and books, highly charged discussions occurred over the morality of public sex, man-boy love and S/M.[90] I will briefly sketch the contours of these conflicts.

Many gay men who came of age in the 1970s struggled to demedicalize homosexuality, or at least to strip the medical model of its negative meanings. Gays asserted that homosexuality is a natural, normal human expresssion. Typically, they took over the sexualization of homosexual identity that was implied in the medical model, but gave to it a positive twist. Indeed, a free-wheeling, polymorphous sexuality was celebrated as the virtual cornerstone of an affirmative gay identity and community.

As part of their struggle to legitimate homosexuality, some gay men produced discourses and representations that sought to take consensual sex out of the realm of morality. By framing sex, including homosexuality, as largely outside the realm of moral judgment, gays wished to advance their claim to social inclusion. Several discursive strategies were employed to strip the moral significance of sex to a bare minimum. First, it was proposed that insofar as sex is a personal affair between consenting adults, it should not be an arena of further moral regulation. The choice of when to have sex, with whom and how, was said to be a private one guided by individual aesthetic preferences.[91] Second, some gays maintained that an open system of sexual exchanges plays a unique social role in the gay community. Through sexual liaisons with multiple partners, bonds of solidarity, from friendships to love relationships to feelings of brotherhood among all gays, are created.[92] In other words, sex is viewed as connected to a logic of social identity and community as its primary meaning and rationale, and not to a narrow personal moral code. Finally, some gay liberationists held that the open, prolific sex system of the gay culture needs to be viewed fundamentally in a political rather than a moral context. Uncoupling sex from an intimate "marital" familial context was thought to expand possibilities for self-expression, pleasure and social bonding; the movement towards eroticizing everyday life was said to prefigure a liberated sexual and intimate culture.[93]

These liberationist discourses did not advocate the end to the moral regulation of sex, but its minimization. They exhibit what we previously called a libertarian ethic. Sex is viewed as having multiple meanings—from procreation to love and pleasure or health—and multiple legitimate social settings—from a long-term committed intimate relationship to a brief encounter. The only moral rule governing sexual desire and behavior should be a norm of mutual consent. This ethic fits, of course, with gays' struggle for rights and social inclusion. A libertarian ethic maximizes tolerance for diverse intimate lifestyle choices. For many homosexuals, it also resonated with the elaboration of a gay male urban community that was, in fact, organized around sexually oriented institutions, e.g., bathhouses, bars, pornography theatres, and sex shops.

A curious alliance formed between some gay liberationists and entreprenuers, who saw in the emerging gay community a potentially rich market. These two social forces promoted a libertarian ideology. Sex was to be stripped of most of its moral weight, and the demand for moral rules beyond consent was often seen as a thinly veiled strategy of social control or homophobia. Judging from surveys like *Homosexualities* and *The Gay Report*, the libertarian ideology articulated well the practices of large segments of this population.[94]

Many gays, however, were deeply troubled by the movement to abstract sex from a moral realm and minimize social restraints. Some gays felt, especially in light of the antigay backlash beginning in the late 1970s, that the free-wheeling, "promiscuous" lifestyle celebrated by many in the subculture provided ammunition to their critics. Still other critics of the libertarian ideology were approaching middle age and wished to settle into a marriage-like arrangement. This was made difficult not only by a sexual culture which proliferated opportunities for sex, but by a liberationist ideology which provided little support for gay unions.

Many gays were, as well, troubled by a sexual ethic that placed no restrictions on sexual expression beyond consent. While these critics of a libertarian ethic appreciated its tolerance towards social diversity, they believed that it permitted the proliferation of forms of sexual and intimate life that were immoral. For example, responding to the heightened visibility of S/M in the gay culture, Craig Johnson asked, "Are there no limits, should there be no limits, no limits at all, on what constitutes legitimate forms of sexual gratification? Or are we obliged to say that we can set no limits so long as the conduct is among consenting adults?"[95] To Johnson, who believed that S/M is "about violence and torture" and is "an unhealthy way of life that threatens us all," the libertarian morality offered no moral guidance.[96] Other gays argued that the libertarian ideology similarly provides no grounds on which to question the pervasiveness of anonymous or casual sex. Yet such sexual exchanges were said to involve a level of objectification and depersonalization that cried out for moral questioning. Responding to not only the pervasiveness of casual sex but its promotion, even celebration, within the gay subculture, Thomas Garrett challenged the conventional wisdom. "Sex is not recreation; it changes things between people."[97] Sex is said to elicit deeply felt emotions and intimate longings that are devalued or denied in the brief encounter. Casual sex promotes superficial and callous ways of relating. It is a defensive reaction to wishes for intimacy and love. Its celebration of pleasure reduces emotionally thick exchanges to one-dimensional exchanges of bodily stimulation. Finally, the heightened expectations for pleasure created in the gay sexual culture renders all potential lovers lacking. The "habit of sex-as-recreation" diminishes gay's capacities to enjoy the benefits of long-term intimacies.[98] Garrett's and Johnson's were by no means isolated voices. Arguably the two most important gay novels published in the 1970s, Andrew Holleran's *Dancer from the Dance* and Larry Kramer's *Faggots*, echo similar concerns about the emotionally and socially deadening quality of life in a culture organized around the pursuit of eros.[99]

Informing these criticisms of a libertarian ideology is a romantic sexual ideology. Sex is understood as involving a dense web of individual feelings and longings. The proper sphere of sex is in intimate committed relationships where the integrity of each individual's feelings is respected. As a medium of intimate bonding, sex should exhibit caring, tender qualities, and individuals should always be treated as complex whole beings. From the standpoint of sexual romanticism, sex that is devoid of the thick emotional and social content of intimate bonds is morally suspect if not outright dehumanizing.

Romanticists have a point. Libertarians offer no moral standards to limit sexual expression beyond consent. Moreover, libertarians have not, to date, clarified the meaning of consent or the conditions that make consent possible. Is consent possible under conditions of inequality or socioeconomic dependency? Is consent possible, as man-boy love advocates believe, in a relationship between an adult and a "minor?" Moreover, even if we agree that the concept of consent can be satisfactorily clarified, does it still follow that consent is a sufficient standard for a sexual ethic? For example, does consent justify "public sex?" Dennis Altman defended consensual gay sex in public places (parks, beaches, public toilets) as an integral part of the liberationist project of eroticizing everyday life.[100] Restricting sex to private settings, including commercial institutions like gay bathhouses or private sex clubs, is said to be repressive. It "reinforces the idea that sex should only occur in special venues, rather than wherever the opportunity arises."[101] However, a code that legitimates sex "wherever the opportunity arises" does not respect the rights of individuals who are involuntarily co-present and who may not share the same sexual and social values. The concept of consent simply does not address many of the key moral issues raised by sexual expression. For example, Edmund White wished to frame sex simply as a matter of pleasure beyond good and evil, given conditions of consent. "Sexual habit [is] ... to my mind ... an aesthetic rather than an ethical issue, a matter (so long as no one is hurt) of what gives pleasure rather than what is good or right."[102] But sex is surely not in postwar America simply a matter of "pleasure"; it evokes a range of powerful feelings, from dependency, to dominance, to longings for love and intimacy. Romanticists may be wrong to assume that sex inherently evokes intimate feelings and longings, but they are right in holding that in our culture, including the gay male one, sex carries complex, ambiguous meanings relating to romance, love and intimacy as well as to gender identity and erotic pleasure. To the extent that individuals cannot screen out meanings unrelated to erotic pleasure, these episodes will be transformed into romantic dramas or dramas of gender identity that carry highly charged significance and expectations. Even if sex could be framed simply as a matter of pleasure, it would still require moral regulation; obligations and mutual rights would need to be clarified, responsibilities within and beyond the encounter would have to be addressed, and rules governing where, when, with whom, and how to have sex would need to be specified. Romanticists have highlighted some shortcomings of a libertarian ethic that cannot specify moral standards beyond consent.

A romantic sexual ethic is no less suspect. As we argued in the previous chapter, the definition of sex as an expression of an intimate bond whose qualities should exhibit nurturing, person-oriented values places unnecessarily severe restrictions on sexual behavior and lifestyle choices. Lifestyles that involve the splitting off of sex from intimacy would be disapproved of or stigmatized by romanticists. This stigma would, of course, be used by critics of the gay culture to de-legitimate homosexuality. For, as had been noted, despite AIDS, research through 1990 indicates that while gay men are reducing the number of sex partners a sizeable proportion apparently have not adopted a monogamous norm—neither in practice, nor in principle.

The susceptibility of a romantic ethic to become repressive is evident in those strains within the gay culture to stigmatize those whose lifestyle involves multiple sex partners or nonconventional sex practices. For example, in his polemic against S/M, Craig Johnson speaks of the spread of S/M as a "virus in our community."[103] Seymour Kleinberg, author of *Alienated Affections*, interprets the attraction of S/M and other nonconventional sexual practices by gay men with an appeal to the psychiatric language of narcissism.[104] Kleinberg argues that gay men are prone to narcissism, and as they become self-absorbed, lose interest in others. Boredom motivates the narcissistic individual to experiment with violence and aggression.[105] In other words, nonconventional sex is said to be symptomatic of a personality disorder. This turn to a medical language to stigmatize nonromantic sex is even more blatant in the appearance of a discourse of sexual compulsion and addiction in the gay community. Articles like "Sexual Compulsion: Problem or Punishment" or "Overcoming Sexual Compulsion," which have appeared in mainstream gay publications, describe nonromantic, nonconventional sex as symptomatic of a psychological disorder.[106] Disregarding the multiple meanings "casual sex" has accrued in the gay male culture, one advocate of the sexual compulsion campaign remarks, "A chief motivation for quick, anonymous sex is the desire to relieve tension, anxiety, depression."[107] Drawing on the growing prestige within the gay community of this medicalizing of nonromantic sex, the gay journalist Thom Willenbecher authoritatively declares that "Like drugs, shadow sex seems to attract people lacking in self-esteem."[108] It was inevitable that some would see in the AIDS epidemic a symptom of sexual or psychological malaise. "Untreated sexual problems are often expressed as a desire for anonymous sex, which, in turn, is directly responsible for the spread of AIDS."[109] Some within the gay community will, no doubt, interpret this push to remedicalize nonromantic sex as a sign of internalized homophobia. I prefer to view it as a sign of the evolution of the gay community to a point where many gays feel that they can be self-accepting, yet also committed to fairly conventional intimate values.

Conclusion

In chapter 3, I sketched a debate among feminists over the meaning and morality of sex. The conflict between feminists who are libertarian in their sexual ideology and those who defend some version of romanticism relates to basic disagreements over what sex is and what its role should be in the broader framing of intimate and social life. In this chapter, our focus centered on the issue of the moral boundaries of legitimate sexual and intimate expression. The question of homosexuality dramatically raises the issue of tolerance of sexual and social difference in the United States today.

It was not until the late 1960s that a truly wide-ranging public debate over homosexuality was initiated. Previously, the homosexual question had been confined largely to medical-scientific circles, although there were some literary interventions in the middle decades of the twentieth century. The rise of a gay movement—with some support from straight elites (e.g., physicians, psychologists, ministers, lawyers, professors)—in the context of broad social liberalization occasioned a different kind of discussion. The medical-scientific and religious control of the discourse on sex gave way to a much more democratized public debate. Young rebels, feminists, gay liberationists and renegades from the scientific, medical or religious establishment claimed a right to speak on issues of sexuality and intimate life. Frequently they spoke a language of tolerance. Although this liberal rhetoric often did not extend to homosexuality, homosexual advocates could draw upon it in demanding the legitimacy of gay rights and social inclusion. They appealed to conventional legitimating rationales, e.g., the "naturalness" of homosexuality, or to medical-scientific concepts of "normality" that were now more credible due to available research indicating no relationship between homosexuality per se and maladjustment. Homosexual advocates drew, moreover, on a broader shift in our culture from an ethic based on the morality of the sex act to one based on the interpersonal exchange. The former assumed that certain forms of desire (e.g., heterosexual desire) and certain practices (e.g. coitus or monogamy) are natural and normal whereas the latter held that the moral qualities of the social exchange should serve as normative standards. Homosexual advocates argued that homosexual acts, like heterosexual acts, should be judged by the moral aspects of the social exchange.

In the context of movements toward social liberalization in the United States appeals to legitimate homosexuality had some credibility. By the mid-1970s, the gay movement had begun to go mainstream. Social space was won to build an elaborate gay community; legal reform extended certain rights to homosexuals; gay lifestyle choices were being marketed for the masses. At least some Americans were willing to accept homosexuality as a legitimate expression of sexual and social life, an acceptance born of the expanding tolerance for different forms of life.

By the late 1970s and early 1980s, many Americans were reconsidering the legacy of the 1960s. I prefer to see this period less as a simple backlash to liberalization than as exhibiting multiple strains, some of which represented a credible reassessment of the movements of the past decade and the direction of the United States. Nevertheless, social conservatism was unquestionably the dominant social current.

In the midst of this heightened social conflict in the late 1970s, the homosexual question was central. The New Right and more mainstream conservatives seized on the new tolerance towards homosexuality as a symbol of the moral and social failure of liberalism in America. These conservative social forces made an antigay agenda a cornerstone of their social program. Their strident anti-homosexual rhetoric often dominated the public discussion and politics of homosexuality through the mid-1980s. They rationalized their antigay politic by appealing primarily to a Judeo-Christian religious tradition and a concept of natural law, both of which were said to be organized around a heterosexual familial order. In a word, antigay forces invoked absolutist rationales that centered a sexual ethic on the morality of the sex act. Heterosexuality in itself was seen as a sign of a natural or divinely created moral order.

As conservatives invoked this metaphysical, absolutist concept to de-legitimate homosexuality, homosexual advocates were often forced to rally behind equally absolutist, essentializing rationales asserting the naturalness, normality and universality of homosexuality. Debate was typically polarized through the 1980s, as these contrasting absolutist claims about the nature of homosexuality were advanced.

To the extent that public discourse avoided these terms of the debate, the discussion shifted to the moral character of the gay subculture. Thus, straight liberals emphasized the social form of homosexuality. Although they generally defended the idea of civil rights for gay citizens, they did not support their full social inclusion or equality. This implied, of course, a less privileged—less natural and normal—status accorded to homosexuality. Liberals have seemed willing to accept homosexuality to the extent that it is guided by romantic sexual norms. For many liberals it is, generally speaking, not the sex act or the gender of the sex partner that is morally important but the social form of sexuality. Liberals value sexual expression only as it is linked to love, intimacy, long-term commitment, household stability, and monogamy.

As we move to the gay subculture, the argument shifts somewhat. Obviously, there is no debate over the legitimacy of homosexuality. There is, however, some disagreement over which conceptual and justificatory rationales to employ, e.g., natural law, medical-scientific, religious, ethnic-minority models, civil libertarian, etc. Moreover, there is debate over the social form of homosexuality. The conflict between libertarians and romanticists reflects a basic division within the gay community over the meaning of sex and its role in personal and social life. Finally, although almost all gays advocate a shift to a morality centered on the interpersonal aspects of sex, there is a division between libertarians, who wish to offer a minimal normative standard—consent—and romanticists, who find fault in a sexual ethic that totally abstracts from the qualitative aspects of sexual expression. Romanticists aim to build in additional normative standards by appealing to the qualitative aspects of the interpersonal exchange, e.g., holding that sex should be caring, intimate, involve commitment, and be respectful of the whole individual. Indeed, many romanticists retain a residual morality of the sex act. Certain acts are defined by them as signs of unnaturalness or abnormality, e.g., S/M, fisting, or a lifestyle including multiple sex partners.

Within gay urban subcultures, as within feminist communities and, I would say, within American culture in general, there is a cleavage in our intimate culture over the meaning and morality of sex. The liberationist concept of sex as a sphere of joy and self-fulfillment tends to underpin a libertarian sexual ethic. Post-liberationists, who underscore the potential dangers of eros, lean towards some version of sexual romanticism. The presence of these two sexual ideologies divides Americans on issues of homosexuality, teen sex, cohabitation, sex education, public sex, pornography, etc. By and large the two sides remain polarized. Yet, as we have seen, each standpoint carries definite liabilities. In chapter 5, I wish to stake out a middle ground.

Notes

A portion of this Chapter initially appeared in *Social Text* 19/20 (Fall 1988).

1. Key articles outlining the distinction between homosexual behavior and homosexual identity or role are collected in *The Making of the Modern Homosexual*, ed. Kenneth Plummer (London: Hutchinson, 1981); also see Michel Foucault, *History of Sexuality*, vol. 1, *An Introduction* (New York: Pantheon, 1978); Jeffrey Weeks, *Coming Out* (London: Quartet, 1977).

2. For example, Foucault, *A History of Sexuality*; Jeffrey Weeks, *Sex, Politics and Society* (London: Longman, 1981). This view has been challenged by John Boswell, *Christianity, Social Tolerance and Homosexuality* (Chicago: University of Chicago Press, 1980); Randolph Trumbach, "London's Sodomites: Homosexual Behavior and Western Culture in the 18th Century," *Journal of Social History*, 11 (Fall 1977–78) and "Gender and the Homosexual Role in Modern Western Culture: The 18th and 19th Centuries Compared," in *Homosexuality, Which Homsexuality?* International Conference on Gay and Lesbian Studies(London: CMP, 1989); David Greenberg, *The Social Construction of Homosexuality* (Chicago: University of Chicago, 1989).

3. See Jonathan Ned Katz, "The Invention of the Homosexual, 1880–

1950" in *Gay/Lesbian Almanac* (New York: Harper & Row, 1983); Carroll Smith-Rosenberg, "The Female World of Love and Ritual," in *Disorderly Conduct* (Oxford: Oxford University Press, 1985).

4. Foucault, *The History of Sexuality*, p. 43.

5. See, for example, George Chauncey, Jr., "Christian Brotherhood or Sexual Perversion? Homosexual Identities and the Construction of Sexual Boundaries in the World War One Era," *Journal of Social History* 19 (Winter 1985).

6. Foucault, *The History of Sexuality*, p. 101.

7. See John D'Emilio, *Sexual Politics/Sexual Communities* (Chicago: University of Chicago Press, 1983); Barry Adam, *The Rise of a Gay and Lesbian Movement* (Boston: Twayne, 1987); Allan Berube, *Coming Out Under Fire* (New York: The Free Press, 1990); Laud Humphreys, *Out of the Closet* (Englewood Cliffs, New Jersey: Prentice-Hall, 1972), and "Exodus and Identity: The Emerging Gay Culture," in *Gay Men*, ed. Martin Levine (New York: Harper & Row, 1979). Studies done in the 1950s and early 1960s document the evolution of a gay culture prior to gay liberation. See, in particular, Donald Webster Cory, *The Homosexual in America* (New York: Greenberg, 1951); Martin Hoffman, *The Gay World* (New York: Basic Books, 1968); Del Martin and Phyllis Lyon, *Lesbian/Women* (San Francisco, Ca.: Glide, 1972).

8. See Seidman, *Romantic Longings*, chap. 6.

9. For example, Gene Phillips, "The Homosexual Revolution," *America*, Nov. 14, 1970; Jack Starr, "The Homosexual Couple," *Look*, Jan. 26, 1971; "The Militant Homosexual," *Newsweek*, Aug. 23, 1971; "Gays on the March," *Time*, Sept. 8, 1975; Sister Jeanine Gramick, "The Myth of Homosexuality, *Intellect* Nov. 1973.

10. See John D'Emilio, *Sexual Politics/Sexual Communities*, chap. 12.

11. See Dennis Altman, *The Homosexualization of America* (Boston: Beacon, 1983); Michael Bronski, *Cultural Clash* (Boston: South End Press 1984). For similar arguments in the straight media, see "How Gay is Gay," *Time*, Apr. 23, 1979; "Gay Impact," *Macleans*, Feb. 18, 1980; "A New Big Push for Homosexual Rights," *U.S. News and World Report*, Apr. 14, 1980.

12. On the antigay backlash, see Dennis Altman, *The Homosexualization of America*; Barry Adam, "The Roots of Homophobia," *Christopher Street*, 103 (1986); Larry Bush and Richard Goldstein, "The Anti-Gay Backlash," *The Village Voice*, Apr. 8–14, 1981; Steven Seidman, "The Case of Antigay Politics: The Failure of the Left," *Dissent*, Fall 1989; Larry Bush, "Homosexuality and the New Right," *The Village Voice*, April 20, 1982; Scott Tucker "The Counterrevolution," *Gay Community News*, Feb. 21, 1981; Sasha Gregory-Lewis, "Unraveling the Anti-Gay Network," *The Advocate* Sept. 7, 1977.

13. On efforts to repeal gay rights ordinances, see "Why the Tide is Turning Against Homosexuals," *U.S. News and World Report*, June 5, 1978; "Voting Against Gay Rights: A Backlash Against Growing Tolerance," *Time*, May 22, 1978; Joseph Gusfield, "Proposition 6: Political Ceremony in California, *The*

Nation, Dec. 9, 1978; James Tracy, "Behind St. Paul's 'Affectional Preference' Vote,"*Commonweal*, July 7, 1978; Arthur Bell, "Why Gay Rights Went Down," *The Village Voice*, Nov. 25–Dec. 1, 1981. "Enough! Enough! Enough!" *Time*, June 20, 1977, Ken Ross, "Gay Rights: The Coming Struggle," *The Nation*, Nov. 19, 1977.

14. Quoted in Bush and Goldstein, "The Anti-Gay Backlash," p. 10.

15. Quoted in Doug Ireland, "The New Homophobia: Open Season on Gays," *The Nation*, Sept. 15, 1979, p. 209.

16. Quoted in Bush and Goldstein, "The Anti-Gay Backlash," p. 10.

17. George Will, "How Far Out of the Closet?" *Newsweek*, May 30, 1977, p. 92.

18. *Ibid.*

19. *Ibid.* Cf. M.J. Sobran, Jr., "Capital M," *National Review*, Mar. 17, 1978.

20. Samuel McCracken, "Are Homosexuals Gay?" *Commentary*, Jan. 1979, p. 24.

21. *Ibid.*

22. *Ibid.*, p. 26.

23. Midge Decter, "The Boys on the Beach," *Commentary*, Sept. 1980. Cf. Norman Podhoretz, "The Culture of Appeasement," *Harper's*, Oct. 1977.

24. *Ibid.*, p. 40.

25. *Ibid.*, p. 38.

26. *Ibid.*, p. 47.

27. *Ibid.* Also, see the letters in response to Decter's article. In particular, the letters in support of an antigay politic came, interestingly, from some prominent figures. See those by Robert Nesbit, Ernest Van Dan Haag and Howen Bradford, all of whom echo Decter's fears of homosexuality as a major national threat. They appeared in *Commentary*, Dec. 1980.

28. See Alan Bell and Martin Weinberg, *Homosexualities* (New York: Simon & Schuster, 1978) and Karla Jay and Allen Young, *The Gay Report* (New York: Summit Books, 1977). See my discussion of gay intimate lifestyles in *Romantic Longings*, chap. 6.

29. See Seymour Martin Lipset and Earl Raab, *The Politics of Unreason* (Chicago: University of Chicago Press, 1978).

30. Morton Kondracke, "Anita Bryant is Mad About Gays," *The New Republic*, May 7, 1977, p. 15.

31. Paul Robinson, "Invisible Men," *The New Republic*, June 3, 1978, p. 10.

32. John Judis, "The Danger of Ideology over Politics," *In These Times*, Feb. 3–9, 1982, p. 10.

33. See Steven Seidman, "The Case of Antigay Politics."

34. See, for example, "Gay Plague has Instituted Fear of the Unknown," *The Philadelphia Inquirer*, June 20, 1982; "New Homosexual Disorder Worries

Health Officials," *New York Times*, May 11, 1982; "Killer Gay Disease Spreads to Kids," *New York Post*, Dec. 11, 1982; "Homosexual Plague Strikes New Victims," *Newsweek*, Aug. 23, 1982; "The Gay Plague," *New York*, May 31, 1982; "The Gay Plague," *Rolling Stone*, Feb. 18, 1983.

35. On the epidemiology of AIDS, see Steve Connor and Sharon Kingman, *The Search for the Virus* (New York: Penguin, 1988); James Curran et al., "Epidemiology of HIV Infection and AIDS in the United States," *Science* 239 (Feb. 3, 1988). Useful overviews are provided in *The Social Dimensions of AIDS*, ed. Douglas Feldman and Thomas Johnson (New York: Praeger, 1986) and Michael Fumento, *The Myth of Heterosexual AIDS* (New York: Basic Books, 1990); Gerald Oppenheimer, "In the Eye of the Storm: The Epidemiological Construction of AIDS," in *AIDS: The Burden of History*, ed. Elizabeth Fee and Daniel Fox (Berkeley,Ca.: University of California Press, 1988).

36. CDC Task Force, "A Study", *Annals of Internal Medicine*, 99 August 1983.

37. See John Martin and Carole Vance, "Behavioral and Psychological Factors in AIDS," *American Psychologist*, Nov. 1984.

38. "A Hard Look/New Worry About Gay Disease," *San Francisco Examiner*, Oct. 24 1982, p. 14.

39. John Fuller, "AIDS: Legacy of the '60s?" *Science Digest*, Dec. 1983, p. 85.

40. Patrick Buchanan, "AIDS Disease: It's Nature Striking Back," *New York Post*, May 24, 1983, p. 31. Cf. William Buckley, "On Handling Gays," *National Review* Mar. 18, 1983, p. 345; George Will, "AIDS: The Real Danger," *Washington Post*, July 7, 1987, p. B7.

41. *Times Union* (Albany, New York), Jan. 18, 1986.

42. Quoted in James D'Eramo, "The New Medical Journal Homophobia," *New York Native*, May 21, 1984, p. 9.

43. Quoted in Cindy Patton, *Sex and Germs* (Boston: South End Press. 1985), pp. 3–4. On efforts by conservatives to use AIDS to promote an antigay politic, see Richard Goldstein, "The Use of AIDS," *The Village Voice*, Nov. 5, 1985; Patton's *Sex and Germs* and Altman's *AIDS and the Mind of America* are very useful in this regard.

44. For example, Mark Starr and David Gonzalez, "The Panic over AIDS," *Newsweek*, May 4, 1983; John Lee, "The Real Epidemic: Fear and Despair," *Time*, July 4, 1983; Gail Appleson, "Litigation Imminent in AIDS issues," *National Law Journal*, July 25, 1983; Michael Daly, "AIDS Anxiety," *New York*, June 20, 1983; William Greer, "Violence Against Homosexuals Rising Groups seeking Wider Protection Say," *New York Times*, Nov. 23, 1986; David Kline, "A Crisis of Mounting AIDS Hysteria," *Macleans*, Aug. 1, 1983.

45. Charles Krauthammer, "The Politics of a Plague," *The New Republic*, Aug. 1, 1983, p. 21.

46. Richard Lyons, "Sex in America: Conservative Attitudes Prevail," *New*

York Times, Oct. 4, 1983; "Homosexuals Find a Need to Reassess," *New York Times*, May 29, 1983; "Homosexuals Confronting a Time of Change," *New York Times*, June 16, 1983; "AIDS Education Takes on an Urgency Within the Homosexual Community,"*New York Times*, Sept. 22, 1985.

47. George Dullea, "Homosexual Couples Find a Quiet Pride," *New York Times*, Dec. 10, 1984.

48. Ibid.

49. Ibid.

50. Michael Callen and Richard Berkowitz with Richard Dworkin, "We Know Who We Are," *New York Native*, Nov. 8, 1982.

51. Michael Callen, letter. *The Body Politic*, Apr. 1983, p. 93.

52. Stephen Harvey, "Defenseless: Learning to Live with AIDS," *The Village Voice*, Dec. 21, 1982, p. 21.

53. Callen et al, "We Know Who We Are,"

54. David Goodstein, Editorial, *The Advocate*, Aug. 6, 1985.

55. Larry Kramer, "1,112 and Counting," *New York Native*, Mar. 14, 1983.

56. Ibid.

57. Quoted in Tom Morganthau, "Gay America in Transition," *Newsweek*, Aug. 8, 1983, p. 33.

58. Goodstein, editorial, *The Advocate*, Aug. 6, 1985, p. 3.

59. Arthur Bell, "Where Gays are Going," *The Village Voice*, June 29, 1982, p. 1.

60. Arnie Kantrowitz, "Till Death Us Do Part: Reflections on Community," *The Advocate*, March 17, 1983; Cf. Margot Joan Frommer, "Coping," *The Washington Blade*, Jan. 21, 1983.

61. Ibid., p. 26.

62. Ibid.

63. Ibid.

64. Steve Marz, "A Quick Look Back and Some Thoughts on The Year Ahead," *The Washington Blade*, Jan. 7, 1983, p. 23. Cf. Frank Lawler, Jr., "Changing Sexual Behavior Via AIDS," *Mom . . . Guess What!* Feb. 1983.

65. Ibid.

66. Ibid.

67. Randy Shilts, *And The Band Played On* (New York: St. Martin's Press, 1987).

68. Ibid., pp. 19, 24, 46, 58, 89, 154.

69. Ibid., p. xxii.

70. Ibid., p. 213.

71. See Simon Watney, *Policing Desire* (Minneapolis: University of Minne-

sota Press, 1987). Also, Cindy Patton, *Sex and Germs*; Richard Kaye, "AIDS Neglect," *The Nation*, May 21, 1983.

72.   Michael Bronski, "AIDing Our Guilt and Fear," *Gay Community News*, Oct. 7, 1982.

73.   Ibid., p. 10.

74.   Dennis Altman, "AIDS: The Politicization of an Epidemic," *Socialist Review* 14 (Nov.–Dec., 1984).

75.   Ibid., p.108.

76.   Dennis Altman, *AIDS and the Mind of America* (New York: Doubleday 1985).

77.   Ibid., p. 172.

78.   Patton, *Sex and Germs*; Cf. Richard Goldstein, "AIDS and The Social Contract," in *Taking Liberties*, ed. Erica Carter and Simon Watney (London: Serpent's Tail, 1989). Also see "AIDS: Cultural Analysis/Cultural Politics" ed. Douglas Crimp *October* 43 (Winter 1987).

79.   Patton, *Sex and Germs*.

80.   Ibid.

81.   Ibid., pp. 17–18.

82.   Tim Vollmer, "Another Stonewall," *New York Native*, Oct. 28–Nov. 3, 1985.

83.   On HIV as the cause of AIDS, see Steve Connor and Sharon Kingman, *The Search for the Virus* (New York: Penguin, 1988) and *The Essential AIDS Fact Book*, ed. Paul Douglas and Laura Pinsky (New York: Pocket Books, 1988).

84.   I have summarized a range of relevant research in *Romantic Longings*, chap. 6.

85.   See Altman, *The Homosexualization of America*; Bronski, *Culture Clash*; John Lee, "The Gay Connection," *Urban Issues* 8 (July 1979); Seidman, *Romantic Longings*, chap. 6.

86.   There is a growing literature documenting changes in gay men's sexual behavior in response to the HIV/AIDS epidemic. A useful overview of this literature is available in *AIDS: Sexual Behavior and Intravenous Drug Use*, ed. Charles Turner et al. (Washington, D.C.: National Academy Press, 1989).

87.   See my *Romantic Longings*, chap. 6.

88.   Research leaves no doubt that gay men have significantly reduced the number of sex partners, but continue to be nonmonogamous. See Charles Turner et al., *AIDS*; John Martin, "AIDS Risk Reduction Recommendations and Sexual Behavior Patterns Among Gay Men: A Multifactorial Categorical Approach to Assessing Change," *Health Education Quarterly* 13 (Winter 1986); Clifton Jones et al., "Persistence of High-Risk Sexual Activity Among Homosexual Men in an Area of Low Incidence of the Acquired Immunodificiency Syndrome," *Sexually Transmitted Diseases* 14 (1987).

89. On safe sex activism in the gay community, see Patton, *Sex and Germs*, chap. 10. Also see her "Notes for a Genealogy of Safe Sex," in Cindy Patton, *Inventing AIDS* (New York: Routledge, 1990).

90. For example, there occurred a heated debate within the gay community over public sex. See Scott Tucker, "Our Right to the World," *The Body Politic*, July/Aug. 1982; Ken Popert, "Public Sexuality and Social Space," *The Body Politic*, July/Aug. 1982; Thom Willenbecher, "Quick Encounters of the Closest Kind: The Rites and Rituals of Shadow Sex," *The Advocate*, Mar. 6, 1980; Pat Califia, "The Issue of Public Sex: Pro," *The Advocate*, Sept. 30, 1982; Eric Jay, "The Issue of Public Sex: Con," *The Advocate*, Sept. 30, 1982; Dennis Altman, "Sex: The New Front Line for Gay Politics"; George Stambolian, "The Sex," *New York Native*, Feb. 15–28, 1982.

91. For strong statements of a libertarian position, see Altman, *The Homosexualization of America*, p. 184, and Charles Silverstein and Edmund White, *The Joy of Gay Sex* (New York: Simon & Schuster), p. 150.

92. See Richard Goldstein, "Fear and Loving in the Gay Community," *The Village Voice*, June 28, 1983; Arnie Kantrowitz, "Till Death Us Do Part: Reflections on Community"; Martin Humphries, "Gay Machismo," in *The Sexuality of Men*, ed. Andy Metcalf and Martin Humphries(London: Pluto Press, 1985); Edmund White, *States of Desire*, p. xiii; Ken Popert, "Public Sexuality and Social Space," *The Body Politic*, July/Aug. 1982.

93. See Altman, *The Homosexualization of America*; Tim McCaskell, "Untangling Emotions and Eros,: *The Body Politic* July/Aug. 1981.

94. Alan Bell and Martin Weinberg, *Homosexualities*, Karla Jay and Allen Young, *The Gay Report*.

95. Craig Johnson, "S/M and the Myth of Mutual Consent," *New York Native*, May 29–June 11, 1985, p.29.

96. Ibid., pp. 29–30. For a contrasting, sympathetic view of S/M, see Edmund White, "Sado Machismo," *New Times*, Jan. 8, 1979; Geoff Mains, *Urban Aboriginals* (San Francisco: Gay Sunshine Press, 1984); Karl Steward, "Knights in Black Leather," *The Advocate*, May 29, 1984; Arnie Kantrowitz, "From the Shadows: Gay Male S/M Activists," *The Advocate*, May 29, 1984.

97. Thomas Garrett, "Not Play, Not Recreation," *New York Native*, March 15–28, 1982. This piece expressed a general feeling among many gay men of the time who wished to connect sex to love and intimacy. This spirit is captured by Neil Allen Marks, "The New Gay Man," *New York Native*, Apr. 12–25, 1982.

98. Ibid.

99. Andrew Holleran, *Dancer from the Dance* (New York: William Morrow, 1978); Larry Kramer, *Faggots* (New York: Random House, 1978).

100. Altman, "Sex: The New Front Line for Gay Politics."

101. Ibid., p. 80.

102. Edmund White, *States of Desire*, p. 37.

103. Craig Johnson, "S/M and the Myth of Mutual Consent," p. 29.

104. Seymour Kleinberg, *Alienated Affections* (New York: St. Martin's Press, 1982), chap. 7.

105. Ibid.

106. See, for example, Yaacov Gershoni, "Overcoming Sexual Compulsion," *New York Native*, Nov. 7–20, 1983; Joe Cockerell, "Sexual Compulsion: Problem or Punishment," *New York Native*, Feb. 11–24, 1985; David Stoven and Jeffrey Leiphart, "Coping with the Kid in the Candy Store," *New York Native*, March 16–28, 1982.

107. Yaacov Gershoni, "Overcoming Sexual Compulsion," p. 28.

108. Thom Willenbecker, "Quick Encounters of the Closest Kind: The Rites and Rituals of Shadow Sex."

109. William Wedin, "Sexual Healing," *New York Native*, July 30–Aug. 12, 1984, p. 26.

5

Beyond Romanticism and Libertarianism: Towards a Pragmatic Sexual Ethic

Sex has moved, in Dennis Altman's words, to the front line of politics in the United States.[1] Conflicts over abortion, teen sex, pornography, AIDS, sex education, homosexuality, public sex, and nonconventional sexualities have stepped into the center of public life. Although these conflicts are often sites for social struggles over, say, gender, race or class, they indicate an underlying moral division in America over sexual values. These sexual conflicts evidence broad disagreements over what sex is and its proper role in personal and social life. They exhibit an opposition between a romantic and a libertarian sexual ethic.

Sexual romantics and libertarians, as we have seen, stand for contrasting sexual regimes. The former connect sex to bonds of affection, intimacy and love. Sex, says romanticists, is a way to express intimate feelings; it always implicates the core inner aspects of the self. It should never be approached casually or with a eye to mere erotic pleasure. Sex should exhibit its essentially intimate nature in its practices. It should be gentle, caring, nurturing, respectful and entail reciprocal obligations. Sex should be person-centered; the individual should always be treated as a full intact person.

A romantic ideology can sanction both heterosexual and homosexual lifestyles, or it can subscribe to an exclusively heterosexual norm. If sex is defined as an intimate expression and bond, why should the gender of the individual matter? Although the logic of romanticism leans towards the removal of sexual object choice as a moral category, romanticists often insist on a heterosexual norm. They appeal to a morality of the sex act. That is, they assume that certain sex acts carry an intrinsic moral meaning. This absolutist standpoint can be articulated in a religious or scientific language. It might be argued, for example, that homosexuality is an illegitimate practice by virtue of violating a religious norm of heterosexuality, or medical-scientific discourses can be appealed to that assert the same norm. Similarly, a romanticist does not need to object, in principle, to public representations of sex, but only to those that encourage one-dimensional hedonistic-expressive or nonromantic sexual meanings. They might argue, however, that since public sexual representations cannot build in enough context and affect to convey a view of sex as an intimate bonding experience, such images ought to be severely limited. This would not, in principle, suggest prudery, but could simply reflect their normative concept of sex. In general, romanticists often fall back upon a narrow morality of the sex act. Those romanticists who argue that sex should be confined to adult, heterosexual, genital-centered, coital, intimate arrangements embrace a conservative sexual ethic whereby the sex act has intrinsic moral significance. Thus nonheterosexual, non-genital centered, nonmonogamous sex is defined as inherently perverse, abnormal, unhealthy, or morally inferior. The more romanticists rely on a morality of the sex act, the more conservative is their sexual ethic. Thus, whereas feminist romanticists like Andrea Dworkin or Kathleen Barry view sex as an intimate bond, they break from a morality of the sex act to the extent that they legitimate same-sex intimacies as long as they are loving. They appeal to a morality of the sex act, however, to the extent that they define, say, hedonistic, body-centered sex for erotic pleasure as alienating or pathological by virtue of deviating from the norm of intimate, loving sexuality. Conservatives like Midge Decter and George Gilder not only rely on a romanticist position to judge sex acts but invoke a morality which excludes virtually all nonheterosexual, nonmarital, noncoital-centered, nonmonagamous sex from the realm of moral legitimacy.

By contrast, a libertarian sexual ethic frames sex as having multiple meanings. Sex may be a medium of pleasure, love or procreation, and sex is said to be legitimate in multiple social settings. Individual choice and consent are considered the guiding norms sanctioning sexual expression. Underpinning a libertarian ethic is a benevolent view of sex. Sex is seen bringing health, joy and happiness to the individual. Although libertarians insist that sex can have multiple meanings, there is an essentialist strain in much contemporary libertarian ideology. Sex is defined, in essence, as a mode of bodily, sensual pleasure. Unfortunately, according to libertarians, dominant social groups impose higher moral purposes on sex (e.g., procreation, love, family, spiritual growth) for social or political reasons. Imbuing sex with heightened social significance produces a cluster of legal and state restrictions and regulations. Sex loses its playful, erotic innocence as it becomes a sign of the moral state of the individual and society. Moreover, as sex accrues these surplus meanings and purposes, rigid moral boundaries crystallize that classify sexual desires and acts into "normal" and "abnormal," and categorize them as good, healthy and right versus bad, sick and wrong. Libertarians intend to free individuals of the excessive social controls that inhibit sexual expression and stigmatize transgressive desires and acts.

Of course, libertarians are not all of one stripe. Some libertarians defend more controls on sexual expression than do others. For example, some will reduce the moral conditions of legitimate sexual expression to a minimum. They legitimate sex in any social exchange where there is consent, regardless of the age of the parties, and without demanding that every exchange entail reciprocity of affection or pleasure. These libertarians argue that so long as sex is freely chosen and consensual, individuals should be free to engage in whatever sexual exchange they choose. Others demand not only mutual consent, but also require that sex be confined to adults in an exchange involving some continuity and commitment. They will argue, for example, that only adults of a certain physical and mental capacity can give consent and are sufficiently mature to be trusting and respectful in a sexual exchange.

Libertarians have abandoned virtually any trace of a morality of the sex act. They assume that sex acts carry no intrinsic moral significance. Any consensual sex act can be morally acceptable depending on its context. It is the moral character of the social exchange which renders sex practices legitimate or not. Thus, sex involving power imbalances or even aggressive, pain-inflicting behavior carries no intrinsic moral meaning. If this behavior occurred in a consensual S/M scene, it would be judged acceptable, whereas if the social exchange involved coercion it would be unacceptable. Particular sex acts involving specific combinations of orifices and organs, or which entail behaviors exhibiting aggressivity, pain, passivity or role-playing carry no intrinsic moral meaning. They receive their moral character from the qualities of the social exchange (e.g., consent, mutuality of affection and pleasure, and expectations), not the qualities of the act.

As a libertarian sex ethic abandons a morality of the sex act, it protests a sexual regime that assigns moral status to sexual and intimate practices on the basis of their inherent meaning. Libertarianism is almost invariably a standpoint of criticism of existing sexual hierarchies. Libertarians aim to free sex from excessive social controls in order to allow individuals to enjoy its pleasurable and expressive possibilities.

In the last two chapters, I have pointed to some merits and weaknesses of each sexual ideology. I argued that the strength of romanticism lie in its attentiveness to the qualitative aspects of sex, i.e., to issues of the emotional and social aspects of the social exchange as well as to considerations of power. This has allowed romanticists to spotlight the perceived dangers of sex. At the same time, this emphasis on judging sexual expression by its qualitative aspects has often led them to be unnecessarily restrictive and intolerant of sexual difference. In this regard, I have praised libertarians for their tolerance of the multiple forms of sexual and intimate expression. Libertarians are to be valued for their role in challenging sexual orthodoxies. But if romanticism is too restrictive, I fault libertarians for failing to provide sufficiently differentiated standards to guide sexual decision making and evaluate sexual practices.

I do not wish to rehearse these arguments. My criticisms of the two sexual ethics, however, begs the question: from what vantage point am I making these judgments? In other words, what set of assumptions guides my moral discourse? And what would a compelling sexual ethic look like in the United States today? Let me spell out what I think should be its guiding assumptions.

Postmodern Premises

I do not believe it is fruitful—or possible—to articulate a universal moral imperative that can guide sexual practice. Claims such as treat others as ends in themselves, or appeals to a utilitarian pleasure/pain calculus, cannot be translated into precise normative guides for specific everyday situations. Moreover, many philosophers and theorists today find these universalistic rationales objectionable on the grounds that they seem unavoidably to mask local, culturally-specific values and interests.[2]

Both romanticists and libertarians appeal to some notion of the nature of sexuality in justifying their ethical standpoint.[3] The former invoke the notion of sex as essentially implicated in intimate, core self-feelings, and on that basis justify the moral imperative that sex be tied to intimate committed social bonds. Moreover, romanticists invoke the notion of a naturally correct sexual order to exclude certain sex acts and intimate lifestyles from the realm of legitimacy. Although there is no conclusive argument one can marshal against such appeals to an absolutist metaphysic which grounds the moral classification of sexual practices, such metaphysical or "foundationalist" discursive strategies have diminishing credibility. From at least the *philosophes*, to Marx, Nietzsche, and Freud to the more recent poststructuralist, postmodern discourses, many of us in the West have concluded that behind constructions of a natural moral order lie ethnocentric projections. Our awareness of social diversity, in particular, the introduction of alternative discursive conventions and perspectives which have accompanied the mainstreaming of marginal groups (e.g., African-Americans, women, lesbians and gay men), has made many of us suspicious of appeals to an absolutist, transcendent standpoint.[4]

In part, libertarians have drawn on the cultural capital of this skepticism. They too, however, make essentialist moves. For example, in arguing against the regulatory apparatus that accompanies the wrapping of sex in higher moral purposes, libertarians often appeal to an essentialist notion that sex is—now and always—simply a bodily, sensual pleasure.[5] They invoke this definition to unburden sex of its restrictive social controls. But this claim is as little redeemable as the romanticist one that sex is, in essence, an intimate bonding experience. How do we know sex is essentially a pleasure? And what does it mean to speak of sex as a pleasure? What does pleasure mean? What model of human experience is presupposed in framing sex as a "bodily, sensual" sensation that does not implicate the self in nonsensual feelings, identities, relational connections? Without pressing this further, assertions about the nature of sex amount to normative claims about how we ought to approach sex. There is, of course, nothing intrinsically wrong with such normative constructions. I take issue, however, with the attempt to disguise these moral claims as simply cognitive ones about the nature of sex. I object to the fact that essentialist appeals to a natural or divine order, made to justify a normative construction, inhibit vital public discussion that would be encouraged by a more pragmatic moral strategy. Finally, I take issue with the attempt to claim universality for what are culturally specific, socially bounded concepts of sex, connected to broader social agendas.

I advocate guidelines for a sexual ethic that repudiates all appeals to a natural, divine, morally given order capable of grounding a particular sexual ethic or moral classification of sex practices and lifestyles. This means abandoning essentialist arguments about the nature of sex that inevitably mask a particular practical-moral sexual agenda. I recommend a sexual ethic that is guided by historicist and pragmatic assumptions.[6] A pragmatic ethical strategy intends less to specify a strict moral casuistry of right and wrong behavior, or a moral hierarchy of feelings, desires, acts, and lifestyles, than the provision of broad guidelines for individual and social regulation.[7]

A pragmatic sexual ethic would grant a minimal respect and legitimacy to the empirical differences in sexual concepts and practices we encounter across social space. Unless we are prepared to exclude all those sexual constructions that differ from "our" own, or to deny difference by interpreting them as minor variations of an identical phenomenon, we must concede that different groups evolve their own sexual culture around which they elaborate coherent lives. If we are to avoid implicating ourselves in a social order that legitimates force to repress significant differences, we must operate under the presumption that empirically given sexual differences carry a certain integrity.

Our starting point should be an understanding of the basic assumptions of a particular society with regard to sexuality, the relationship between sex, identity, and private and public life. The existing sexual and social patterns of the society one is addressing need to be accorded a certain respect and legitimacy; these patterns should be seen as growing out of, and fitted in some useful way, to the lives of the various individuals and groups who share a history, culture and social structural position. A minimal level of respect therefore needs to be accorded existing patterns as they reflect, in part, a creative adaptation to individual or group life.

Respect for the conventions and practices of a society presupposes an understanding of them. More is needed than a passing knowledge based on superficial, external sources. Being knowledgeable presupposes reliance to some extent on the self-descriptions of those who support the conventions and practices in question. We need to grasp the complex ways in which conventions and practices fit into the lives of particular individuals or groups, to see what needs they satisfy in relation to the structural position and history of the individual or group. In a word, being knowledgeable about a practice entails grasping it in relation to the meanings accorded to it by agents in their specific social context. Only by understanding sexual behavior in its context, and relying to some extent on the meanings with which agents imbue their action, can we achieve a minimal level of understanding of social differences.[8]

To the extent that a sexual ethic builds in the norm of being knowledgeable of existing realities, it will inevitably encounter the wide diversity of sexual and intimate patterns in the contemporary United States. We live in a society where there is not simply one sexual culture or lifestyle pattern. There are diverse intimate conventions, arrangements and normative orders depending on considerations of gender, sexual orientation, race, socioeconomic standing, cultural status, religion, age and so on. To take, say, the patterns of middle-class, middle aged, white heterosexual men as normative for white, middle-class, middle aged women or white, middle aged, middle-class, gay-identified men ignores the important differences between these groups that reflect divergent psychological, social and cultural dynamics.

Once we acknowledge this empirical diversity, it can be almost overwhelming. Differences proliferate as combinations of age, race, sexual orientation, gender, class, physical ableness, and ethnicity are seemingly infinite. Of course, a moral discourse does not need to record and take into account every nuanced variation in sexual meaning or behavior. Nor am I denying the presence of important continuities between groups. To the extent that these sexual variations obtain in the same society where there are shared cultural traditions, commonalities among social groups will be evident. There may, for example, be overlap between middle-class, middle aged heterosexual men, women and gay men in the United States today with respect to the importance of free choice, consent and the mutuality of pleasure. Indeed, as socially powerful groups or classes are able to translate their social power into cultural power, they may create a national sexual culture which expresses their own cultural values at the expense of the sexual values of others. Thus, it is probably not far-fetched to argue that since at least the 1930s, and surely from the 1950s, a middle-class liberal culture which emphasized binding sex to love and pleasure has achieved a certain cultural authority in the United States. Yet, it is equally incontestable that while certain broad sexual and intimate values and conventions may have achieved a level of national consensus or legitimacy, their concrete form and articulation continues to vary significantly along the dimensions of gender and sexual orientation and perhaps age, race and class as well. For example, evidence suggests that while gay-identified men in the 1970s shared with the wider culture the importance of linking sex, friendship and romantic love in one, inclusive, intimate relationship, a unique gay subculture emerged that often separated these three components.[9] That is, some gay men of this period looked to friendships for long-term social support and to casual sex with multiple partners for sexual pleasure, while intermittently combining friendship and sex in short-term romantic affairs. In this regard, studies show that a typical gay male pattern in the 1970s subculture involved long-term, intimate, loving relationships that would be desexualized with sexual expression centered in casual sex with multiple partners. The key point is that a sexual ethic needs to be attentive to significant variation, by which I mean differences in meaning, expectations, and intimate arrangements that would have to be considered in understanding any specific population. This is an important issue. In order for a sexual ethic to avoid authoritarian implications, its descriptions and judgments of a group's practices must be expressed in a language-capable of being understood and contested by that group.

The liberal pluralistic premises of my argument would lead me to reject moral standpoints which dismiss a whole sexual culture or way of life. Judgement to the effect that a entire cultural pattern is narcissistic, anomic or immoral for whatever reason (e.g., promiscuous, product of "high" rates of divorce or illegitimacy) do not exhibit the minimal level of respect and knowledgeability of social difference that I take to be a condition of a moral judgment. Dismissive judgments of a whole way of life presuppose some absolutist standpoint that is, in certain key ways, external to the social patterns being evaluated. Such global critiques devalue a way of life to the point of sanctioning its elimination and stigmatizing those who participate in it. Totalizing critiques strike me as authoritarian and dangerous. By failing to accord any legitimacy to a social pattern, and thus failing to grasp its adaptive aspects, these absolutist moral judgments function as dangerous hegemonic strategies.

Both libertarians and romanticists are suspect in this regard. Romanticists appeal to an essentialist concept of sex to judge current sexual patterns while largely ignoring the social context, social position, particular history and indigenous local meanings of those whose conventions sharply deviate from the stated ideal. Romanticists propose, on the grounds that sex is, in essence, an intimate social bond and an expression of the core inner self, that those individuals, groups, or subcultures that deviate from this normative concept are psychologically, socially, or morally inferior if not outright sick, perverse, sinful, or dangerous. Thus, romanticists tend to see in hedonistic-expressive, body-centered sex, whether expressed in pornographic representations, casual sex or in S/M sex, little more than psychological or social pathology. Typically, the self-descriptions of the agents are either ignored or discounted. To the extent that they are considered at all they are dismissed as expressions of self-deception, bad faith, false consciousness, or male-identification. Thus, when feminist romanticists encounter lesbian S/M practitioners who describe their practices as consensual and valued for their spiritual, health, and psychologically releasing qualities, they invariably ignore these descriptions or discount them by characterizing them as self-deceptions, e.g., instances of male-identification.

I recommend a sexual ethic that acknowledges a minimal level of respect for current social patterns. This implies little more than the assumption that a given sexual and intimate pattern crystallized in part as an adaptive response by agents, for whom these practices are meaningful. Unless we want to deny that individuals are purposive, decision making agents, capable of being knowledgeable, insightful and trustworthy in their decisions, we must accord existing patterns a level of integrity. We must begin, then, with the forms of life that moral agents have created. This means acknowledging observable differences and according sexual variation at least a minimal level of legitimacy. A pragmatic sexual ethic renounces the task of making global judgments. It strives only to provide guidelines. Its judgments will be tentative, and somewhat ambiguous; it will offer less an imperative or a moral calculus than broad guidelines that individuals draw on to weigh various considerations and make judgments. It seeks less to impose a moral order from the high ground of expertise or moral authority than to contribute to an ongoing conversation about private and public life.

Choice and Responsibility: Normative Guidelines for a Pragmatic Sexual Ethic

I have put forward certain principles or, more correctly, urged certain normative guidelines: respect for existing patterns and the acknowledgment of social differences, knowledge of the practices to be judged, reliance on the self-understanding of those being addressed, and abandonment of global judgments. These guidelines do not, however, provide us with norms to assess our conventions or practices. The question remains: what standards or norms should guide our decisions and judgments?

What kinds of general norms or standards can allow us to respect sexual and social diversity while providing limits that reflect the real dangers sex carries for many contemporary Americans? The libertarians provide us with a beginning: consent. We—contemporary adult Americans—would agree, I think, that no matter what our disagreements over particular sexual practices and arrangements, a necessary condition of their moral legitimacy is that they be based on free choice, and that the parties to the exchange should have voluntarily agreed to it.

Of course, free choice and consent is, in light of the traditions of Marxism, Freudianism, feminism and poststructuralism, suspect. Thus, some radical feminists argue that lesbian S/M cannot be consensual despite practitioners self-descriptions to the contrary. If, as some radical feminists assume, women value sex that is nurturing, tender and person-oriented, then women who practice S/M are by this logic either not women, or are not acting like women. These women are said to be male-identified, to have so thoroughly internalized male controlled gender codes that they reenact them without realizing that they reproduce their own oppression. Thus, critics of lesbian S/M say that consent is absent in these practices since in a male-dominated society women are under the control of men whose power extends to shaping gender images in a self-serving way. There is, in this account, no consent given to lesbian S/M, given radical feminist assumptions regarding male domination, female and male sexuality and S/M as a gender dynamic. Male identification or some form of false consciousness render apparent acts of consent into residues of power dynamics.

Of course, this type of argument could be applied to virtually any practice, that is one of its weaknesses. Libertarians could rejoin that the same accusation of false consciousness is true for heterosexual marriage or lesbian "unions." Straight or lesbian women may appear to consent to marriage or a lesbian union, but in fact they can be seen as enacting the dominant sexual, intimate romantic code which, it might be argued, contributes to reinforcing male dominance, heterosexism or a restrictive intimate ideal. One can appeal, then, to structural or cultural factors which involve no reference to individual choice to explain heterosexual marriage or lesbian unions as easily as S/M.[10] Indeed, to the extent that our culture has been formed by traditions such as Marxism, feminism, Freudianism, and nonindividualistic social science, the assumption of free choice and consent is easily put into doubt. We can always explain away individual consent with structural conditions; we can always trace consent to power effects. Moreover, if we assume that power imbalances rules out consent, is there any intimate social exchange that can be said to not involve coercion?

I believe that we need a concept of consent to function as a general norm. The notion of consent provides one basis for a very general moral classification of sexual practices that would seem to be consistent with widely shared liberal cultural traditions in the United States. For example, an appeal to a notion of consent allows us to proscribe acts of sexual coercion such as sexual abuse and rape. Similarly, the norm of consent renders sex between adults and children illegitimate, even if the issue of the age of consent can be legitimately contested.

I believe a concept of consent can be defended if it is abstracted from its individualistic contractarian context. If we accept the premise that to understand and judge sexual practices we must place them in their indigenous setting and grasp the meanings they have for the acting agents, we can assess whether a specific act involves consent. This will not typically be a simple judgment, our actions are never a matter of absolute freedom or coercion. Attributing consent to a practice would be, as I see it, a matter of determining whether there are any compelling reasons to believe that an agent made a decision in which there was an understanding of the meaning of the act, and the possibility of choosing an alternative action. For example, to the extent that a woman is able to say why she married, and that her reasons make sense in light of her social and cultural status, we would have some grounds to describe her behavior as consensual. The description of her behavior as consensual would be enhanced if we could demonstrate that she had alternatives available. If we could make a plausible case that this woman could have chosen to remain single or cohabit with a man or a woman, the claim that her decision to stay married was voluntary would gain considerable credibility.

Attributing consent to an act does not mean that we surrender critical judgement. As I said above, sexual and social practices in general are neither pure acts of choice nor coercion. Consent, to say it otherwise, is not synonymous with free choice or absolute freedom. Individual choice always occurs in a context of constraint, stemming from internal processes (e.g., biology, personality structure, self-identity) and external factors (e.g., social position, cultural codes), all of which place definite limits on an individual's ability to exercise choice. A social analyst would be well advised to examine how, say, class or gender dynamics structure—and restrict—individual intentions and behavior. To assess whether and to what extent consent is given by (say) women who marry and stay married, it would not be sufficient to establish intentionality or choice. We would need to consider those factors external to individual willfulness that *constrain* choice, e.g., women's economic position, the realities of violence and harassment, and cultural constructions that bind femininity to the roles of wife and mother. Ascertaining structural constraints to behavior is in no way a denial of individual agency and the possibility of consent. Invoking constraining factors does not fully explain away an individual's mediating role—as a reflective, knowledgeable, object-defining agent—in action.[11] I will not, however, try to ground this position by some appeal to the nature of human action or social process. I appeal only to the moral implications of my argument. To invoke structural, cultural, or biological factors to explain away individual intentionality and choice would be to implicate oneself in an authoritarian social order. To project a social order as a product of what are, in the end, unconscious processes is to deny individual responsibility and reduces humans to objects. It is these moral and, broadly speaking, ideological implications of the critique of consent to which I appeal in contesting them.

Defending consent as one normative standard that guides sexual choice does not mean it alone is sufficient. We have already seen the limits of a narrow ethic of consent. Consent and its opposite, coercion, are not absolutes. Practices cannot, typically, be described by either both. The acute social analyst can, at best, examine the conditions limiting choice but to the extent that intentionality can be identified and alternative courses of action reasonably be claimed to be available, we must attribute some degree of consent. The alternative is to endorse a position where, in virtually all situations, the intentional aspect of action can be explained away. We therefore end in endorsement of an epistemological position that withdraws from individuals their ability to be subjects, i.e., to make choices and to assume responsibility for their acts. In denying individual agency we implicitly endorse authoritarian social and political values.

Consent is, in my view, a necessary element of a sexual ethic in the contemporary United States. Ascertaining consent allows, as I have noted, only for very provisional and modest ethical judgments. As a normative guide, consent is further limited in that it does not provide moral guidelines for a range of everyday situations, practices and conflicts that must be addressed by a sexual ethic. For example, decisions relating to the legitimacy of public sexual expression and what kinds of expression, conflicts over the morality of body-centered, hedonistic sexual practices, which entail a heightened sexual objectification and instrumental orientation, disagreements about the appropriateness and the norms of sexual expression for teenagers, and conflicts over the morality of casual sex or nonmonogamy are not given moral clarification by invoking the norm of consent. Furthermore, this norm does not adequately address the various risks sex has for different populations. A woman who has to decide between the potential pleasures of sex and the risks of pregnancy, sexually transmitted disease or stigmatization as a "loose or lustful woman" will find no clarification in an appeal to the concept of consent. A libertarian sexual ethic that stipulates the legitimacy of sex so long as there is mutual consent neglects vast domains of everyday practice that are implicated in an apparatus of moral regulation.

If libertarians—with their focus on the formal aspects of the social exchange of sex—offer the concept of consent as the chief normative standard, romanticists—with their emphasis on the qualitative aspects of sex—look instead to the quality of the exchange. Just as the libertarian's minimalistic ethic fails to provide sufficiently differentiated ethical guidelines, romanticists—as the mirror image of the libertarians—have been found wanting for being too restrictive. Many romanticists wish to limit legitimate sexual expression to ongoing, intimate, loving relationships in which sex itself responds to the whole individual and exhibits the intimate qualities of the social bond. But this substantive ethic inevitably has the consequence of creating a vast category of deviant, stigmatized sexual and intimate practices. In some conservative romantic discourses virtually all nonmonogamous, nonromantic, body-centered-hedonistic, casual, and homoerotic intimate arrangements are proscribed. Yet we need, I believe, to retain from romanticism something of its more discriminating, fuller moral language.

This, then, is the dilemma: how to arrive at a sexual ethic that preserves what Gayle Rubin calls "benign sexual variation," yet articulates norms that allow us to make the kinds of moral judgments that are routinely made in everyday life.[12] The libertarian concept of consent allows for "benign sexual variation" but it does not provide sufficient closure or grounds to make the kinds of decisions that have to be made. I wish to propose that the concept of responsibility might be able to provide further moral guidelines while respecting sexual diversity.

I believe that the concept of sexual responsibility has strategic value as a way of articulating a sexual ethic that affirms variation, yet offers standards to limit choice. Romanticist strategies appeal to a morality of the sex act to limit sexual choice; they argue that sex is in essence an intimate act and therefore that this essence should be exhibited in its expressive qualities. The concept of responsibility makes no such appeal. It is, like the idea of consent, a strictly formal, relational concept. It does not, moreover, look to the qualitative aspects of sex practices to articulate limits. As a normative standard, it is, accordingly, less susceptible to creating stigmatized practices, desires, identities, and communities. The concept of responsibility preserves sexual variation yet has the capacity, I will argue, to limit choice and to serve as a useful guide to sexual decision making and social regulation.

The concept of responsibility is, to be sure, a rather slippery one. The word seems to have two implications in current usage in the United States. It refers to the notion of an individual who is obligated to others by virtue of occupying a specific social role (e.g., a father's duty to his children, or a teacher's duty to his or her students). An individual may also be said to act "responsibly" when the anticipated impact of an action on the welfare of others is taken into account. I take the latter meaning as the basic, more inclusive one. Responsibility in the sense of fulfilling social role obligations assumes that agents act as they do because they have in mind others' interests. Thus, responsibility suggests an awareness that what one does influences the world of objects—human and otherwise—and that one has a moral obligation to consider these consequences in deciding on whether and how to act. Deployed as a normative standard, responsibility implies a pragmatic ethical standpoint. Acts or practices carry no intrinsic moral meaning but get their moral significance from their consequences or impact on the individual, society, and the world of natural and cultural objects. This means assessing the morality of acts by situating them in their specific social historical context, and analyzing them not only in terms of whether they include choice or intentionality, but in terms of these consequences. The concept of responsibility, like the idea of consent, compels us to view acts in relation to the meanings of those engaged in the acts, as well as in terms of their effects.

If we are to evaluate the morality of an act by its consequences, then we need to raise the question of how we evaluate behavior, since any single act can generate a multitude of consequences. In principle, all the possible consequences of the act should be considered that are at least likely to be meaningful in light of the cultural traditions of the society. This includes considering the effects on the physical, psychological, and social condition of the agent. For example, in the case of casual sex one might reasonably ask, as many individuals undoubtedly do, how might sex outside an intimate bond affect me? I might consider potential health risks or risks of violence. How might such behavior affect me personally or emotionally? Will I feel shame, adventurous or empowered? How might it effect me socially, e.g., how, if at all, will it impact on my relationships? Will it create positive social ties, or disappointments and antagonism? What kinds of values and social ideals of individual and social life am I promoting in this behavior? An ethic of responsibility would also entail assessing the consequences of an act on others affected. This would involve the same considerations as above, e.g., the act's effect on others—physically, psychologically, and socially. The focus on others should center, however, on the potential harm of an agent's action. An individual should not assume that what one judges to be beneficial will be similarly assessed by others. By focusing on the harmful impact of an act, there is, at least, a greater possibility that an agent will acknowledge and preserve whatever difference exists between the other and oneself. Thus, I would urge that, in assessing the consequences of behavior for others, the moral agent focus primarily on the act's potential harm.

If, as I have argued, we evaluate the morality of an act by its consequences, from whose vantage point do we assess the effects? The moral assessment of practices will vary depending upon the vantage point of the moral agent. In light of whose values or interests should the agent (or critic) assess the morality of sexual behavior? It seems reasonable that in assessing the morality of a practice, the agent will initially consider its consequences in light of his or her own values and interests. Yet this represents a limited moral standpoint and contains an authoritarian logic: a logic of identity which may easily

translate into one of domination. The moral agent needs to acknowledge sexual and social diversity; individuals and groups hold different
values, interests and standpoints towards the world. The moral agent
should consider the standpoint of the other as potentially different
from his or her self and evaluate the consequences of behavior from
that vantage point as well. The consequences of behavior for different
groups or populations who are differently situated or socially positioned with regard, say, to class, gender, sexual orientation, or race,
would perhaps vary considerably. For example, casual sex may have
had a set of meanings and consequences for gay men in the 1970s that
was very different from those for heterosexual women. There may be
further variations in the social and moral significance of casual sex
between white middle-class Americans and working-class African-
Americans. To assess the morality of sexual practices I would argue
that we need to understand the meaning and consequences of that act
for those individuals or populations implicated by that act.

The concept of responsibility is, as I use the term, a complex relational one. It implies neither a particular concept of sex nor a specific
substantive sexual ethic; nor does it authorize any particular sexual
practice, e.g., heterosexuality, marriage, or monogamy. Responsibility, like the concept of consent, requires that we analyze practices in
their immediate social setting being attentive to the meanings the act
has for various agents and its multiple consequences. We are speaking
of a set of guidelines which individuals can use in making decisions
about sexual practices and which we—as social analysts or moral
critics—can use to assess the morality of social rules and norms that
regulate sexual expression and practice. From this pragmatic standpoint, notwithstanding acts in which coercion is obvious (e.g., rape)
or irresponsibility evident (e.g., an agent knowingly engaging in sex
acts that carry a high-risk of transmitting sexual disease to an unsus-
pecting partner), most sexual practices will partake of degrees of
moral legitimacy or illegitimacy. The moral agent—individual decision maker or critic—will not be able to appeal to the concepts of
consent and responsibility to legitimate particular sex acts or intimate lifestyles in some simple global way. Rather, he or she could
appeal to these formal norms to serve as moral guides aiding individuals to make choices in light of conflicting moral claims.

The sexual ethic I am proposing departs from a substantive ethic
that is typically connected to an essentialist concept of sex and absolutist values. From my postmodern, pragmatic standpoint, particular
sex acts and intimate arrangements carry no intrinsic moral significance. Acts of moral judgment will take the form of assessing the
personal and social consequences of various practices or conventions.

Such calculations will in turn appeal to the values and cultural traditions that shape moral life. The morality of sexual practices should then be almost always a matter of conflict or contestation. Change with respect to sexual morality would be expected as our understandings and power balances change. This flux and fluidity of moral life would be, to some extent, limited by the retained norms of consent and responsibility, which would serve to constrain or circumscribe the range of rhetoric that could be appealed to in order to legitimate particular practices.

A brief illustration will further clarify my position. Take the case of "cross-generational" sex, in which the younger partner is a minor or below the age of consent (which varies from state to state). A substantive ethic might proscribe this practice by appealing to a medical discourse which defines this behavior as intrinsically indicative of a type of perversion or abnormality—pedophilia. I would withhold judgment until I was more knowledgeable about the particular context in which such practices took place. From my vantage point, it would be of critical importance to know, for example, the age of the persons involved, their gender, the kind of relationship they had, the particular sex acts involved, and, of course, the broader social conventions governing sexual practices.[13]

Let us assume that the exchange was between a contemporary American adult aged 40 and an 8-year-old child. I would ask, first of all, whether this was an exchange where mutual consent is possible. Presuming the absence of physical coercion, is it reasonable, given American conventions, to assume that an 8-year-old could consent to a sexual exchange with an adult? It is certainly possible, I would argue, for an 8-year-old to have an understanding of sex in the sense of involving certain acts and meanings (e.g., pleasure, play, intimacy). Yet, a suspicion about the legitimacy of this practice would also be reasonable, since American conventions do not typically entail expectations of sexual knowledge and behavior (beyond autoerotic behavior) at this age. We could, in other words, legitimately contest the claim that a child of 8 could be sufficiently knowledgeable about sexual meanings to understand what his or her behavior meant. We could be even more doubtful about this child's capacity to choose an alternative action, i.e. refuse sex. Given the authority adults carry in a child's world in the United States, most Americans would, I think, consider it reasonable to cast serious doubt on the premise that a child could act in an autonomous fashion. In other words, the authority adults have over children would be considered likely to render any decision a child made about a sexual exchange at least, in part, a decision made out of fear, a desire to please or as a result of a child's perception that the behavior was expected and natural. It would, for example, be difficult to imagine a child being able to refuse sex if the adult soliciting it was, say, a family member, friend, or an adult known to the child in a role of authority (e.g., a teacher or doctor). It is not the power imbalance per se between the adult and child that raises serious doubts about the child's ability to consent but the imbalance in an exchange in which reasonable doubt already exists about the child's capacity to act intentionally, to understand the meaning of this behavior both for him/herself and for the adult partner. If the issue of consent left any doubt about the legitimacy of this sexual exchange, applying the norm of mutual responsibility leaves none. Even if we could somehow defend the notion that an 8-year-old child could give consent, we could not reasonably expect such a youngster to understand the manifold consequences of sexual behavior and take these into account in deciding if, and how, to act. We could not reasonably expect a contemporary American child to be knowledgeable with respect to issues of sexually transmitted disease and risks of physical or mental harm, or expect a child to understand how sex might elicit complex feelings of aggressivity or intimacy, or how it carries levels of meaning he or she could not possibly make sense of. This argument would apply regardless of whether it was the adult or the child who initiated the sexual exchange. Some man/boy love advocates have argued in this regard that often it is the boy who intends and initiates sex or intimacy with an adult man.[14] The question of who initiates sex is irrelevant to the extent that the boy is incapable of acting responsibly, i.e., understanding and assessing the possible consequences of his behavior for himself and his adult partner.

I would not conclude from the above that all cross-generational sex between an adult and a minor is illegitimate. I do not subscribe to a type of sexual ethic that classifies particular sex acts as right or wrong or normal and abnormal according to absolutist sexual values; thus, I could entertain the possibility of a legitimate exchange between an adult and a minor. What if, for example, the exchange involved a 15-year-old boy and a 28-year-old girl? Given current American conventions and practices, it would be reasonable to believe that a 15-year-old boy understands complex sexual meanings. We could, I think, reasonably assume that such a boy could refuse sex with a 28-year-old woman without serious fears of reprisal. Furthermore, a boy of 15 could be expected to grasp the manifold consequences of sex and to assess his behavior in light of these. Thus, a somewhat cogent case could be made for cross-generational sex between an adult and a minor.

Of course, as the age differential between the adult and the minor narrowed so that it was no longer cross-generational—say, between a 15-year-old and a 18-year-old—the possibility of the exchange realizing the conditions of mutual consent and responsibility would be further enhanced. Whatever legitimacy could be accorded such an exchange would be provisional until our knowledge of the arrangement was also enhanced. If, say, we learned that the boy was financially dependent on the adult woman, or that he has learning disabilities, his capacity to choose an alternative action or act responsibly by assessing the consequences of his behavior would be called into question. Moreover, even in the absence of these complicating factors, legitimate doubts could be raised about the ability of a young American teenager to understand and assess the potential psychological, social and physical consequences of his sexual behavior. How emotionally and intellectually capable is a young teenager of understanding the effects of sex on himself and his partner? How able is he or she to take precautions to prevent psychological, physical or social harm? My point is that questions of legitimacy or normative rightness with respect to cross-generational sex which involves a minor will often involve contested claims.

Questions of legitimacy apply to sex between teenagers and, indeed, between young adults, though sex among this population has achieved a high degree of acceptance in post-World War II United States. The issue here is, as I see it, less a matter of consent since, except for cases of rape, teenagers can reasonably be said to act with intentionality and understanding of their behavior. The ability of teenagers, especially younger ones, to assume sexual responsibility is, to my mind, much more contestable. We would, I think, need to concede that this is no less true of many adults, as is evidenced by, say, the rates of illegitimacy among adults or the failure of many divorced or separated men to provide financial and parental support to the children they have fathered. Surveys and ethnographic studies of teen sex relate a mixed tale of sexual responsibility, of boys and girls who clearly do not act with adequate sexual knowledge or understanding of the manifold consequences of sex for themselves and others. Yet, these same documents also show young people who grasp the risks and benefits of sex and who can be insightful with respect to the consequences of their behavior.[15] To the extent that we have sufficient reason to believe that teenagers can grasp the multiple meanings of sex, analyze its effects and make reasonably informed decisions about sexual practices, I would defend their right to have sex. That does not mean that I would give blanket legitimation, or assign equal value, to all teenage sexual exchanges not involving coercion. The following considerations would favor extreme caution in extending any general legitimation to teen sex. Teens are typically not psychologically, socially and economically independent; they often do not have access to important sexual information and contraceptive devices; and they will frequently not be in a position to deal effectively with the unexpected consequences of sex.

From a policy standpoint, however, given the realities of teen culture and the ability of teens in general to give consent and act responsibly, I would oppose policies that favor a norm of abstinence. A certain level of respect for current practices is, as I have maintained, an essential condition of a sexual ethic. Calling for abstinence is inconsistent with the conventions of teen culture as well as those of the broader mainstream. I would recommend, as an essential starting point, that policy makers understand teen sex practices and accord them a level of legitimacy. What is needed, I would think, is sex education courses that relate directly to the teen subculture, i.e., that provide information, encourage both sexual and social skills, and clarify choices and their consequences in ways that are meaningful to them. In addition, I would defend making birth control and contraceptive information available to teenagers so that their choices can be safer and more responsible.

Conclusion

Every society sets out rules regulating sexual expression. These rules tell us when to have sex, where, with whom, and how frequently. They regulate sexual representations as well as private behavior. These sexual rules presuppose basic ontologies of sex, i.e., definitions of sex that relate it to gender, self-identity and public life. These sexual concepts and rules are embodied in law, public representations, medical and scientific institutions as well as popular culture, everyday maxims and custom; they amount to a sexual regime. This sexual regime inevitably privileges particular desires and acts while disapproving and penalizing others. Individuals whose chief practices are transgressive will suffer while conformity will confer legitimacy.

Sexual romanticism and libertarianism project two variant regimes. The former projects a moral hierarchy in which desires, acts and lifestyles are evaluated in terms of their conformity to an intimate, loving, monogamous, genital-centered, privatistic, adult sexual life. Romanticism proscribes practices that involve, for example, public sex, casual exchanges, multiple partners, and body-centered hedonistic values. Romanticism creates a vast culture of stigmatized desires, identities, networks and even communities. Its intolerance of sexual variation is what libertarians challenge. Libertarians aim to defend "benign sexual variation" by abandoning a morality centered on the intrinsic moral nature of sex acts. They aim to expand legitimate sexual expression or to reduce state and social controls, by advocating for a minimalistic ethic: sexual exchanges acquire legitimacy to the extent that they are mutually consensual and perhaps entail mutual pleasure or affection—though this factor is almost never theorized. Libertarians may aim to defend transgressive sexualities that they see as socially innocuous in order to diminish sexual oppression, but their minimalistic ethic fails to provide useful guidelines for sexual decision making or sufficiently differentiated norms to assess sexual rules.

My sympathy lies with the libertarian defense of sexual pluralism. Individuals should have wide latitude in choosing their sexual practices and intimate arrangements so long as coercion is absent. However, I would argue that the concept of choice alone is insufficient as a moral guide. Libertarians tend to invoke a highly individualistic liberal concept of free choice to legitimate practices. Unfortunately, this is dubious in light of the theoretical critique of liberal individualism, e.g., Marxism, feminism, structural or cultural social science. Moreover, libertarians' implicit individualistic liberalism is betrayed by their failure to incorporate into their moral reflection a communitarian concern with the relation of individuals to one another and to a broader social community. I have sought to remedy the liberal individualistic bias in this sexual ethic by introducing the concept of responsibility. As I use the term, it presupposes viewing the individual as implicated in a social community to whom he or she bears obligations. My effort to sketch a socially rich notion of responsibility represents the communitarian aspect of my standpoint. Sex should be viewed not simply as entailing a self-relation, but relations to others and to the community with whom we each share a common world.

The pragmatic formalistic sexual ethic I have proposed attempts to retain the strong defense of choice and pluralism of the libertarians while abandoning the naive notion that a sexual ethic can address only the private individualistic aspects of sex expression. Libertarians would, of course, be the last to deny the political and public character of sexuality. However, they do not, in my view, incorporate this insight into their theorization of a sexual ethic. A compelling sexual ethic must, it seems to me, address sex's implications in a complex web of social and political connections.

My proposal for a pragmatic formal ethic intends to provide a socially richer and more useful moral language than does libertarianism. I wish to suggest rules for decision making and to offer a critical vantage point from which to assess the existing sexual regime. My aim is to preserve the expanded notion of choice and diversity of the libertarians without surrendering a critical standpoint. This requires, it seems to me, a pragmatic, formalistic ethic which is unlikely to produce the discredited, stigmatized identities characteristic of a substantive ethic that relies on some sexual ontology.

Notes

1. Dennis Altman, "Sex: The New Front Line for Gay Politics," *Socialist Review*, 65 (Sept.–Oct. 1982).

2. Richard Rorty, *Philosophy and the Mirror of Nature* (Princeton University Press, 1979), *Consequences of Pragmatism* (Minneapolis: University of Minnesota Press, 1982), and *Objectivity, Relativism and Truth* (Cambridge: Cambridge University Press, 1991); Bernard Williams, *Ethics and the Limits of Philosophy* (Cambridge: Harvard University Press, 1985). *Relativism, Cognitive and Moral*, eds. Michael Krausz and Jack Meiland (Notre Dame: University of Notre Dame Press, 1982).

3. Cf. Ann Ferguson, *Blood at the Root* (London: Pandora Press, 1989).

4. The argument against foundationalist justificatory strategies is occurring in a number of disciplines. The work of poststructuralists like Derrida or Foucault, as well as the American pragmatist Richard Rorty, has been pivotal. Several anthologies have materialized which provide easier access to some of the key debates. See, for example, *After Philosophy*, eds. Kenneth Baynes et al. (Cambridge: MIT Press, 1987); *Social Science as Moral Inquiry*, eds. Norma Haan et al. (New York: Columbia University Press, 1983); *Feminism/Postmodernism*, ed. Linda Nicholson (New York: Routledge, 1990) and *Postmodernism and Social Theory*, eds. Steven Seidman and David Wagner (Cambridge: Basil Blackwell, 1991).

5. See, for example, Michael Foucault, *The History of Sexuality:* Vol. 1, *An Introduction* (New York: Pantheon, 1978), p. 157.

6. Cf. Jeffrey Weeks, *Sexuality and Its Discontents* (London: Routledge, 1985); Gayle Rubin, "Thinking Sex: Notes for a Radical Theory of the Politics of Sexuality," in *Pleasure and Danger*, ed. Carole Vance (Boston: Routledge, 1984).

7. My argument runs parallel to that developed by Jeffrey Weeks. Weeks describes his position with the term "radical pluralism." "Its aim is to provide guidelines for decisions rather than new absolute values, but two inter-related elements are crucial: the emphasis on choice and relations rather than acts,

and the emphasis on meaning and context rather than external rules of correctness." See *Sexuality and Its Discontents,* p. 218; also see his *Sexuality* (London: Tavistock, 1986). Abandoning a morality of the sex act, Weeks intends to assess the morality of sex by understanding the meaning agents give to their acts in specific social settings. The moral lens focuses on individual choice, contextual meaning and the character of the social exchange. While Weeks wishes to defend human sexual diversity by this strategy, he insists that this approach does not amount to libertarianism since by attending to power dynamics and social constraints on choice he can provide a critical standpoint. In the course of applying his radical pluralistic approach to public sex or pornography, I find a finely nuanced understanding of these phenomena but the only norm he appeals to in order to register reservations is that of choice or consent. While Weeks urges that we grasp the meaning of sex acts by situating them in their context and relating them to the intentions of the agent, only the issue of choice versus constraint guides his moral assessment. The pragmatic concern with the consequences of the act plays no role in his moral standpoint. But why should we concern ourselves only with whether agents choose or were constrained to act as they did while ignoring the moral implications of the effects of their action?

8.   See Pat Califia, *Sapphistry* (Tallahassee, Florida: Naiad Press, 1980), p. 107. Also see the recent literature on homosexuality which makes the point regarding the variation in the meaning of same-sex behavior as a central part of its constructivist approach. See, for example, Michel Foucault, *The History of Sexuality;* Jonathan Katz, *Gay/Lesbian Almanac* (New York: Harper & Row, 1983); *The Making of the Modern Homosexual,* ed. Kenneth Plummer (London: Hutchinson, 1981); Jeffrey Weeks, *Coming Out* (London: Quartet, 1977).

9.   See my *Romantic Longings,* chap. 6.

10.   Cf. Pat Califia, "Man/Boy Love and the Lesbian Movement," in *The Age Taboo,* ed. Daniel Tsang (Boston: Alyson,) p. 138; Rubin, "Thinking Sex," p. 304.

11.   Cf. Jeffrey Alexander, *Theoretical Logic in Sociology,* Vol. 1, (Berkeley: University of California Press, 1982) and Anthony Giddens, *The Constitution of Society* (Berkeley: University of California Press, 1984).

12.   Gayle Rubin, "Thinking Sex," p. 283.

13.   I have profited from the discussion by Jeffrey Weeks, *Sexuality and Its Discontents,* chap. 9; Pat Califia, "The Age of Consent; An Issue and its Effects on the Gay Movement," *The Advocate,* 30 Oct. 1980; Kate Millet, "Beyond Politics? Children and Sexuality," in *Pleasure and Danger,* ed. Carole Vance; Kenneth Plummer, "Images of Paedophilia," in *Love and Attraction,* eds. M. Cook and G. Wilson (Oxford: Pergamon, 1979) and "The Paedophile's Progress: A View From Below," in *Perspectives on Paedophilia,* ed. Brian Taylor (London: Batsford Academic and Educational LTD, 1981). In particular, the essays in *The Age Taboo,* ed. Daniel Tsang.

14.   See *The Age Taboo,* ed. Daniel Tsang; Tom O'Carroll, *Paedophilia* (Lon-

don: Peter Owen, 1980); *Semiotext(e) Special: Large Type Series: Loving Boys* (Summer 1980).

15. My understanding of teen sexual beliefs and values in postwar America relies upon a range of survey data available from the 1970s through the 1980s. In particular, I have found helpful the following works: Melvin Zelnik and John Kantner, "Sexual Activity, Contraceptive Use and Pregnancy Among Metropolitan-Area Teenagers: 1971–1979, *Family Planning Perspectives*, 12, (Sept.–Oct.); Melvin Zelnik, John Kantner and Kathleen Ford, *Sex and Pregnancy in Adolescence* (Beverly Hill, Ca.: Sage, 1981); Anne Pebley, "Teenage Sex," *Family Planning Perspectives* 14 (July/August 1982); Robert Coles and Geoffrey Stokes, *Sex and the American Teenager* (New York: Harper & Row, 1985). As a corrective to the somewhat limited views of teen sex available from surveys, I recommend ethnographic studies such as Sharon Thompson, "Search for Tomorrow: On Feminism and the Reconstruction of Teen Romance," in *Pleasure and Danger*, ed. Carole Vance; Joyce Canaan, "Why a 'Slut' is a 'Slut': Cautionary Tales of Middle-Class Teenage Girls' Morality," in *Symbolizing America*, ed. Hervé Varenne (Lincoln, Neb.: University of Nebraska Press, 1986. See the essays in *Changing Boundaries*, ed. E. Allgeies and N. McCormick (Palo Alto, Ca.: Mayfield, 1983). Also, although he studies a slightly older population, Michael Moffatt's *Coming of Age in New Jersey* New Brunswick: Rutgers University Press, 1989), an ethnography of American college culture, offers some wonderful insights.

Epilogue

Consensus about the meaning of sex and the moral boundaries of legitimate sexual expression has been seriously fractured in post-World War II America. Although postwar prosperity and the trend towards social liberalization may have promoted anomic strains in our sexual culture, the elaboration of a youth culture and the rise of the new social movements in the 1960s has played a key role in shaping current conflicts over sexual meanings and morality. From the feminist challenge to dominant images of female sexuality, to lesbians and gay men framing homosexuality as both a natural lifestyle alternative and a social identity, to the countercultural wish to eroticize everyday life, the exclusive legitimacy of a heterosexual, romantic, marital, monogamous norm has been challenged. The postwar period witnessed the proliferation of diverse, often conflicting, sexual discourses and lifestyles. Such conflicts intensified from the mid-1970s on as marginalized communities (e.g., feminists, gays, the counterculture) began to enter the mainstream and meet with resistance.

The sexual struggles of our time do not neatly fold into dualisms of young versus old or Left versus Right. Thus, while feminists generally contest constructions of female sexuality that, say, privilege vaginal orgasm, they are internally divided over the meaning and role of pleasure, over the legitimacy of public sexual representations, and the link between sexual and gender politics. Nor can we reduce current conflicts in the United States to a battle between the forces of sexual freedom and repression, as it is the very meaning of choice, expression, restraint, diversity, and so on that is being contested.

Current sexual conflicts cannot be reduced to struggles over, say, gender or class.[1] The battles over defining and regulating sexual desire and practice are, to be sure, linked to struggles around gender, race, class or party politics, but they cannot be reduced to them. Conflicts over the meaning and legitimacy of homosexuality, or over what forms of desire and sex acts are permissible, at what age and in what kind of social setting, are battles on the front lines of sexual and not gender or class politics. Moreover, sex—like gender, ethnicity or religion—has become a sphere of identity for Americans. We define ourselves as heterosexual, homosexual, swingers, sadomasochists, man/boy lovers, fetishists. For some of us, sexuality is a domain of community building—as it has been for lesbians and gay men and to a lesser extent for swingers or some S/M practitioners. To this extent sexuality must be analyzed in its own terms, as having its own social dynamics, cultural codes and politics. A political sociology of sex would need to evolve its own vocabularies to explain the formation of pleasures, intimacies, sexual identities and communities, and to comprehend the struggles over sexual definitions and norms that occur in diverse media and in the legal, medical, scientific and governmental institutions.[2] I have not tried to provide such a political sociology of sex. Instead, I have sought to outline some very broad ideological conflicts in contemporary America. I intended to engage these discursive struggles as a participant to this moral and political conflict.

I have argued that underlying many of the social conflicts around sexuality in the contemporary United States—the struggles around pornography, abortion, homosexuality, cohabitation, divorce, and teenage, cross-generational, public and nonromantic sex—is a conflict between two broad concepts of sexual meaning and ethics. American's are divided between a romantic and a libertarian sexual ethic, two constructions which serve as master frameworks through which Americans think about sexuality. They represent antagonistic sexual ideologies. Romanticists frame sex as implicating the core inner self; they project sex as a sphere of love which should entail long-term intimate bonds. They are critical of those who view sex as a mere pleasurable or self-expressive act since this is said to reduce individuals to mere objects. Not only is this instrumentalization of the self said to do harm to the individual, but it is presumed to weaken intimate ties. Libertarians, on the other hand, defend the multiple meanings of sex, although many of them frame sex as a bodily pleasure which is legitimate in virtually any consensual exchange. They see in the exclusive romanticization of sex an occasion to impose unnecessarily restrictive sexual norms.

As we edge towards the mid-1990s, I do not anticipate the disappearance of either sexual ideology. Despite the rhetoric of a sexual counter-revolution and a coming era of repression often heard on the Left today, or the announcements by conservatives and liberals of the dawning of a new era of spiritual intimacy and romance, I expect less a dramatic break from the recent past than an intensification of these conflicts.[3] The two sexual constructions are culturally and socially rooted in America. For example, mainstream Judeo-Christian religious traditions in the United States as well as secular liberal and romantic traditions, are chief carriers of sexual romanticism. Similarly, libertarian currents linked to cultural modernism and radical social visions as well as to Antinomian Protestant traditions would seem to ensure the continuation of a hedonistic-expressive, libertarian sexual ethic and politics.[4] There are, as well, social structural supports for these two sexual constructions that seem unlikely to change in the near future. The commercialization of everyday life promotes a strain towards separating eros from intimate bonds as a new sphere of profitability, e.g., pornography, gay bathhouses, massage parlors, escort services, phone sex, etc.[5] Yet, at the same time, an elaborate institutional, legal and governmental apparatus continues to ensure the dominance of romantic sexual meanings and politics. I do not anticipate an end to the conflict between romantic and libertarian sexual frameworks in the near future.

I have sought to stake out a moral space intermediary between these two orthodoxies. I have introduced a pragmatic moral language that offers general directives, not imperatives or hard and fast moral rules of action. I think a move away from a substantive ethic anchored in some ontology of sexual and human nature is crucial to breaking from the current impasse. If the movements of change in the 1960s and 1970s and the reactive movements of the 1980s tell us anything, it is that a great diversity exists in sexual concepts, conventions and lifestyles across America today. Instead of invoking absolutist sexual values derived, say, from particular religious or medical-scientific traditions to morally classify desires and acts, I suggest that we begin to think of sexual ethics more as loose guidelines, structured by some general norms that leave both individual judgment and social ambiguity intact. I can invoke no substantive or essentialist concept of sex or human nature to warrant my preference. I can, however, invoke the many suspicions that today surround essentialist, foundationalist strategies. Compelling arguments have been made that these justificatory strategies mask local or ethnocentric interests and values. My approach appeals instead to those American traditions that respect individual judgment, social diversity and the capacity of individuals to regulate their own lives, especially in the private sphere.

I acknowledge there is a downside to my standpoint. The premises and the norms I have offered—e.g., according of limited respect to

existing diverse practices; mutual consent, mutual responsibility—
are at best, very rough guidelines that permit a wide latitude of
legitimacy to practices that may be correctly perceived to have negative personal and social costs. They provide, moreover, neither hard
and fast rules of conduct nor unambiguous standards of moral judgment regarding sexual behavior. They are at best regulative norms
and ideals. The regime I recommend demands more tolerance of excesses and more fluid moral boundaries. Yet what we gain more than
compensates for this ambiguity and excess: a wider tolerance of social
difference; a respect for individuals as moral agents; and a reinvigo-
rated public realm where contested moral claims need to be redeemed
through argumentation.

My approach will make it much more difficult to label specific
desires, acts or lifestyles as deviant or perverse. Since I have abandoned the notion that there is a right sexual practice or a set of
absolute sexual values that we can appeal to, it will be much more
difficult to articulate some kind of rigid moral hierarchy of sexual
correctness, and therefore to label transgressive acts as bearing a
stigmatizing identity. This would mark a crucial step away from an
automatic interpretation of sexual desires or acts as signs of an essential personal identity. To the extent that sex acts need to be understood
in their immediate context from the vantage point of the individual,
and to the extent that moral judgment amounts to a complicated
calculus weighing considerations of choice, constraint and consequences, there will, perhaps, be less of a moral gradient between acts.
Sex acts may be less likely to be taken as self-revelatory. Sexual
practices will at the very least lose some of the moral weight they
carry as signs of personal or social health and virtue. The defense of
a sexual regime that allows individuals more freedom in framing the
meaning of sex and defining its relation to identity and a public social
sphere without, however, permitting the individual to ignore the enormous burden of responsibility that he or she bears, is the moral hope
that informs this book.

Notes

1. Cf. Gayle Rubin, "Thinking Sex: Notes for a Radical Theory of the
Politics of Sexuality," in *Pleasure and Danger*, ed. Carole Vance (Boston:

Routledge, 1984); Eve Kosofsky Sedgwick, *Epistemology of the Closet* (Berkeley: University of California Press, 1990).

2. The most convincing case for a political sociology of sex has been made by Rubin, "Thinking Sex."

3. I am not denying that trends in the 1980s underscore important developments. In *Romantic Longings* I highlighted movements to spiritualize sex and intimacy, some of which were closely tied to a restrictive sexual politic. I am denying, as I did less emphatically in my previous book, that these trends mark a reversal of the "dualistic" intimate culture that has evolved in the twentieth-century United States.

4. See, for example, Daniel Bell, *The Cultural Contradictions of Capitalism* (New York: Basic Books, 1976); Richard Sennett, *The Fall of Public Man* (New York: Alfred Knopf, 1977); Bernice Martin, *A Sociology of Contemporary Cultural Change* (Oxford: Basil Blackwell, 1981); Daniel Yankelovich, *New Rules: Searching for Self-Fulfillment in a World Turned Upside Down* (New York: Random House, 1981); Peter Clecak, *America's Quest for the Ideal Self* (New York: Oxford University Press, 1983).

5. Cf. Dennis Altman, *The Homosexualization of America* (Boston: Beacon Press, 1983); Barbara Ehrenreich and Deirdre English, *For Her Own Good* (Garden City, New York: Doubleday); Tim McCaskell, "Untangling emotions from eros," *Body Politic*, July/Aug. 1981.

Index